BUTCHART
GRAND CANYON TREKS

12,000 MILES THROUGH
THE GRAND CANYON

Sullivan Peak from the west, Nankoweap. (Photo: Harvey Butchart)

BUTCHART

GRAND CANYON TREKS

12,000 MILES THROUGH THE GRAND CANYON

EDITED & DESIGNED
BY WYNNE BENTI

Spotted Dog Press

GRAND CANYON TREKS

Published by Spotted Dog Press
Bishop, California

First Edition 1998, Spotted Dog Press

Cover: Harvey Butchart in the limestone narrows of Two Hundred and Nine Mile Canyon by Scott Baxter
Back cover: Coronado Butte by Michael Quinn
Book typesetting, production, and maps by Spotted Dog Press

Library of Congress Cataloging-in-Publication Data
Butchart, Harvey, 1907-
         Grand Canyon Treks/Harvey Butchart: edited by Wynne Benti
– 1st ed.
                P. Cm.
Includes bibliographical references and index.
Prev. Eds.: Glendale, Calif.: La Siesta Press, 1970-1984
        ISBN 0-9647530-2-2
1. Hiking – Arizona – Grand Canyon National Park – Guidebooks.
2. Trails – Arizona – Grand Canyon National Park – Guidebooks.
3. Grand Canyon National Park (Ariz.) – Guidebooks.
I. Benti, Wynne. II. Title.
GV199.42.A72G734 1998
917.91'320453 – dc21

                                              97-36947
                                                CIP

Printed in the United States of America

A Note About Safety

*Various aspects of hiking and canyoneering have certain risks
and hazards associated with them.
Some of these hazards include, but are not limited to,
adverse weather conditions, loose rock and rockfall, exposed rock,
rugged terrain, unpredictable flash floods, stream crossings,
potential for insect, snake or animal bites, hypothermia, heat stroke and
heat exhaustion, hyponatremia and dehydration.
The editor and publisher of this guide make no representations as to the safety of
any hiking route described in this book. Always check ahead with the
Back Country Office of Grand Canyon National Park for pertinent information,
including permit reservations, before you travel into the backcountry,
as conditions are constantly changing.
The Grand Canyon is not the place for one's first hiking experience,
and a book is not a substitute for maps or mountaineering skill
nor can it make climbing or hiking safe for those who do not practice
or are uneducated in the principles of safety. Those who are inexperienced in
desert backcountry travel are encouraged to seek training provided by
various mountaineering clubs and outdoor organizations.
There is no substitute for experience, skill and knowledge of safety procedures.*

A Word About Archaeological Sites and Artifacts

*Archaeological sites and artifacts are protected by
the Antiquities Act of 1906
and the Archaeological Resources Protection Act of 1979.
All historic and prehistoric sites on Federal lands
are protected and defacement, removal, excavation or destruction
of such antiquities is prohibited by law.*

Table of Contents

"In wildness is the preservation of the world."

HENRY DAVID THOREAU

Acknowledgments

Walt Wheelock was the first to set *Grand Canyon Treks* in motion by encouraging Harvey Butchart to write a book based on his Canyon trail notes. Grand Canyon National Park Museum Curator Carolyn Richard, photographer Michael Quinn and the staff of the museum helped to broaden the original scope of this book by providing access to museum archives. We are very grateful to Bil Vandergraff, United States Park Ranger/Back Country, Grand Canyon National Park who reviewed work-in-progress. Lon Ayers provided review. Janet Balsom of Grand Canyon; Linda Martin, United States Park Ranger, Mesa Verde National Park; and Jeff Burton, Archaeologist, National Park Service also provided helpful information.

Jorgen Visbak, who spent years hiking with Harvey Butchart, made available his personal photographs of the early days spent hiking with Harvey and company. Scott Baxter provided cover photography. Joseph Hall contributed the only known photograph of Dr. Butchart making a jumar ascent. Edward Zdon provided technical review. Ski Camphausen, R.N. reviewed terminology. Andy Zdon, my husband and Northern Arizona University alumnus, who like many of us was inspired by Dr. Butchart's hiking legacy in college, contributed information on Canyon geology.

The most remarkable part of this project was time spent with Harvey and Roma Butchart, and especially having the opportunity to work with Harvey on his classic book. With a mathematical mind as quick as a whip, he hasn't forgotten the details: from intricate route descriptions and events, to his hiking companions idiosyncrasies, or what they carried in their packs on the days he hiked with them. He inspired endless dreams with his adventurous exploits, and he will continue to be a source of inspiration to those who follow his story throughout the magnificent landscape of the Grand Canyon as told in the pages of *Grand Canyon Treks*.

"Dr. Butchart had driven up that morning from Flagstaff, where he heads the Mathematics Department at Arizona State College. He had started down the Tanner Trail from Lipan Point, then had turned left off the trail to seek a possible new route down the face of the Redwall; he had found only one, and later had discovered a new way down the cliffs of Tapeats Sandstone as well. Reaching the River he had turned west and followed its bank... ...and arrived at our camp on schedule and apparently unwearied. In the morning he would climb the vertical mile to the rim by the Hance Trail. This, for Harvey Butchart, was only a mildly strenuous hike... ...I once told him that he must know the Canyon's inner fastness as well as the native bighorn sheep or wild burros did. But when he showed me his topographic maps crisscrossed in ink with the routes of his favorite hikes, I realized I had underestimated him. No individual bighorn or burro ever had traveled so much of the Grand Canyon.

FRANÇOIS LEYDET
Grand Canyon: Time and the River Flowing

FOREWORD
by Harvey Butchart

This may be the place to say something about my role in Grand Canyon lore. When our daughter developed hay fever in Iowa, I welcomed the opportunity to teach mathematics at Northern Arizona University in the dry desert climate. At first, the Canyon was just another place to hike along with the Rockies and the San Francisco peaks in the Flagstaff area. However, the challenge of discovering new routes through the cliffs became an obsession, and finding ruins, waterfalls and natural bridges became the lure. I felt like I was part of a chain that dated back to prehistoric Indians and Spanish explorers. I read all the books about the Canyon that I could find, while "Dock" Marston and Plez "P.T." Reilly gave me suggestions for doing the legwork for their chronicles. By 1963, Colin Fletcher referred to me as the one who really knew the Canyon and had kept a journal of what was to be enjoyed there. John Annerino called me the "father of modern Grand Canyon hiking." The park rangers were always appreciative since I gave the research library a copy of my hiking logs and large maps showing where I had been. I only wish that my predecessors — Hance, Bass and the Kolbs had left such records, and I certainly regret that my immediate mentor, Merrel Clubb, hadn't documented his trips.

Walt Wheelock was the initial inspiration for my effort to get something in print about my Grand Canyon wanderings, and Wynne Benti proposed to give it new form and a new lease on life. I was glad to accept Wheelock's offer to publish what I had learned, as it was my hope that what I had learned would not die with me. Still, my book is intentionally sketchy so the reader might have to do a little guessing about the details.

I dedicate this book to all who enjoy the Grand Canyon, and to those who may use this book to enhance their own Canyon experience.

INTRODUCTION
by Wynne Benti

When the *Grand Canyon Treks* series was first published in the early 1970's, it was the only substantive guide to the remote back-country wilderness of the Grand Canyon. Today this fabled collection of trail notes, which represents nearly a half-century of hiking records and route documentation, has established its place in history by providing a contemporary perspective on remote backcountry travel in the Grand Canyon. While men and women spent most of the twentieth century making history on the Colorado River, Butchart explored the canyons and plateaus of this immense wilderness rarely, if ever, meeting another person along the way.

Only a few thousand people visited the Grand Canyon each year when Harvey Butchart first started hiking there. Many of those early visitors rarely ventured below the Rim unless it was in the guarded safety of a guided mule train. Over the years, their numbers have grown dramatically, with nearly five million people a year now visiting the South Rim alone. Of those, approximately 60,000 make it into the Grand Canyon's backcountry — more than 1.2 million acres of wild and rugged terrain, where traditional trails are virtually non-existent, and are replaced by cross-country routes through serpentine chasms carved out of rock hundreds of millions of years old. The closest thing resembling a trail might be an old, winding prospector's track which hasn't seen a man-made improvement in almost a century.

Many of Harvey Butchart's routes drop down cracks in steep ravines and traverse narrow ledges with nothing more than meager finger-holds with which to balance one's weight. They follow faint game trails, tight twisting side canyons and boulder clogged, vertical-walled creek beds. There are dead-ends at dry waterfalls and false starts at a canyon's edge. In many cases, back-tracking is

Harvey Butchart near Mineral Canyon, Hance Trail (Harvey Butchart Collection)

required. Water is very scarce; and, at least three quarts to four gallons, depending on the route and trip duration, should be carried if springs are unreliable or unknown.

Nature, powerful and unsettled, is constantly changing the appearance of these routes. Over the years, floods and fluctuating water flows on the Colorado River have changed the landscape along the river itself. Beaches are created and swept away. Debris flows may fill the mouth of a canyon with boulders and rocks standing twelve feet high, only to be washed away by a flash flood a few months later. Rockslides have wiped away portions of old foot trails or blocked them with slabs of fallen rock.

Experienced canyon hikers or mountaineers who have hiked in rugged desert terrain will understand what it takes to plan and commit to a trip in the remote backcountry of the Grand Canyon. The ability to read a 7.5 minute topographic map and to use a compass for navigation; experience in route finding; good physical conditioning and endurance; carrying the right equipment; competent

Days gone by: in camp at Two Hundred and Fourteen Mile Canyon. Wood fires are now prohibited below the rim due to extreme fire danger. (Photo: Jorgen Visbak)

climbing ability; comfort on exposed rock and the ability to decipher vague routes through the constantly changing shape of the land are just some of the skills needed for this kind of travel. Hiking with companions, experience and skill can make the difference between life and death. Long hard days, heavy loads of water, and challenging, rugged terrain — these are the primary characteristics of Harvey Butchart's routes.

In the autumn of 1945, as the aspen trees turned gold on the Colorado Plateau and the Second World War came to an end, Harvey Butchart took what was to be the first of hundreds of hikes in the Grand Canyon. During the next forty years, he would walk over 12,000 miles, log more than 1,000 actual hiking days and record his experiences in a notebook. He developed a keen eye for being able to identify routes through uncertain terrain and hiked to places in the Grand Canyon that no contemporary had previously visited or has been to since, according to many. Even today, Harvey Butchart continues to influence generations of canyon hikers who follow in his footsteps. There is no question — the mathematics professor from the heartland is the father of contemporary Grand Canyon hiking.

Nearly four thousand years ago, prehistoric people who were the descendants of the Paleoindians, the oldest known cultural tradition in native North America, made the first impression on the Grand Canyon. Subtle reminders of these ancient people and those that followed them are hidden within the vast, endless miles of inner gorge, vertical cliffs and blue-green water — a hand print on the overhang of a cliff, a split-twig figurine in the dark recesses of a cave, or steps cut into a vertical wall of rock.

John Wesley Powell's exploration of the Colorado River in 1869 was responsible for initiating a flurry of activity in the Grand Canyon throughout the second half of the 19th century, and well into the 20th. Men and women attempted to turn dreams into personal fortune or fame often at the Canyon's expense, and many met with disillusionment or tragedy. Prospectors, developers, railroad men and every possible kind of promoter wandered through the Canyon with the thought of turning its immense natural beauty into personal fortunes and glory. Tourists and hikers eventually discovered the Grand Canyon, and many of these later visitors, unlike their predecessors, came solely for the experience of enjoying its awesome natural beauty and solitude.

During the years of the Great Depression, exploration of the Grand Canyon backcountry was sporadic at best, with attention still focused on the water — the Colorado River. It wasn't until the end of World War II, that a new age of backcountry discovery and exploration prevailed.

Harvey Butchart and his wife, Roma, with their two children, moved from Iowa to Flagstaff with the expectation that the drier climate of the Arizona desert might cure his daughter's asthma. Harvey had accepted a position as a mathematics professor at Arizona State College at Flagstaff, which would later become Northern Arizona University. Not long after arriving in Flagstaff, he made his first trip to the Grand Canyon.

For the next forty years, Harvey would spend nearly every day off, weekend and holiday driving from Flagstaff to the Grand

Canyon. Until he was 70, he hiked in the Grand Canyon throughout the year, though there were times when, despite the fact that he seemed to tolerate heat better than most, he was so weakened by it that he had to sit down for awhile beneath whatever shade he could find. In later years, most of his Canyon hiking was done during the cooler temperatures of winter. His knowledge of elusive springs was so thorough, that he rarely carried more than two gallons of water as a buffer between them. With the exception of water, lightweight was the way he preferred to travel. He didn't carry a tent, preferring to sleep on an air mattress beneath the starry skies. He ate sandwiches of white bread and margarine, snacks of peanuts and prunes. The heaviest object in his pack was a flannel-lined Dacron sleeping bag, the kind used for car-camping. He eventually upgraded to a lightweight down bag. When it did rain, he covered himself with a plastic tarp and slept safe and dry on his air mattress while the water puddled around it. At night, while lying in his sleeping bag, he listened to the mice scamper across the pots and pans.

Harvey Butchart climbed 83 of the 138 or so named Grand Canyon summits. Twenty-five of those were first ascents. Credited with finding some 116 approaches to the Colorado River, he kept detailed trail notes and marked his routes on a set of Matthes-Evans Grand Canyon maps, the only complete map of the area available at that time (significant updates have been made on more recent maps). Of all the trails he hiked, the engineering of the Kaibab impressed him the most as did the beauty of the North Rim Trail. Nankoweap Mesa provided his most solitary wilderness experience. Scattered pot sherds and the absence of man-made cairns suggested that he may have been the first to walk the mesa since the ancients. His favorite personal achievement was being able to locate Royal Arch Creek, which wasn't on the old Matthes-Evans map. He had great physical endurance and speed, and could complete in one day, what would take most people two or three.

One of the old Matthes-Evans maps vividly illustrates the extent to which Harvey Butchart hiked. He meticulously hand-penned his routes in black ink and created a detailed map like this for each area that he hiked in the Grand Canyon. Over the years, inaccurate and unauthorized copies of his maps have been "recreated" and sold to the unwary.
(Photo: Michael Quinn, Grand Canyon Museum Collection, 12786)

Through the years, Harvey met, at one time or another, nearly everyone who had become a part of the Canyon's contemporary backcountry history. Harvey discussed route information with Emery Kolb whose photography studio and home, which he shared with his brother Ellsworth, was and still is located on the edge of the South Rim, just west of the Bright Angel Lodge. Otis "Dock" Marston, whose first trip on the Colorado River was with the great Norman Nevills, and who later became a river runner, was a dedicated collector of Grand Canyon and Colorado River history. He spent years exchanging hiking information and route ideas with Harvey.

In the mid 1960's, Colin Fletcher sought out Harvey for detailed information during the planning stages of his three month journey through the Grand Canyon which would become the basis of his book, *The Man Who Walked Through Time*. Fletcher spent countless hours with Harvey studying maps and routes attempting to determine if it was possible to hike from Supai in the west, to the Nankoweap Trail on the eastern side of the Canyon. Fletcher wrote:

"...At the very start of my year of waiting I had begun trying to gather information about foot travel through those parts of the Canyon away from the river and the Rim-to-Rim tourist trail. I inquired of park rangers, packers, geologists and men who had "run" the river several times. But before long it dawned on me that when it came to extensive hiking in remote parts of the Canyon, none of them really knew what he was talking about. So I set about tracking down the experts on foot travel. In the end I discovered that they totaled one: a math professor at Arizona State College in Flagstaff. But Dr. Harvey Butchart, I was relieved to find, knew exactly what he was talking about."

Harvey Butchart was born May 10, 1907 in Hofei, China to missionary parents just a few years before the Chinese Revolution. In 1920, four years after his father died, Harvey's mother returned to the United States with her children, taking residence in Vermont, Illinois. Eventually, the family moved to

Filling the canteen on the way to Royal Arch from Enfilade Point. (Photo: Jorgen Visbak)

Eureka, Illinois so Harvey's older brother could have his teeth straightened by a proper dentist. Harvey attended Eureka College, the alma mater of former President Ronald Reagan. It was during his freshman year at Eureka, in Latin class, that Harvey met Roma Wilson, daughter of the college president. Harvey graduated Summa Cum Laude with a Bachelor of Science degree in Mathematics. Roma graduated Magna Cum Laude with a degree in French. He went on to receive his Ph.D. from the University of Illinois. They married on July 28, 1929 and spent their honeymoon camped at Starved Rock State Park in Illinois, ironically and perhaps appropriately named for recent college graduates light on cash near the onset of the Great Depression. Harvey spent about twelve years teaching at various colleges in the midwest, including three years at Grinnel College in Iowa before accepting a position teaching math at Arizona State College at Flagstaff. It was there that Harvey discovered the Grand Canyon and became the sponsor for the school's hiking club.

The surplus-style frame pack that Harvey carried during his many years of hiking in the Grand Canyon and his hiking boots are now part of the permanent collection at the Grand Canyon National Park Museum. The photograph on the previous page shows Harvey, dressed in a khaki-colored shirt and pants, kneeling at the edge of a water pocket filling his army surplus canteen in the brown silty water. There were times when Harvey carried up to two gallons of water, particularly on hikes where water sources were either unknown or non-existent. Often times, he carried only a gallon, relying on water pockets, seeps, or groundwater which had to be scooped out from the sandy beds of washes. More desperate measures called for drinking out of a cattle tank with one or two cow patties floating unappealingly on the surface. Many of his hiking companions drank the Colorado River water without treating it. He never developed a tolerance for the river water which he always had to treat. Once, while camping below the North Rim, a rock slide came tumbling down from the cliffs above, and landed on top of Harvey's sleeping bag. Though Harvey narrowly escaped injury by running for cover when he initially heard the rockfall, a large rock put an impressive dent in his favorite half-gallon canteen.

He rarely carried a rope, perhaps less than a dozen times during his years of hiking. He would resort to bringing a rope only after he had been stopped getting where he wanted to go by some unforeseen obstacle. Even then, as he looked for a place to set up a rope, he would discover a way around the obstacle and find that a rope wasn't needed at all.

Jorgen Visbak, a Danish chemist who moved to the United States after World War II, was one of Harvey's closest hiking companions. Jorgen noted that they rarely hiked the Grand Canyon in summer because of the triple-digit temperatures. Most hiking was done between October and April, while summers were spent boating the Colorado River or Lake Mead.

Many of the old trails built by the prehistoric Canyon inhabitants and prospectors have all but disappeared, victims of flash

Jorgen Visbak (front) with Harvey on the Colorado River between Separation and Spencer Canyons. (Photo: Jorgen Visbak Collection)

floods and erosion. One of the seemingly endless challenges for Harvey was to locate these old routes. While following an indistinct track, perhaps a prehistoric footpath to Powell Plateau, Harvey noticed faint outlines on the surface of the rock. Upon his return to the rim, he notified park anthropologist R.C. Euler who went to investigate and found forty-five different prehistoric house ruins.

His favorite part of the park was the Eastern Grand Canyon. Harvey studied his turn-of-the-century Matthes-Evans map to get a general idea of the route he wanted to explore. The maps, with their enormous and somewhat unwieldy scale, never really came close to showing the subtle nuances of a route. Even today's 7.5 minute topos are very limited in their scope of detail. Harvey would often return to an area several times before locating the correct starting point of a particular route or a passageway around an obstacle. He enjoyed trying to locate the settings of the famous Kolb brothers photographs.

Harvey with Homer Morgan (left) at Spencer Canyon. (Photo: Jorgen Visbak)

Most of this exploration was done on foot through rugged terrain — narrow ravines, precipitous dry waterfalls, exposed ledges where a faint trail might end at a vertical cliff of Redwall. On occasion, a rope was carried and used for protection on exposed routes where there was a risk of falling and being injured.

In those days, Harvey and his hiking companions did a lot of things which, by today's standards, would be considered dangerous and discouraged, if not prohibited by the Park Service. One of these was to use an air mattress to cross the Colorado with the intention of continuing a hike on the other side of the river or in a downstream canyon. The river was not an obstacle to Harvey Butchart. In 1956, when he was 49 years old, he floated down the San Juan River from Mexican Hat to Last Chance Creek on an air mattress, followed by a trip down the Colorado River from Lee's Ferry to the Bass Trail. He was very careful to portage around all of the major rapids including Lava Falls. Harvey and Jorgen sometimes made these small voyages without the safety of life-jackets. Instead, they wrapped the contents of their packs in plastic bags — the idea being that the airtight bags would pro-vide floatation in case of an upset in the rapids. Sadly, the flaws of this system came to light when a companion drowned, having let go of his air mattress in a rapid. Converts to this method of downriver transport later strapped lifejackets to their backpacks in addition to their air mattresses.

Harvey did not spend forty years hiking in the Canyon with-out at least one or two close calls. One cold winter day, while climbing alone in Nankoweap, he set up a fixed over-hanging rappel rope to lower himself down a vertical wall, with the expec-tation of climbing back up the same rope using jumar ascenders. On the return trip, when he was about nine feet above ground, the old goldline rope began to spin out of control and soon, he was upside down with his feet strapped tightly in the jumars. With some intense finger work, he freed himself from the rope by untying his shoelaces and slipping out of his shoes. With no flashlight and little more than a flannel shirt for warmth, he walked all night, and for the greater part of the following day to get back to his car.

On a trip to remote Royal Arch with Jorgen Visbak, Chuck Johnson and Doc Ellis, he jumped over a pool of water. An awk-ward landing resulted in the bruising of the Achilles tendons in both heels. So severe was the injury, that he was unable to stand without doubling over in excruciating pain. They decided to send Chuck for help. Walking at a determined pace, he reached the South Rim a day and a half later. There, he notified the Park Service and a helicopter rescue was arranged. Their location back at Royal Arch was so inaccessible that when the helicopter came by on its first pass there was no place for it to land. The only suit-able landing site was on the top of Royal Arch. With rangers pushing him along, Harvey crawled on his hands and knees to the top of Royal Arch where, in a daring maneuver, he was picked up by the helicopter.

Harvey Butchart on the beach at the mouth of Spencer Canyon.
(Photo: Jorgen Visbak)

In 1993, when Harvey was 86 years old he was invited to run the Colorado River, one of many such invitations he had received over the years. At the helm of the self-bailing pontoon boat was Cameron Stavely, the grandson of Norman Nevills. As Harvey held on tight, they floated from Lee's Ferry to Diamond Creek on what was perhaps, his last trip down the Colorado. Almost exactly forty years earlier, Harvey, Jorgen and Dock Marston boated down the river when it flowed freely through what is now Lake Powell and Glen Canyon Dam.

Harvey celebrated his 90th birthday in 1997, amid a flurry of activity which included interviews with reporters, photo sessions, subsequent articles in magazines, and many luncheons with various organizations. Perhaps, the most memorable occasion was a tribute at Northern Arizona University where many of the people whose lives had been touched by Harvey Butchart gathered to honor his achievements as a Grand Canyon backcountry adventurer.

During an interview, Harvey was once asked:

"Why did you do it?"

He replied:

"I hadn't thought a lot about why I did it, but when I did, I analyzed it by categories. The first was physical fitness. Of course there are lots of ways to achieve that. Another was to enjoy the scenery, aesthetic appreciation of scenery. The third was based on scientific curiosity — what's over beyond the next ridge? Where can I find an Indian ruin or something that I might be interested in, like a natural bridge or a waterfall — a scientific curiosity about what's not shown on the map, but might be there? The fourth was sociability, enjoyment of company when backpacking. The last one was contrary to all of that — and that was to go by myself and work up a reputation for being an expert."

Between games of chess with Roma, visits with family, and the routine of daily life, he thinks about that tireless question, "Why did you do it?" And, he ponders for awhile.

"I loved the adventure of it all, the thrill of overcoming obstacles and the challenge of staying safe."

A GRAND CANYON GEOLOGY PRIMER
by Andy Zdon

This introductory primer on Grand Canyon geology describes the principal formations that the Grand Canyon traveler can expect to encounter. Some familiarity with the names of the geological formations within the Grand Canyon is necessary in understanding the routes described by Harvey Butchart. However, numerous more localized or discontinuous formations are not described. The Grand Canyon traveler who wishes a more extensive knowledge of Grand Canyon geology is referred to such excellent references as *Grand Canyon Geology*, edited by Stanley S. Beus and Michael Morales or other geological references on the area.

The rim of the Grand Canyon is formed by the Kaibab Formation which is easily recognized as the tan limestone cliff that drops off immediately from the rim. The Kaibab Formation was deposited in a shallow, marine environment, and careful observation of these limestones will usually reward the hiker with numerous fossils consisting of corals, sponges, and other ancient lifeforms.

The forested, buff-colored slope beneath the Kaibab Formation is the Toroweap Formation. The Toroweap Formation gradually changes from sandstone in the eastern Grand Canyon (especially around the Little Colorado River) to limestone in the western Grand Canyon toward Lake Mead. The hiker is not likely to identify much in the way of fossils in this formation, and most fossils that are found will be in loose limestone rocks that are derived from the Kaibab Formation and have fallen from above.

Beneath the Toroweap Formation, the Coconino Sandstone presents a formidable cliffy appearance, and is one of the most conspicuous geologic formations in the Grand Canyon. Upon closer inspection, it contains easily recognized cross-beds, which are evidence of ancient sand dunes. Fossils found within the

Coconino Sandstone are not like those found in the Kaibab Formation, but consist of "trace fossils." Trace fossils are simply the marks of early lifeforms such as footprints that have been fossilized in the sandstone. Fossil footprints of animals that ranged in size from primitive reptiles to small spiders can be found.

The next layer consisting of the Hermit Shale and the Supai Group (a series of geological formations grouped together) makes up the red slopes and bench-like cliffs beneath the Coconino Sandstone. These "red-beds" primarily consist of alternating shales and sandstones, and are usually dotted with pinyon and juniper. Hiking routes within the Hermit Shale and Supai Group are generally easier to follow than in the overlying Coconino Sandstone or in the magnificent cliffs of the Redwall Limestone below.

The Redwall Limestone forms a magnificent and easily recognizable cliff below the redbeds. However, the red appearance of the Redwall limestone is only a facade. The reddish color is caused by iron-oxide staining from the Supai Group above, and is only a surface feature. Unstained Redwall Limestone actually presents a grayish appearance. This is the formation within the Grand Canyon in which the hiker is likely to find large caves. Fossil corals and shells are also frequently found in the Redwall.

The Muav Limestone blends into the bottom of the Redwall, and is only conspicuous to the hiker reasonably well-informed with Grand Canyon geology. However, the Bright Angel Shale underlying the Muav Limestone presents a dark greenish shale that is easily identified by all. The Bright Angel Shale contains fossils of "trilobites," tiny marine creatures that scurried along the sea floor.

A large bench called the Tonto Platform is present at the base of the Bright Angel Shale. This is the bench that hikers at Plateau Point are standing on, and on which the Tonto Trail runs along its length. The Tonto Platform represents the top of the Tapeats Sandstone, a brown, resistant, cliff-forming sandstone unit. The Tapeats Sandstone is the oldest of the easily identified sedimentary formations within the Grand Canyon — with one exception. At certain localities within the inner gorge, shale and sandstone beds that are brightly colored and are obviously dipping at a far steeper angle than the other sedimentary rocks in the canyon consist of the "Grand Canyon Supergroup." The Grand Canyon Supergroup contains some of the oldest sedimentary rocks in the entire Colorado Plateau.

The steep and ragged cliffs of the inner gorge generally consist of the older Precambrian metamorphic rocks that make up the Vishnu Schist, the Zoroaster Granite (actually gneiss), and other lesser known units.

As stated earlier, this is not an exhaustive description of the geologic formations in the Grand Canyon; nor, is every rock type likely to be found mentioned. As an example, basaltic lava flows are found in parts of the Grand Canyon, though they are not included in formations listed in this primer. A working knowledge of the formations in the Grand Canyon will provide a greater perspective of the Canyon's magnificence.

The Grand Canyon

"There are two reasons for me to do something.
The first is that someone has already done it.
The other is that no one has done it."

HARVEY BUTCHART

What a grand place to take a hike! This is undoubtedly the thought of the small percentage of visitors to the Grand Canyon who also happen to be backpackers. Little has been written concerning the old non-maintained trails. Still, the number of hikers who venture away from the thirty miles of modern, well-maintained trails has been increasing from year to year. There is a thrill in finding the unexpected, but both for safety and the maximum satisfaction, most outdoorsmen will welcome a briefing.

Hiking in the Grand Canyon is mountaineering with essential differences. The main differences include the summer heat, lack of water and the fact that the uphill portion of most trips is usually done on the way out, when one is the most tired. Everyone who hikes in the Canyon should discover their own personal tolerance to the heat and steep terrain by at least a short apprenticeship on the Bright Angel and Kaibab Trails. Only then should they branch out to the more challenging prospector trails.

The history of the Grand Canyon is full of stories about unforeseen weakness due to heat and dehydration. For instance, a riverman with much experience in Glen Canyon wanted to take his first party through the Grand. The skipper promised the family of a seventeen year-old on the trip, that the young man would walk around all of the bad rapids. Between Hance Rapids and Bright Angel Creek there are rapids where walking the bank is

Looking down on Lava Falls. (Photo: Jorgen Visbak)

impossible, so the guide figured that he and the boy would walk the Tonto Trail to Phantom Ranch in one long day, while the rest of the party continued on downriver. If the guide had known more about the Tonto Trail, he would have taken the boy up to the South Rim and then back down the Kaibab Trail to the bottom. Instead, they hiked during the hottest part of the day which almost resulted in disaster. They were unable to find the water where springs were indicated on the old map, and no one can walk the whole route in a summer's day. The river guide was taken to Phantom Ranch on a mule. He remained weak, so the party went on without him. A number of men have been killed by similar conditions of heat and dehydration.

Bright Angel Trail

The Bright Angel Trail follows what was first, a prehistoric Indian route from the South Rim to the Colorado River. During the late 19th century, prospectors improved the trail and charged tourists a toll for its use. Coconino County maintained it for a time and then the National Park Service took it over in 1928. The Bright Angel Fault lifted the strata to the west and it is this break through the cliffs that makes the route possible. Just below the rim, the trail goes through the first of two tunnels. About thirty feet above the trail just west of the first tunnel, the wall and ceiling of an overhang are decorated with Ancestral Puebloan pictographs of deer and other designs in red clay. This protected ledge can be quite easily reached from above, yet it is unfortunate that vandals have added their own spray can graffiti.

Indian Gardens, the oasis 4.5 miles down the trail, is recognized by its majestic cottonwood trees. Early pictures show that this grove has grown dramatically since the arrival of the first tourists. The Havasupai Indians once grew crops here. From the early days of tourism along the South Rim, to the 1960's, the water from the springs was collected and pumped to the South Rim. However, there were major water shortages during the main tourist season. The problem was remedied by the construction of a multi-million dollar pipeline from Roaring Springs near the North Rim. The pipe was buried beneath the trail, crossing the Colorado River under a foot bridge built in 1965. Just as the project neared completion in December of 1966, the Canyon was covered by a remarkably wet storm. Several inches of rain fell on two feet of snow. For days, as much water came down the Bright Angel Creek as that which flowed in the Colorado River during the very low stage, about 3,500 cubic feet per second. Long sections of the North Kaibab Trail were swept away and the pipeline was destroyed.

Rebuilding the pipeline took longer and cost more than the original job. It was the flood, not of the century, but of the millennium.

Along the Bright Angel Trail, 1.5 miles above Indian Gardens and three miles below the rim, drinking fountains are turned on during the hot season. Water is available and the restrooms are open all year at Indian Gardens. Below the Gardens, the trail forks, one branch going to Plateau Point where there is a spectacular view of the Colorado River 1,300 feet below. The other branch continues down beside Garden Creek and gets below the Tapeats Sandstone in a narrow gorge. A sign used to point the way to the base of the Tapeats west of the bed where one could find some ruins and place a hand on the "unconformity" – the time gap between deposition of the rock units. The upper half of your hand will be on rock five million years younger than rock touching the lower half of the same hand.

The nonstratified rock of the inner gorge is commonly called granite although most of it is schist: greatly deformed, and metamorphosed sedimentary or volcanic rock. At the top of these 1.8 to 2.0 billion year old rocks, Garden Creek enters an impossibly steep chute and the trail veers to the east. The old "Devil's Corkscrew" section of switchbacks still shows, but the modern route swings farther to the east as it drops to the bed of Pipe Creek. To get a quick idea of a really wild part of the Grand Canyon, go up the bed of Pipe Creek for five or ten minutes. One can even climb out of this forbidding narrows into the basin surrounded by the Tapeats cliff. Along the easy route to the Tonto Trail to the east, an overhang shelters an Ancestral Puebloan pictograph, and a miner's cairn points the way to the rough scramble through the Tapeats to the west. When you continue on toward the Colorado River down the Bright Angel Trail, note Garden Creek again as it falls to join Pipe Creek.

There is often a trickle of water in Pipe Creek, but it usually disappears into the gravel before reaching the river. One hot and dry day, I saw two men who had come down the Kaibab Trail and were going up the Bright Angel. They were digging for water in

Plateau Point (Photo: Andy Zdon)

the bed and waiting for their shallow pool to clear. Just around the next corner were pools.

On hot days, hikers often sit down in the Colorado River at the mouth of Pipe Creek. This is refreshing, but one should use discretion. Once, an eighteen-year-old girl waded out too far and was drowned.

The original route from the South Rim to Phantom Ranch was via the Bright Angel Trail, along the Tonto, and finally down the lower part of the Kaibab Trail. More recently, the spectacular River Trail was blasted from the solid rock to connect the lower ends of the two main trails. The new footbridge furnishes another cutoff on the way to the ranch, as it is no longer necessary for one to follow the River Trail east to the Kaibab Suspension Bridge.

On our way from the ranch to the Bright Angel Trail, we once came upon bare human footprints. They continued all the way to Indian Gardens. There we overtook a hiker who had tried to swim across the river with his clothes and shoes in one hand. In the middle of the river, he had to drop everything and swim for his life. Thus, he was clad in his underwear until he could borrow more suitable attire.

It is 7.8 miles from the South Rim down the Bright Angel Trail to the Colorado River and about 2.5 more to Phantom Ranch. The return by this route takes most hikers from five to eight hours. There is no water on the Kaibab Trail, so it is preferable to go up the Bright Angel in hot weather. Even so, one should carry some water. Once, I met a young Englishman on the steep trail above Indian Gardens. He confessed that he was "a trifle parched," and he handed my canteen back, a pound lighter.

Bright Angel Campground

After crossing the river on the new bridge, one passes by some buildings belonging to the government and used for general maintenance. One building was a lab for the engineer who took daily samples of the Colorado River water. To get these specimens, he sat in a little car dangling under a cable above the middle of the river. Before Glen Canyon Dam was built, the river was very irregular in transporting silt. For years, the rangers would tell you that the river carried one million tons of silt per day. Then without fanfare, the rate was cut to half a million tons per day. The river still looks brown about half of the time, especially when the Paria and the Little Colorado are in flood stage. Most of the silt is now trapped in upper Lake Powell behind the dam, and even when the entire river appears brown, a cupful is fairly clear. Some people feel no ill effects from drinking the water untreated, but there are many instances of enteritis, and sometimes even giardia. Filtering the water before drinking is highly recommended. The campground is provided with purified tap water. Fires are prohibited below the rim and you must carry out what you carry in, including trash.

In December of 1966, a massive flood swept away all the willows growing beside the creek, and cut away the terrace at the lower end of the area. No trace was left of the comfort station. Many of the buildings at Phantom Ranch were also damaged by the flood. Strangely, a rock pavilion thirty yards to the north was left intact.

One myth that circulates from time to time about the Inner Canyon is that it never rains at the bottom of the canyon. According to this colorful rumor, the air is supposed to be so warm that the raindrops evaporate before they reach the ground. This statement has about as much truth in it as does the one about the

Phantom Ranch trail crew bunkhouse after the 1966 flood
(Grand Canyon Museum Collection, 5097)

snows of winter never reaching the river. Pictures of snow on the Kaibab Bridge refute the latter, and during severe winters, plumbing in the structures along the river has been broken by freezing temperatures. Where the river splashes spray, I have seen the rocks coated with ice throughout the day in January.

The rainfall at Phantom Ranch averages about eight inches per year and most backpackers don't bother with a tent. A light air mattress keeps me above the surface water runoff, and I carry a big plastic sheet that will cover my sleeping bag on a rainy night. If there are only two or three people in the party, they can often find shelter under overhanging ledges, though this is not recommended during electrical storms. During one short but vigorous shower, I moved into the rock pavilion at Bright Angel Campground. This was better for experience than for sleep because the other people were playing a flashlight on a little skunk and a ringtail cat, who were darting in and out of a crack in the cliff behind the building.

There used to be a public swimming pool at Phantom Ranch. It was a great way to beat the heat and relax after a long, hot hike from the rim. Unfortunately, people started complaining about the lack of a filtering system, so Fred Harvey responded to their complaints by simply filling in the pool. Cold drinks can be obtained at the ranch if you arrive before eleven in the morning or late in the afternoon, when the commissary is open. It is too bad that there is such a big temperature difference between the rim and the bottom of the canyon in summer, which averages about twenty degrees. The bare rock walls of the inner gorge act like a giant reflector oven for the high summer sun.

Early visitors who told of the canyon bottom being in a perpetual twilight with little sunshine, no birds, and hardly a green leaf were giving way to their fears. They let the fall of a rock, poor footing near a cliff, or the sighting of a rattlesnake get blown way out of proportion. My average encounter with a rattlesnake was one about every forty days of hiking, and I rarely, if ever, saw them on the main trails due to the high number of people. Of course, this doesn't mean that you won't see a snake, but the odds of seeing one are about equal to getting near a bighorn, and sheep sightings in the canyon are a very unique and rare experience. Then again, most of my canyon hiking was done during the winter when snakes were hibernating. Only once during my more than 1,000 days of Canyon hiking did rocks fall nearby. A small slide fell with absolutely no warning while we were in camp. All we heard was a hiss and the thud as it hit the ground just a yard away from my sleeping bag.

Kaibab Trail

To get to the Kaibab Trail from the East Rim Drive, take the Yaki Point turnoff and then turn on the first paved road heading west. The South Kaibab Trail is just north of the parking area at the end of the road and is well marked. It is approximately 6.3 miles from the rim to the Colorado River, which is the only source of water found anywhere near the trail. The Kaibab Trail crosses the Canyon from the South to North Rim as one continuous trail and was completed by the Park Service in 1928, as a direct route to Phantom Ranch from the South and North Rims, following years of unsuccessful attempts to assume management of the Bright Angel Trail from Coconino County. Ironically, the same year work was completed on the Kaibab, the Park Service finally assumed control of the Bright Angel. Distant views are better than they are along the Bright Angel Trail since much of the Kaibab Trail is on a promontory. Mileposts are hard to maintain against the depredations of souvenir hunting vandals, but a few are left, especially along the lower half of the trail. The laziest and weakest hikers seem to be the most eager to record their achievement by tearing down the markers nearest the trails.

Just north of the Cedar Ridge picnic area, about 1.5 miles below the rim, one sees a butte of red Supai Sandstone whose top is at the level of the picnic area. It is O'Neill Butte and it has been climbed at least twice, but this is for experts. The butte is named after Bucky O'Neill, the former sheriff of Yavapai County. As a Rough Rider for Teddy Roosevelt, O'Neill lost his life in the Spanish-American War.

Down to the west from the Kaibab Trail, one can see the Tonto Trail connecting the Kaibab to the Bright Angel. During the years of 1965 and 1966, the Bright Angel Trail below Indian Gardens was closed for the construction of a pipeline. The Tonto

Confluence of Bright Angel Creek and the Colorado River (Photo: Andy Zdon)

Trail from the Bright Angel to the Kaibab Trail was improved and used by people who wished to start down the Bright Angel Trail and then go to the river. A cabin where the trail crosses Pipe Creek was partially crushed by a phenomenal snow in December 1967. Where the Tonto Trail meets the Kaibab near the rim of the inner gorge, a sign gives the mileage over to Indian Gardens as 4.3 and promises no water. Actually, one can almost always find a trickle in Pipe Creek.

The bay to the east of the Kaibab Trail is Cremation Canyon, where Indians cremated the remains of their dead on the rim and pushed the ashes over into the canyon. Out of sight, on the east arm of Cremation, are several caves. One of them contained split twig figurines — little effigies of deer that have been dated from 3,000 to 4,000 years old by the Carbon 14 method. Across the bay, below the Redwall Limestone, one can see two small clumps of green trees. The one to the north is a fairly reliable seep spring.

The distance from the rim to Phantom Ranch is 7.3 miles. An average hiker who wants to enjoy the scenery and take pictures should allow about three hours for the trip. Getting back to the rim will separate the men from the boys. The boys make it in about five hours while the men will need at least another hour. These times are for average hikers. Speed demons have trotted from the rim to the river and back in less than three hours.

The North Kaibab Trail

As you go up from Phantom Ranch to the North Rim, there is no need to carry much water. However, it is recommended that water be filtered or treated before drinking, as the stream is only a few yards away from the trail. On occasion, I have poured water down my back or dipped my shirt to cool off on a warm day.

About 0.3 miles north of the ranch is the beginning of the Clear Creek Trail. It switchbacks to the base of the Tapeats Sandstone, and then levels out above the river before getting through to the Tonto Platform. The views up and down the inner gorge are extremely rewarding from this point if one decides to go no farther along the trail.

Continuing north along the main trail, one goes through an impressively narrow corridor in the granite. The junction with Phantom Canyon is about a forty-five minute walk from the ranch. The flow of this creek is perennial, but much less than Bright Angel Creek. Fording the main creek can be a problem during the high water of late spring or after a summer storm. Progress is easy up Phantom except where one passes pools. Either wade or crawl along the smooth, sloping granite. At the end of this granite gorge there is a waterfall in the Tapeats that can be bypassed by a short rock climb about thirty yards east of the fall on the south side. Farther east, a ravine can be climbed on the north side. Breaks in the north wall may be also used to get up to the valley above. In May, the open valley above is a wild flower garden. Excursions up the two arms of the canyon will reveal the complicated geology, Indian ruins, and at the end of Phantom in the Redwall, a narrow slot beneath a fall. Near the lower end of the valley on the north side is an overhang which has been used as a campsite. Before this was a national park, cattle were left here for winter pasture and Edwin D. McKee, one of the leading authorities on Grand Canyon geology, used to tell about a lone steer that lingered after the last roundup.

There are two somewhat easier routes to the open valley of Phantom Creek. One can go up the scree and granite slope from the north end of Bright Angel Campground. From the ridge, one can see the break in the Tapeats, then proceed along the Tonto Platform to the saddle east of Cheops. One usually runs into a slight trail from there, down into Phantom Creek Valley. The third route is direct if you were coming down from the North Rim, and it is the only trail possible for stock. About a half mile downstream from Ribbon Falls, cross the creek and one finds an obscure trail going up to the Tonto Plateau and then around into Phantom Canyon. It comes down the valley near the old camp under the overhang.

Returning to the main trail, continue upstream. It is easy to see why bridging the creek crossings has always been difficult. When this route was pioneered by prospectors and the surveyors under USGS geologist, Francois Matthes, it was necessary to cross the creek ninety-nine times. During the extensive trail work of 1928, the route was improved so that there were only seven creek crossings. At first, loose boards were propped up on stepping stones and these were replaced after each flood. Then suspension bridges were supported a few yards above the water, but big floods would wash these away. Steel beam bridges were then tried, but the superflood of 1966 took these out as well.

About 5.5 miles north of Phantom Ranch, a spur trail leads west to where Ribbon Creek comes out of a slot high above and spatters down on a mossy tongue of travertine. Cool off by jumping behind the veil of water, or climb up beside the travertine and walk behind the fall. The light is often poor and a good picture of Ribbon Falls is a prize.

A fine side trip is the visit to the valley above Ribbon Falls via the trail that leaves the main trail about one hundred yards north of the Ribbon Falls spur. This trail leads to Upper Ribbon Falls. To the south, at the base of the cliff, are a number of ruins.

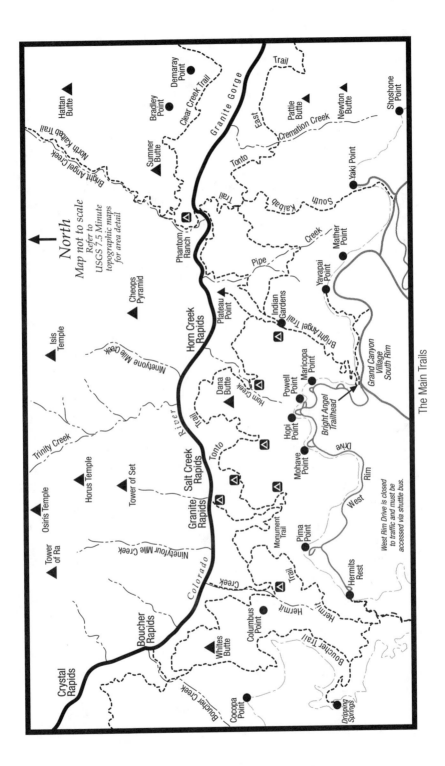

The Main Trails

Farther to the southeast is a route by which you can scramble up to the more remote valley above the upper falls. Views of the surrounding peaks are inspiring. One can truly experience the feeling of being in a remote area even though the main trail is just an hour's walk away.

Cave explorers talk enthusiastically about climbing up into Wall Creek, another good tributary of Bright Angel Creek. Another fine side trip is to go up the slope south of Wall Creek to a break in the Redwall south of a promontory. Careful route finding will get one to the top of Deva Temple. This is a non-technical ascent, but I spent ten hours away from Bright Angel Creek on the round trip. From the saddles to the north and south of Deva, there are routes down to Clear Creek. One can also go to the North Rim by following Hermit Shale over to Obi Canyon and then up.

Some interesting petroglyphs and pictographs are at the base of the Coconino just west of Obi Canyon. Once, while doing an aerial survey from a helicopter, R.C. Euler, former Grand Canyon National Park archaeologist and later museum curator of the Northern Arizona Museum in Flagstaff, located some ruins halfway through the Supai Formation on the southeast side of Deva near a spring. I found a way through the Redwall on the north side of Brahma. The ravine is narrow and steep and I had to crawl behind a big chockstone through a hidden hole. If one has the time to look, there may be an easier bypass.

A landmark on the main trail is Cottonwood Camp, a ranger residence which is used occasionally by trail workers. Branching off to the northwest a bit upstream is "The Tempest," another tempting detour. When I was out there in late May one year, little streams were splashing over high falls. Ouzels and wrens added to the magic of the ferns and redbud trees. I could climb the Redwall in the east fork at the end of the canyon, and a better climber has gone up the Redwall on the other fork. At the North Rim, they tell of two girls who were startled while getting a full-body suntan when a man appeared above them on the rim of the Coconino, five-hundred feet below the campground. Up Bright Angel Creek from

"The Transept" is an east side tributary called Manzanita Canyon, a fine place to engage in additional investigation.

The buildings at the junction of Bright Angel Canyon and Roaring Springs Canyon were built to supply water and power to the North Rim settlement. Water came down through a wooden penstock to run a generator which was managed by an engineer who lived here all summer.

The creek from Roaring Springs is by far the largest tributary of Bright Angel Creek. The cave from which the water flows has been surveyed and has 11,000 feet of passageways. The cascades below the cave put on a fine show and the roar of the water is easily heard by tourists at Bright Angel Point on the rim thousands of feet away. This is the water that is also taken by the pipeline over to the South Rim village. The Kaibab Trail goes up the canyon across from the falls. A particularly spectacular section was blasted out from the face of the cliff. The finest pictures of the upper section are taken in autumn when the aspens and maples are in their full red and golden glory.

Travel on the Kaibab Trail is done for various reasons. Allyn Cureton, who had been over the route several times, decided to set a speed record. He walked and ran the entire 20.6 miles of the trail from the North Rim to the south in three hours and eight minutes. He and others have crossed the canyon from the South Rim to the North and back again in much less than 24 hours. Two weeks may be spent in this one area alone if one wants to see and thoroughly experience all of the interesting detours.

Another fine side trip is up Bright Angel Creek to its source and a little farther. One encounters a fine fir forest at this relatively low elevation. There are beaver cuttings and the fishing is fine. Well below the source of the main creek, the Old Kaibab Trail branches to the northwest. Near the top, the old trail is well-hidden in the scrub oak. I have also come down to this part of the old trail by following the valley from where the Point Imperial branch of the scenic drive leaves the Cape Royal Highway. It is all marvelous wilderness.

Grandview Trail

During the late 19th and early 20th centuries when the Grand Canyon was first becoming known as a tourist destination, the South Rim, from Grandview Point to Moran Point, was better known and more popular than the present village area. John Hance developed two trails, the earliest between the Sinking Ship and Coronado Butte and the other east of Coronado Butte. Copper was found at the base of Horseshoe Mesa and by 1892, Pete Berry was building a trail to the mines. Most of the route is cut into the clay slope or along rock ledges, but at two places they had to construct cribs of logs wired to the face of the cliff. Between 1950 and 1970, sections of retaining wall had fallen away. Most of the trail is still in good shape, and this section has become increasingly popular with hikers. The scenery may have been as strong an attraction to the miners as the ore, and the former is as fine as ever.

Long before the El Tovar Hotel was built and Grand Canyon Village developed on the South Rim, the Grandview Hotel stood near the head of what was the Berry Trail. Renamed the Grandview Trail, it was the easiest way down to the mines on Horsehoe Mesa. Stagecoaches with relays of horses brought tourists from Flagstaff in a single day. With a mule train bringing water from the spring 3,000 feet below, the enterprise was a leader in the tourist business. Eventually, the railroad came through from Williams to what is now Grand Canyon Village, and a whole new era of tourism opened up on the South Rim. With the new train service bringing in droves of tourists, business on the South Rim boomed and people all but stopped visiting Grandview Point. The Grandview and Buggeln Hotels eventually went out of business and were torn down. The mines became unprofitable and the old ore carts were left to the wilderness seekers.

The Grandview Hotel, circa 1905. (Grand Canyon Museum Collection, 12091)

The Trails Illustrated Grand Canyon National Park map shows the Grandview Trail from its beginning on the rim to its end at the Tonto Trail. The only time that one might lose the trail would be in late winter when it is under two feet of snow. There is no water along the route however water can be found in two places below Horseshoe Mesa. A vestige of the original Grandview Trail forks to the south from the present trail near the bottom of the Kaibab Formation. It contours along the east side of Grandview Point going to the rim not far from the old hotel site.

An impressive amount of trail construction is seen in the Coconino where the trail was paved with rock fitted edgewise. Looking down Grapevine Canyon to the northwest, one might think it would be simple to walk right through the Redwall. It is an interesting route, but there is some exposed hand-and-toe climbing in the lower third of the Redwall. Some care is also needed to find the route through the Coconino directly below the trail. Indians and prospectors must have known about this route. An unbroken prehistoric pot was found in a shallow cave below the Redwall rim to the northeast and there is a miner's camp still farther east.

One spring day, I saw what appeared to be a peach orchard in bloom down in Grapevine Canyon. I soon realized that I was looking at the finest grove of redbud trees I have ever seen. A trickle of water in the Tonto section supports a dense stand of wild grapevines. Some have said that the name was given to this canyon because of the tangle of rocks at its mouth. More likely, it comes from the actual vines hanging above the Tonto Trail.

Coming back to the main Grandview Trail, we could look down through a notch at the bottom of the Coconino into the west arm of Hance Canyon. The apparent ease of descent here to the southeast is not deceiving. One can readily go down and cross the valley. It is also possible to find a way through the Redwall on the other side and climb out of the canyon south of the Sinking Ship.

There are a few places where slides have hurt the trail, but most hikers should be able to reach Horseshoe Mesa and the mines in less than three hours with a full pack. The main tunnels were closed off to the public several years ago because of the obvious danger associated with having visitors walk inside potentially unstable mine workings. When they were open, the tunnels extended well beyond the limit of daylight, so lights were needed for their exploration. Just east of these mines is a very steep, loose spur trail which drops down to Page Spring below the Redwall. The trail is easy to miss at first glance and might intimidate those new to canyon hiking. The miners carved a neat basin in the soft shale at the spring which is worth seeing. There is a lot of algae in this pool, but it is the nearest water to the old mine shacks on the mesa. Water can also be found in Cottonwood Creek on the west side of Horseshoe Mesa, but there is a drop of about 1,200 feet of elevation just to get down to the creek. The Grandview Trail continues down to the east and joins the Tonto Trail at the rim of the Tapeats Sandstone.

Directly north of the mine shacks is Horseshoe Mesa Butte, a ridge of red sandstone. When we first climbed it, I had to accept a boost from a tall companion. On top, we found two old cairns.

We returned by a different route at the east end and made an interesting loop trip out of it. The Grandview Trail continues north of the mine area and is clearly shown on the map going west of the butte.

A vague spur track, which can be easily missed, goes west below the Redwall rim to a fine cave, with high ceilings decorated with stalactites. With 1,000 feet of mapped passageways, it is by far the most accessible of all the caves in the park.

The main trail continues north and descends to the Tonto inside the west prong of the horseshoe. One can cross the Tonto Platform near the rim of the inner gorge and go down to the river at the lower end of Sockdolager Rapids.

Instead of going down to the foot of Sockdolager, one can turn east at the base of the Tapeats and go down into Hance Canyon. It is only a steep scramble down to the junction of the side canyon and the Colorado. The beginning of Sockdolager (named by the Powell Expedition after an old boxing term for a "knock-down blow") is at least as impressive as its lower end. Frederick Dellenbaugh, who accompanied Major John Wesley Powell on his second expedition down the Colorado River, described the rapids in his classic book, *A Canyon Voyage*:

"The boats rolled and pitched like a ship in a tornado, as we flew along... then the mighty waves smote us. The boat rose to them well, but we were flying at twenty-five miles an hour and at every leap the breakers rolled over us. 'Bail!' shouted the Major, — 'Bail' for your lives!"

The Old Hance Trail does come down Hance Canyon, yet it is much more difficult than the route described above.

Back on the Tonto, we followed the old trail around into Cottonwood Canyon west of Horseshoe Mesa. Water is sometimes found in the bed near the Tapeats, but if not, there is always water in the west fork of the south arm. Near this spring are signs of a former camp, a wooden floor and some piping. Perhaps, the Grandview Hotel people came here for water. O'Neill Spring, shown on the map south of the trail and up the west side of the mesa cannot be trusted. Neither can the spring on the map in the west arm of Cottonwood.

There are several ways to the river near the mouth of Cottonwood Creek. A ravine on the east side cuts through the Tapeats well north of the Tonto Trail. One can get through the same cliff in the west arm where the Tonto Trail crosses. In either case, follow the base of the bed near the river. There are several impassable falls in the bed higher up. A third route is to stay on the Tonto Trail until it turns east away from the rim of Cottonwood. Here the extension of the Grandview Trail to the river cuts through the Tapeats. One can go east just below the Tapeats and get to the bed of Cottonwood as before. In the bed you can stand at the lip of a sixty-foot waterfall and look down at the river. Backing away a few yards, you can climb over a low wall and walk down a talus slope to the river.

The trail through the Tapeats west of Cottonwood was shown on the old Matthes-Evans East Half Map continuing down to the river away from Cottonwood Canyon. Several of us were convinced that this was an error until I read the map more carefully and made allowances for a section of the trail that had fallen away. The trail became distinct again, and at the bottom I was able to identify the exact locations of photographs and illustrations from the old books.

Following Grapevine Canyon to the river is another project. The springs shown on the map can generally be trusted and there should be more water up Grapevine above the Tonto Trail. One can get down through the Tapeats just west of the springs. Grapevine in the Archean rock is free of barriers until one is near the river. A major fault accounts for the general alignment of Grapevine and Vishnu Canyons but the lowest part of Grapevine veers away to the west. One can, rather precariously, bypass the waterfall on the left. However, at the very end there is a drop of fifteen or twenty feet into the river. Where the bed turns away from the fault, one can climb up and over to the river. When Allyn Cureton and I did this we found something modern.

On the Grandview Trail. (Photo: Andy Zdon)

Under a slight overhang, was a box containing some old clothes and some pop bottles. Near them, on the top of the spur, some newspapers, that were folded and weighted with pebbles, spelled out the word "NO." We guessed that some river adventurers had given up on a river trip here, and that the message was to tell aerial searchers that no help was needed.

Boulder Canyon, west of Grapevine, has been tried more than once as an access route to the river, but even good climbers have been baffled here. If the Lonetree Canyon spring is dry, look for water in the bed below the Tapeats. R.C. Euler, spotted some Indian ruins from a helicopter on the west side of Lonetree where the hanging valley meets the inner gorge. Jim Sears was able to climb down to the river west of the high waterfall. Sears graduated from NAU in geology and received his doctorate from the University of Wyoming. He had a good mantle technique that I was unable to duplicate. Like all of us, he had an intense love of the canyon and was hesitant to divulge information about his favorite hikes to inquiring authors, because he disliked seeing other people's tracks.

If one were to go down the Grandview Trail and along the Tonto to the Kaibab Trail without any detours, two days would be a safe time allowance. However, in very hot weather or if the springs were dry, this route is absolutely dangerous. The experience of the river runner attempting to walk from Hance Rapid to Phantom Ranch via the Tonto Trail in one day was just one ill-fated example. Another near tragic case involved two young men whose hiking had been limited to the mountains and who had absolutely no experience in a desert environment. They each carried a sixty pound pack which included equipment one would use in the Sierra Nevada — even parkas and a camp axe — but they had only a quart of water apiece. They were unable to locate a water source and threw away everything — empty canteens, even expensive cameras. One panicked and insisted on trying to go down Cremation Canyon to the river while the other continued west along the Tonto and finally reached Phantom Ranch.

The desperate man tried to make his way down Cremation. He slid down a chute of granite and was trapped in a deep pool of stagnant water. He was found and pulled out several days later.

In the upper end of the east arm of Cremation, one can climb into the cave where the split twig figurines were found. There is also an easy route through the Redwall to the top of the promontory dividing Grapevine from Cottonwood. The miner's camp is about halfway between the heads of these two routes at the top of the Redwall. Once can climb down to the spring in the wet arm of Cottonwood from the west, but the route isn't a bit obvious. It is easy to see the route through the Redwall on the spur separating the two forks of the south arm. There are also numerous routes through the Redwall along the rim of Horseshoe Mesa.

Not to be confused with the cave that is reached from the trail along the top of Horseshoe Mesa, is a cluster of caves near the bottom of the Redwall north around the corner from the trail down the west side of the neck. A branch of the trail ends at the foot of a scree slope that leads up to the caves.

Marble Canyon Area

River runners know that Marble Canyon is at least as beautiful and impressive as the better known parts of the Grand Canyon, but only a small number of hikers ever visit the area throughout the year. There are only a few trails scattered across the canyon and one must be prepared for rugged, slow walking. There are some routes from the rim to the river, and a few hikers have traversed below the rim from Lee's Ferry to Nankoweap. Kenton Grua spent ten days walking along the left side of the Colorado from Mile 7.8 to President Harding Rapids using caches of food he left on a boat trip from Lee to Pearce Ferry. Others have walked sections along both sides of the river. Ron Mitchell, with different companions on some of the five legs of the trip, has walked all the way from Lee's Ferry to Nankoweap. He also had the honorable distinction of being the first man to have walked from Lee's Ferry to Havasu Creek.

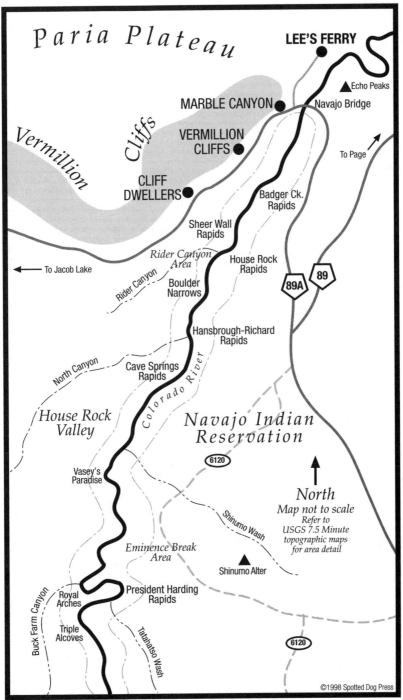

Marble Canyon area – Lee's Ferry to Tatahatso Wash.

Lee's Ferry

There are many fine hikes in this area. The best known and most challenging is through Paria Canyon, about thirty-seven miles one way. One should not attempt it in less than two days and only when flash floods are unlikely. There is plenty of wading so winter is a bad time. Even at Thanksgiving one group had to stop repeatedly to build fires. The snow water and slush ice were more than their feet could stand. The canyon is a spooky one, like the narrows of Zion, but without that much water.

A shorter trip worth taking is up the Spencer Trail just east of Lee's Ferry. If the lower end of the trail is not immediately visible, it can be found up in the talus. There are superb views of the Vermillion Cliffs, the Echo Peaks, and the Colorado River. One can walk east across the plateau to Ferry Swale, an ancient meander of the Colorado River formed eons ago, which is now hundreds of feet above the present bed.

Mileage along the Colorado River is measured both upstream and down from Lee's Ferry. Ferry Swale ends at a sheer cliff above the river at Mile 10.8. At Mile 10, there is a place where a man can get down to the water. Great care in route finding is needed and one should allow extra time for false moves. Upstream from the base of this route, one can find the inscription "F.G. Faatz, Nov. 16, 1892." Higher and to the east, are some very ancient petroglyphs of animals and abstract designs. One could carry an inflatable boat up the Spencer Trail, across the plateau and down to the river at Mile 10, then row back down the river to Lee's Ferry. It is a charming part of the river and it is possible to see swimming beavers on occasion. There is a spring on the left at Mile 8.7. An old road was built along the left side of the river to Mile 3, dating back to the time when a southern California power company was studying a potential dam site in Glen Canyon.

Major John Wesley Powell near Flagstaff, circa 1891.
(Grand Canyon Museum Collection, 17230)

Hikers can get across the river and use this road to visit canyons at Miles 1.5, 2 and 3. All three soon stop the hiker with absolute barrier falls, but they are very scenic. Between the first two canyons is a shallow cave with a number of names cut in the back wall. John Hislop, civil engineer and member of the first Stanton railroad survey party of 1889, carved his name in large letters inside the cave which now bears his name, "Hislop."

Echo Peaks

Across the river, from the boat landing at Lee's Ferry, are the rugged Echo Peaks. When the second Powell party was waiting for supplies in 1871, three of the group climbed the northernmost of the three summits. While on the summit, one of the men shot his revolver into the air which resulted in at least twenty-two echoes. From this incident the peaks received their name. The easiest approach is to cross the river from the paved road or drive off the highway south of Navajo Bridge and walk from the end of a dirt road. The south peak is the highest summit and to climb it, walk up a sand slide and then turn right. In 1965, there was no evidence of a previous ascent. The middle peak can be climbed from the same saddle from the top of the sand slide. To climb the north peak, one must go down the west side, and around to the northeast side of the peak, then climb up a ravine that leads to a chimney blocked by a chockstone. The men from Powell's party helped each other around this obstacle. I got around it by bracing my feet on one wall and pressing my shoulder blades against the other. There were two cairns on top. In one, was a jar with a note describing how Harry Aleson had brought his dog to the top via an easier route on the east side. Aleson, who was one of the Grand Canyon's first true river rats, was the fellow who brought Georgie White to the Colorado River at the end of World War II. Georgie later pioneered commercial float trips, using rubber Army surplus rafts. In the other cairn, was a rusty baking powder can containing some indecipherable writing. Names were written on a postmarked envelope dated 1911. One of the climbers from that party drowned in a ferry accident less than six months later. It was my thought that the baking powder can was left by the Powell party and that the later party of 1911 had removed Powell's original note.

Lee's Ferry to Soap Creek

It is possible to walk within the canyon from the mouth of the Paria to Soap Creek with the exception of about the first two hundred yards. We had to walk along the rim of the rising ramp until we reached a break down to the riverbank. Most of the footing crosses over broken rocks or through the sand between them. Sometimes one must push through thickets of willows and tamarisks. At one place, we had to step very carefully along a narrow ledge where the cliff rises out of the water. There is a side canyon at Mile 2.7 where one can go out to the road. It has some eerie narrows and interesting bypasses for barrier falls. Less than a mile upriver from Navajo Bridge, the cliff comes down into fairly deep water. To bypass this, we had to climb up about thirty feet and get down with meager hand and toeholds. This nearly vertical descent was difficult enough to turn back two of a party of four men. Once under the bridge, we had to follow a bench higher and higher away from the riverbank, but before we reached a side canyon, we walked down a rockslide to the river.

There is a place at Mile 6.2 where we were able to leave the canyon by walking up another rockslide to the high bench and then proceeding south to a hanging valley at Mile 6.5. There were no real barriers between us and the highway. By continuing down along the river, the way was clear to the mouth of Soap Creek. Badger Creek Rapids is a major one, and walking up Badger Canyon is very impressive. One can go about a mile before coming to a dry waterfall that requires a twenty-foot pole or ladder to surmount. Badger Creek has been accessed from the highway by several parties of excellent climbers using ropes to bypass several barrier falls. For years, Soap Creek has been used as an access route to the river. The people at Cliff Dwellers Lodge used to keep a fixed rope at one drop. The north fork leads to a high fall and only an expert climber can get out there. For a quarter of a mile, the south fork is a jumble of great blocks. There are many places where the hands must be used. Where the bed levels off, the route soon goes up a short side canyon from the north. At a quick pace, one can walk from the river up to Cliff Dwellers Lodge in less than two and a half hours. Both Badger and Soap Creek Rapids give boaters a quick initiation to violent water beset with rocks. The wild side canyon and the power of the water make the trip down from the highway most rewarding. Kenton Grua walked the left bank from Badger Creek to President Harding Rapids, and then walked from Badger Creek to Pearce Ferry in thirty-six days, staying on the left side.

The left side of the river below Lee's Ferry is also interesting. There were three places that were used as ferry sites at different times. Only a few vestiges of the road which came along the base of the Echo Peaks are now visible. One can see the cut in the solid rock, the dugway, that comes down to the shore on the left below the Paria Riffle, the rapids below the mouth of the Paria. Walking the immediate riverbank is impossible until one is about half mile upriver from the bridge, where a Navajo sheep trail has been constructed down through a ravine.

The next access is via Jackass Canyon at Mile 7.8 opposite Badger Creek. Coming down to the river here is attractive because of the spooky narrows and overhangs. At one barrier fall, we were thankful that someone had fixed a cable for a handline. Jackass Canyon was easier to walk down than Soap Creek, and Badger Creek Rapids was the most accessible of the Marble Canyon area rapids.

The next route from the left rim was via Salt Water Wash at Mile 11.9. The head of this canyon was hard to distinguish from the ravines leading into Jackass Canyon, but once we were well started, the way was direct and not difficult. There were some cairns and signs of trail construction. Walking on the talus slopes was tricky among the fallen blocks, but we found that it was still easier walking than in Soap Creek. Frank Mason Brown, a member of the

Stanton railroad survey party of 1889 and the promoter who wanted to build a railway through the canyons of the Colorado to Los Angeles, drowned just below the mouth of Salt Water Wash at the head of Soap Creek Rapids. With prospector-trapper Harry McDonald at the oars and Brown as passenger, their boat flipped as it crossed into the fast current from an eddy. Unfortunately, when Brown originally ordered the boats and other supplies for the survey party he forgot to order life jackets. McDonald was able to grab onto a river rock. Meanwhile, the other men watched helplessly as Brown bobbed up and down in a swirling hole, unable to free himself from the churning hydraulics. Peter Hansbrough, who was at the helm of Stanton's boat just behind Brown and McDonald, aimed his craft for the hole upon the fervent direction of McDonald who was gesturing from the rock, but they were too late. Brown was gone, most likely pulled under by the powerful current. For two days the survivors searched the riverbank for any sign of Brown, but retrieved only his personal journal and the boat, which was found floating calmly downstream in a shoreline eddy. During those two days, Peter Hansbrough carved an inscription recording the tragedy on the lefthand wall just a few yards above low water level, facing downriver. Six days later, Hansbrough and Henry Richards, one of two African Americans on the trip, perished when their boat rolled on Mile 25 Rapids. Hansbrough's inscription can be seen today, but must be looked for carefully as it is easily missed.

Soap Creek to Rider Canyon

In 1960, I interrupted a float trip through Marble Canyon to go up the Supai Narrows into the open shale valley of Rider Canyon. At that time, I failed to locate the only known route through the rim cliffs. A year later, Ralph Haynes, a prospector and gas station attendant at Cliff Dwellers Lodge, told me how to get through a crack in the limestone rim.

About eleven miles west of Cliff Dwellers, we followed a dirt road through a gate on the south side of House Rock Wash past Kram Ranch. Not all of the dirt roads are shown on the Emmett Wash 7.5 minute topo map, but one can drive within a mile of the break in the rim, about due west of the "P" in the name "Rider Point" on the map. I knew that some student hikers had walked down Soap Creek Canyon and came out at Rider in two days, so I guessed that Ken Walters and I could do it in one.

I drove to a dry cattle tank about a mile from the crack in the south rim of Rider. My wife, Roma took the car back to Cliff Dwellers where we hoped we would come out that evening. My recollection of the route down to the right was fourteen years old and I was happy to find a cairn at the head of this defile. We scouted a bit to locate the best crawlway under the jam of chockstones. I recognized the nine-inch vertical crack in the wall where fourteen years earlier Allyn Cureton and I had noticed a strong breeze blowing out of a subterranean cavity. To find a safe route down to the bed of the broad valley, we had to look around a bit. It must have taken more than an hour to go from the car to the bed of Rider.

Coming to where the bed drops steeply into the Supai Narrows, I elected to stay on the Supai rim while my friend, Ken Walters, decided to go down into the bedrock slot with the idea that he could climb out to the Supai rim farther on. My route was rather slow but continuous, while Ken had to backtrack and follow me. I thought that we would average a mile an hour, judging by what I had done on the other side of Salt Water Wash to Hot Na Na. We walked these six miles in three hours and forty minutes.

A river runner once told me that a boat could be left on the river, and one could find a trail up the Supai rim on the left near the mouth of Tanner Wash. From our vantage point, there appeared to be a possible descent on the east side of Tanner to a ramp that sloped toward the water upstream. Unfortunately, at the end of this bench there still seemed to be a ten-foot drop to the river, so I soon discarded the idea. On the right bank, one can reach the water about a mile below the mouth of Soap Creek. My optimistic prediction concerning our speed proved to be correct. We reached Cliff Dwellers at 4:20pm, just an hour before a big thunderstorm.

I had been from Rider Canyon to South Canyon and from Saddle Canyon to Nankoweap. Ron Mitchell and Dana Gable, a student at NAU, later gave me helpful information about this area. Ron had found a break in the rim of the nameless canyon downriver from South Canyon. It could be called "Mile 36.8 Canyon" from the location of its end at the river. Dana Gable had spotted a break in the rim at the head of Buck Farm Canyon. When Ron Mitchell and Dale Graham went off the rim at this break, I accompanied them down to the Supai. Near the top of the Coconino was a spot where the Ancestral Puebloans had piled rocks for a step. Mitchell and Graham tried going down through the Supai on the north side of the wash, but had to give up more than halfway down.

More recently, Bob Dye discovered that the first tributary on the south side goes through to the Redwall. Mitchell and Graham started on their four-day trip along the top of the Supai, while I took a day hike under Buck Farm Point. From where I turned back, I could see a scree-filled ravine that might be a possible route down to the Redwall.

Next, I went down Mile 36.8 Canyon with Jorgen Visbak and Ed Herrman, a climber from Las Vegas, to see the Bridge of Sighs. From the map we saw that we could park at the best approach to the rim break on the south side near the head of the canyon.

My guess was correct — that we would be able to get to the Redwall after walking the Supai rim for a mile to the east along the north side. A little way into the Redwall were neat overhangs that could be used for a night's shelter, and accessible in the slot below a permanent rain pool. Leaving our packs at this point, we went upriver along the Redwall rim to see the Bridge of Sighs. If we had gone down a steep slope into a bay we could have seen it, but Ed and I contoured while Jorgen went out to a point on the south side of the bay. When Ed and I had overshot the bridge by a half mile, we turned back at some fantastic curving tunnels through the Redwall rim. Although we had missed seeing the bridge, we noticed a possible route through the Redwall to the river across from the bridge.

With water and a good campsite in Mile 36.8 Canyon, I was ready for a two-day trek from Buck Farm Canyon to South Canyon with Jim Ohlman. Letting him out of the car at the head of South Canyon, I parked with the intention of going down Buck Farm Canyon. Below the Coconino I went to the south and made it through the Supai by the route that Bob Dye had found. Going upriver along the Redwall rim, I reached the campsite about a half hour before Ohlman arrived from the head of South Canyon. He had done more than half the trip the first day.

On the second day, he followed my route, over and out of Buck Farm Canyon and then brought the car to the head of South Canyon to hail me as I arrived at the rim around four in the afternoon. There are numerous things of interest along this route — the seep spring at the base of the Coconino in the bed of Buck Farm Canyon; a curving tunnel; and a jug handle arch near the rim of the Redwall north of Buck Farm Canyon. Trash left by a surveying party was found on the west side near Redwall Cavern and at the tram anchorage across the canyon.

I had a good view of a river party that stopped at Redwall Cavern. I was also careful not to miss seeing the Bridge of Sighs, but decided it would take a long rappel to reach the foot of the bridge. R.C. Euler had inspected a prehistoric ruin on the right bank south of the Bridge of Sighs while his helicopter pilot hovered with one skid resting on the outside edge of the shelf. Trying to go down a ravine south of the one for the bridge, I had to give up about one hundred and fifty feet above the river. The Ancestral Puebloan must have reached their dwelling from across the river.

Rider Canyon Area

It's slow going, but it is possible to walk along the top of the Supai on both sides of the river below Salt Water Wash. Here, the Supai starts forming a cliff into the river and the next place to get through the Supai to the river is at Rider Canyon on the right and at Mile 21.8 on the left. Allow about two and a half hours at a quick pace, for the 2.5 miles from Salt Water Wash to Tanner Wash. There are some good seep springs in the bed of Tanner through the Hermit Shale and in the freezing weather, the icicles are fantastic. The way out of the lower valley up through the Coconino is to the west and the easy way to do this requires some scouting. Above this steep climb, one contours along the base of the Kaibab into the bed of upper Tanner and from there the walking is easy to the highway at Bitter Springs.

Another loop goes down Tanner, along the rim of the Supai to Hot Na Na Wash, and then back up to the plateau. The river cuts an impressive trench between the Supai walls. The footing is rough and slow and the way up through the Coconino in Hot Na Na is hard enough to be interesting. When one is north of the narrow upper canyon, a cave at the base of the cliff on the east side is visible. It is most noteworthy for a large pile of owl guano about ten feet long by two feet wide and over five feet high. A shelf above the entrance has been the perch for many generations of owls. The floor around this pile is littered with bones of rodents. Down Salt Water Wash and up Tanner or down Tanner and up Hot Na Na are both good, long one-day hikes.

Following the Supai rim along the right bank from Soap to Rider may be slower still than the walking along the left, but several hikers have done it. It is possible to walk down the bed of Rider Canyon through the Supai to the river and one can also climb out of the upper open valley of Rider to the plateau through a break in the Kaibab. A fault has split a big block away from the main wall and it is necessary to crawl under a huge chockstone. This is the canyon where Franklin A. Nims, the photographer for the Stanton party, was carried out after he suffered a near fatal fall. Stanton and several of his men found that they could go from the river up through a narrow canyon to the open valley. There is an impassable fall at the upper end, but they found a cleft in the south rim. One has to use a crawlway under some chockstones to get out on top.

While other members of the party returned to the river, Stanton walked all night to reach Lee's Ferry to find help for Nims. Stanton returned with Warren Johnson of Lee's Ferry and Johnson's young son, in a wagon which they drove thirty-one miles to the south rim of Rider. In the meantime, the day after they found the route, the men lashed Nims to a stretcher and, using ropes at certain places, got him up to the rim. They got to the top in the afternoon, but waited through a snowy night for Stanton and Johnson. The semiconscious Nims had blankets, but the others shivered around little sagebrush fires that night. Johnson took Nims back to Lee's Ferry where he drifted in and out of consciousness for a week. A small group of Mormons happened through and were able to transport Nims to Winslow, Arizona where a doctor attended to his injuries.

Downriver from Rider

One can walk the right bank downriver from Rider. At Mile 18.5 is Boulder Narrows, so named from the great rock lying in the middle of the current. A huge driftwood log on top shows how high the water used to get at flood stage before the dam was built. At Mile 19 you can climb on through a ravine that cuts the Supai. Then you angle to the west and south to get through the Coconino. And a little farther south you can climb through the Kaibab to the rim. A fossil footprint in the Coconino on this route is as big as a man's palm and clawmarks were also preserved in the rock. This route from the rim to the river is a bit easier than the way through Rider Canyon.

If you try to follow the riverbank down to North Canyon, you have to go along a ledge that rises away from the bank. According to Ron Mitchell, you can get into the bed of lower North Canyon, then get back down to river level. One can also contour along the Supai rim from Mile 19 to North Canyon and get down through the Supai to the river about 2.5 miles beyond North Canyon. One can get down the bed of North Canyon to the Supai, but there are impassable falls in the upper part of the latter formation. Some of the footing along the top of the Supai downriver from the bed of North Canyon is precarious, across steep bare gullies in the shale. I have toyed with the idea of using an ice axe to cut footholds in such places, but they can be crossed if one is careful. Progress along the riverbank is sometimes slow, but it is safer than the Hermit Shale. It took most of a day to go from the water pockets in the Supai of North Canyon to our campsite at Mile 25.5 next to Cave Springs Rapids.

The caves here have sandy floors and are pleasant in cold weather, but remember that the river level can change at night. I once went to sleep with the river ten feet below the mouth of the cave and woke up at midnight with the water only five feet beneath where I was sleeping. I moved to a terrace fifteen feet higher for the rest of the night. The generators at Glen Canyon are used according to the need for "peaking power" and there is a pattern of rising and falling water all the way to Lake Mead. In one of the caves at Cave Springs Rapid, a 1923 survey party found some tools and traps. Some of this jetsam is still there.

Walking speed improves along the top of the Redwall when it begins to show about Mile 23.3. It forms a cliff above the river and from Cave Springs south you can get down to the water only at Mile 26.7 opposite Tiger Wash. At Mile 30.4, one has to go down and up to cross a fault ravine. Going to the river here is easy and a trail comes down to the water across the river. The current, however, makes crossing difficult. Good climbers have gone up through the Supai on the west via two different ravines. There is a bad chockstone to pass in the main ravine, but Jensen, the rancher who owned the ranch in Rider Canyon, said that another ravine to the south of this is easier. Above these Supai breaks, one can go south to a Coconino route and then to the right to a final ravine through the Kaibab. A pot sherd and an old time can along here prove that this route was once used by Indians as well as by prospectors.

An easier way out of the canyon is to follow the Redwall rim into South Canyon. Shortly before you reach this canyon, you can get down through the Redwall to the attractions at Vasey's Paradise. This is where Stanton led his party out, on his first expedition in 1889, following the drowning of three men. After passing the junction of South Canyon and Bedrock Canyon, they scrambled up the north side of South Canyon. One can also walk to the end of South Canyon and get out, but the most direct route goes into Bedrock and then up the fault ravine to the northeast. On the Esplanade, one can walk east around the promontory and up to the rim, or go clear around to the route at the top of Mile 30.4, as described above. A more challenging way is to continue up the fault ravine directly above Bedrock Canyon. This way is also the shortest.

One of the many luckless victims of the Canyon discovered by a USGS party.
(Photo: Emery Kolb, Grand Canyon Museum Collection, 17198)

The most interesting attractions of all Marble Canyon are near the mouth of South Canyon. Just upriver from the mouth on a terrace are some prehistoric ruins and higher, at the end of a well-traveled path, is a headless skeleton. This was found in 1934 by the Swain-Hatch party, but no one knows whether the bones are those of an Indian or a luckless prospector. Getting up the bed of South Canyon through mud, water, and two chockstones is a challenge for the best climbers. From South Canyon, a trail leads downriver and up to Stanton Cave which is quite a large opening, about one hundred and twenty feet above the river. It goes in about forty yards, well past the reach of daylight, and is interesting enough to have attracted cave enthusiasts who have mapped it. It is known for the profusion of split twig figurines that have been found there, more than the combined total from all other sites. These effigies of game animals, probably sheep or deer, were made by splitting a willow wand and bending the two parts to form the legs and body of an animal. According to the Carbon-14 dating method, they are from 3,000 to 4,000 years old. These artifacts, probably charms to insure success in hunting, are the only evidence to show that the Grand Canyon was inhabited so long ago. Archaeologist R.C. Euler has conducted excavations of the floor. George Beck, who had received $20,000 of helicopter time as a gift from a wealthy aunt, would fly around the canyon with Euler in a piloted chopper. Together, they found bones that were identified as coming from extinct animals and birds, namely a kind of goat and a condor. Euler had some of the driftwood dated. The results of the dating indicated that the river had flooded the cave, one hundred and thirty feet higher than its present level, some 40,000 or more years ago.

John Wesley Powell gave the name "Vasey's Paradise" to the area. What arrested his attention was the spring that gushes out of the wall. He was charmed by the greenery that contrasts so sharply with the miles and miles of red walls everywhere else. The serpent of this paradise is poison ivy which constitutes most of the rich, green growth. Cavers have had many days of adventure while climbing and mapping the cave system connected to this spring. Only an expert can climb into the dry hole beside the spring which leads to 12,000 feet of passageways — a spelunker's paradise. When they are farthest in, the map shows that they have more solid rock overhead than they would in any other American cave. A little more than a mile downstream is Redwall Cavern. Hikers have walked the right bank far enough to look across the river at this huge overhang where Powell once said that fifty thousand people could be seated. His exaggeration factor was only about ten.

Left Bank Below Mile 21.7

The Navajo Reservation side of Marble Canyon has many points of interest. Based on observations he made from the air, P.T. Reilly suggested the possibility of getting through the upper cliffs near the nameless wash at Mile 21.7. He also called attention to a deep cave near the north rim of this canyon. Legend has it, that following a skirmish with a group of Navajos, a small band of Hopis retreated to the edge of the canyon where they entered a cave that led 2,000 feet down to the riverbank. They then escaped across the river. According to another version of the rumor, they were able to follow the cave into a dry tube clear under the river. Reilly thought that this cave might be the basis for the legend, so he named it "Refuge Cave." Expert cavers have now mapped this cave completely. Formed by faulting rather than by solution, it goes down through the Coconino and is the deepest cave in Arizona. Donald Davis was the first to follow Reilly's lead, and found the names Herb McLaughlin and Art Greene inscribed inside the cave with the date 1946. They had been brought here by a Navajo. Far below the daylight, Davis found arrow shafts, residue from torches and other artifacts. When he was conducting two archaeologists through the cave, he spotted three unbroken pots. The air seemed fresh at the bottom, but he could not find a way for a man to escape from below. Cavers from Phoenix have since been back and explored the cave, mapping it in great detail. However, at least one of their party was nearly killed by rockfall inside the cave and reported that constant rockfall was indeed a problem. Perhaps the Navajos pursued the Hopis to the vicinity of the cave and then didn't notice that they escaped down the bed of the canyon possibly through a steep, narrow slot distinguished by one very precarious move.

At the time of this writing, there was trail construction going on and some directional barriers had been put into place to help Navajo sheep reach a waterhole. The narrow canyon opens out on Marble Canyon at the top of a sixty-foot waterfall down the Coconino. One can go left along a narrow ledge to a place where the sandstone is broken. After some careful study, we found a ropeless route to the talus below. The Supai is impossible in the main canyon, but the next ravine to the south looks promising. Lower down, this is also impossible, but there is a way to get down at the end of the north wall of this minor ravine. This route, thanks to Alan Doty needs no rope, but is a challenge to follow. There were signs of former use, perhaps by the Hopi during their escape. If one prefers a less sporty route, it is possible to go south along the Supai rim to Mile 23.3.

One can follow the riverbank along the left side for miles, both up and down. There is evidence of beavers. Once, I saw a mother and her kit dive when I was within fifteen feet of them, and watched them swim for thirty feet or so in the clear water. About a mile upriver from Cave Springs on the left bank, is a limestone platform. Stanton called this isolated little butte the "Marble Pier" and he suggested using it as a bridge support for the railroad. Opposite Cave Springs, the Redwall starts to form a consistent cliff which makes the river inaccessible. The only sources of water during the winter months are infrequent rain pools, unreliable in summer, which can be used in a pinch until the river is reached at Mile 30.4. There was a rain pocket in Tiger Wash at Mile 26.7.

Compared to most of Marble Canyon, the Redwall rim from Mile 25.5 to Shinumo Wash is relatively easy walking. A constructed trail, in bad repair, comes down from the rim. Its head is on the left rim of Shinumo Wash about one and a half miles back from the angle of the plateau above the mouth of the wash. There is a cairn at the trailhead. We followed a shallow depression north to the big jump where the trail goes off the rim. The trail was improved years ago so that the Bureau of Reclamation could get horses to the river. After it reaches the bed of Shinumo Wash it becomes obscure. One can go down the bed to the Redwall, but the old trail seems to stay on the left slope. Downriver the trail is still quite clear. A spur goes to the river at Mile 30.4 while the main trail goes on several miles. There is a good view across to Stanton's Cave and Vasey's Paradise. Hikers have reported the presence of an old shack. The climb is rough down the Redwall to the river where the trail ends. At least one hiker, Jan Jensen from Sedona, has continued along the Redwall rim all the way to the route off the rim, to President Harding Rapids at Eminence Break. There is no water along the route making it very dangerous to attempt. Only when the rain pockets are full of recent rain water should it even be considered, and then only by fast, experienced canyon hikers. Jensen could also have gone up to the top through Tatahatso Canyon. A crack behind a Toroweap block makes the route possible. A loop trip down Tatahatso Canyon along the Redwall rim and up the Eminence Break route would probably require two days.

Eminence Break Area

All of Marble Canyon is interesting and beautiful, but the area around President Harding Rapids is particularly appealing. The name of this rapid comes from the following incident. When the 1923 USGS survey party heard about President Harding's death, they rested here during the official day of mourning, then named the rapid to honor the postwar president.

Upriver from President Harding Rapids at Mile 40, the Arizona Power Authority maintained a trailer camp on Buck Farm Point. For several months, men went down to the river to test the rock for a dam, commuting to work each day by helicopter. Previously, the Bureau of Reclamation had worked at two dam-sites following the construction of aerial tramways, one of which came down from the rim of Tatahatso Point on the opposite side of the canyon. Thirty years later, pilot Lynn Roberts, was taking men down to the river every day. He was also flying R.C. Euler around to do salvage archaeology both at sites which might be submerged and or vandalized when and if the dam were built. During the course of these flights, a young surveyor named Gordon Denipah, noticed a particular platform or bridge of poles in a niche high above the river at the base of the Redwall on the right at Mile 43.3. This structure had received some publicity in the Flagstaff paper and I asked Lynn Roberts about it. He said, "Any friend of Bob Euler's is a friend of mine. The motor is warm. Get in and I'll give you a ride."

If you have been in a chopper that lifts a foot or so and then swings forward and you suddenly see the ground a thousand feet below, you experience a thrill you don't get on a fixed wing flight. Lynn dropped rapidly and flew past the platform of poles and then followed the river right over the rock that splits President Harding Rapids. He then began climbing and we looped up

Ruins near Vasey's Paradise, above Eminence Break.
(Photo: Michael Quinn, Grand Canyon Museum Collection, 9569)

through Saddle Canyon where I had been unable to get through the Coconino and where I also tried to find a prehistoric ruin. We didn't find it from the air either, but he took me over the buffalo herd that belongs to the state. We were so low that the herd stampeded down a slope and up the other side, a sight I had only imagined happening in the old Wild West.

On this flight I had seen where the fault called Eminence Break comes to the rim on the south side of Tatahatso Point. It looked like a real possibility for going down from the rim to the river. Soon thereafter, I was trying to find Tatahatso Point by car. After numerous wrong turns, I finally came to the road that leads down the steep grade and out to the old tram site. The road is now so eroded and rocky that only a truck or jeep should be taken down the grade.

There are three fissures in the rim that from above, look like possible routes. The one that goes clear through is now marked with a cairn. In the Kaibab, there is some hand and toe climbing and one needs to watch for rolling rocks for much of the way. About one hundred and fifty feet down from the rim, a thirty-foot tower of rock toppled over and jammed into both walls without breaking, making it possible to walk beneath "Fallen Tower Bridge."

Near the top of this route, I picked up a piece of ordinary pottery that dated back to the main occupation of the canyon, 1,050 A.D. to 1,200 A.D. Lower down, I spotted a fresh looking sherd with yellow glaze and black decorations. Euler called it Jeddito Black on Yellow and was most interested in its appearance here. It confirmed that this route was used between 1,450 and 1,600 A.D. Another feature of this route dates back to the Permian age, over 230 million years ago. These are some of the most distinct fossil footprints that have been found in the entire Marble/Grand Canyon area. They are on the east side of a big block of Coconino Sandstone that has rolled down the slope. There are several types on the biggest block and on neighboring blocks. The largest are bigger than any I have seen in the old park area. They are the size of a man's open hand and are clear enough to make good casts.

The best route seems to be down the bed of the wash in the top part of the Supai and then to the south along a shelf where a cairn has been placed. Beyond a ravine or two a broken slope leads down to the Redwall in the bed. At the junction with another fork, we climbed a minor ravine to the south and continued to where a broken slope takes a recognizable trail down to the river below President Harding Rapids.

Shinumo Wash
to Tatahatso Canyon

Earlier, I described how I had been down the Shinumo Wash Trail to the river at Mile 29. On that trip, I had followed the trail as far as a point across from Vasey's Paradise. Other hikers have since been to the end of this trail at the lower end of the former tram on the Redwall rim near Redwall Cavern. Jan Jensen hiked on along the Redwall rim and reached the river at President Harding Rapids. He had the idea that one should be able to come down Tatahatso Canyon to the Redwall. After some study, I found a break on the south side of a semicircular wall near the top. Below the Toroweap Formation, one could go along a bench to the left and reach a scree-filled ravine where the Eminence Break Fault fractures the Coconino.

Getting through the Supai is just a lot of scrambling over and around boulders. Some rain pools, many redbud trees, and spectacular towers to the north make this an attractive route. At the Redwall rim, I turned north to check out a possible route to the river opposite the Bridge of Sighs. A fantastic feature, was perhaps, the most impressive fresh-looking rockfall in the entire Grand Canyon. The scar on the cliff was huge and what had been a valley was now bulging with yellow rock fragments clear to the river's edge.

I was uncertain as to where to start down to the river. On a false start, I got a good view down 36 Mile Rapids, and came to a minor ravine that had been formed along a fault. An excellent view of the Bridge of Sighs soon confirmed my decision to descend. Surprisingly, a prehistoric ruin on a shelf about thirty-feet above the river has been above all the floods of the past 800 years. I missed the ruin that Euler had found on the opposite side of the river south of the Bridge of Sighs. The site really intrigued me, so I returned with a small inflatable boat. Looking at the rough water of 36 Mile Rapids, I soon gave up the idea of floating down the river to visit Buck Farm Canyon.

I found that one could walk a shelf near the water about halfway upstream to the mouth of Nautiloid Canyon and see the fossils in the rock by using a boat in the eddy. Bob Packard and Ken Walters had carried an eighteen-pound inflatable down here, with the intention of going downriver to climb out the Eminence Break Route from President Harding Rapids.

Now that I knew where to camp on a two-day trip down Shinumo Wash and up Tatahatso, I was eager to complete the traverse. Jim Ohlman was delighted to accompany me. By now, travel along the trail down Shinumo Wash and then along the Redwall rim to the base of the tram had become routine. In the bed near the Redwall, I watched for something that I had noticed on my first trip.

A jet of air had been coming out of a hole in the gravel that was little bigger than a pencil. It was a blowhole connecting an underground cavern with the surface. Gravel and sand must have since plugged the orifice. At Mile 30.4, the Redwall is broken, and a spur trail connects with the river. The way to the water on the other side is also easy, though the current was so swift here that a crossing seemed hazardous. If one were to be swept away at the immediate landing, one might be able to get out to the right bank a little above the mouth of South Canyon. If one should try and fail in crossing from west to east, it would be better to float down to the prehistoric ruin opposite the Bridge of Sighs before leaving the river. Several imposing towers are located in this area.

Saddle Canyon
to Buck Farm Canyon

With this gap filled in, I would have completed in total, the route from Lee's Ferry to Nankoweap. Following my nearly fatal accident involving jumar ascenders in Saddle Canyon which I recount in the route description for Buck Farm Canyon to Nankoweap, I walked all night to get to Nankoweap and on around to Saddle Mountain. I knew how to leave the rim via the Boundary Ridge Route directly east of Saddle Mountain, but the walk from there to Buck Farm Canyon would require two days and would definitely overlap my long night's walk. The trip started with a long rappel in the lower Coconino of Saddle Canyon. My wife, Roma, and our friends, the Roths, came to see me off on the day hike from Saddle Canyon to Buck Farm Canyon.

We all walked together from the car at the end of House Rock Valley Road to the rim above lower Saddle Canyon. Eldon Roth came along down the deer trail to the bed above the Coconino. Part of this route was along a horizontal ledge where previously I had spent a very wet night beneath an overhang. I had been there looking for a way to reach a ruin and a mescal pit that R.C. Euler had seen from a helicopter in lower Saddle Canyon. Years later, Bob Packard found the ruin by going farther east along the ledge. On my first visit I located the eighty-five foot rappel site where I had the accident using jumars. Now with Eldon's help, I used a rappel for a convenient way to start the walk over and out of Buck Farm Canyon.

After I was down, Eldon carried the rappel rope back to the car and drove around to the head of Buck Farm Canyon where I planned to come out in the late afternoon. The walk along the top of the Supai was uneventful, but the scenery was beautiful. In the distance, I saw a window through the rim of the south side of lower Saddle Canyon. Water was still flowing from the tributary on the south side in the upper Supai, but I missed the mescal pit and the granary that had been discovered from the air. After a rough scramble through the Kaibab break at the head of Buck Farm Canyon, I reached the car on the Buck Farm Point Road.

Ron Mitchell, who pioneered the routes in this section of Marble Canyon, was skeptical about finding water and would try to carry enough for two or three days of dry camping. He and Dale Graham also cached several gallons in plastic jugs along the proposed route. In the cool of the year, the water situation is not too bad. There are often rain pools in the Redwall section of South Canyon and one could reach the river at Vasey's Paradise. There is a rain pool in a Redwall slot of Mile 36.8 Canyon and a seep in the bed of Buck Farm Canyon at the base of the Coconino. In Saddle Canyon there is a reliable spring in the southside tributary near the "Y" of the same canyon on the Nankoweap 7.5 minute topo.

There is the route to the river at Mile 49.9 that I have called the "Boundary Ridge Route." I failed to find a way through the Redwall from lower Little Nankoweap Canyon, but Bob Dye, desperate for water on a past trip, found a way through the Redwall between two arms of Little Nankoweap. Packard, Walters, Ohlman and perhaps others, have followed Dye's lead here. Packard said not to try it without a rope. Ohlman has been up from the river through the Redwall of Little Nankoweap by more than one route. These difficult routes are not to be confused with the simple deer trail from the top of Redwall into the upper valley of Little Nankoweap.

The old Matthes-Evans map misled me into thinking that I could walk up Little Nankoweap as easily as I could get through the narrows of Nankoweap Canyon. Trying this route from the river to the Nankoweap Trail on Tilted Mesa, I first checked out the north fork. After giving up here, I climbed a thirty-foot fall in the main bed. Ahead, around a curve was the end, an eighty-foot perfectly smooth wall. An inch-thick hemp rope was partially buried in the gravel at the foot of the fall. Strangely, I later learned who had abandoned this rope — a party of three from Las Vegas who had indeed run out of water and nearly died while trying to get down Little Nankoweap in search of a water source.

Along the River
to Buck Farm Canyon

As previously mentioned, I had seen lower Saddle Canyon at Billingsley's suggestion, and now wanted to do the same for Buck Farm Canyon. Rather than ride on my little inflatable through the rough water of Thirtysix Mile Rapids, I decided to go down to President Harding Rapids and cross on the quiet section of river above. I still had a little trouble finding the right road to the Black Spot Reservoir, but I was able to drive across the dry bed. From there I had no difficulty in getting to the parking above the grade and down to the beginning of the Eminence Break route.

The Fallen Tower Bridge and fossil footprints in the Coconino are among the many interesting sights along the trail. Starting down into the Supai, I noticed some more footprints which I had missed on previous trips. That night, I slept on the bank above the rapids near a river party with whom I had a pleasant visit. In the morning, I walked upriver along the left bank past the place where a school teacher from Iowa had found the unbroken pots cached near a prehistoric ruin, and on beyond the bridge of poles high in a niche across the river. It was easy to cross the river in the quiet water, and walking was much easier along the right bank. There was a good deer trail and I followed a buck for about ten minutes. The deer must swim the river and range through Marble Canyon clear down to Nankoweap. Near a bend in the river, I passed a big alcove called Royal Arches where swallows build their mud nests on the ceiling.

There is an impressive short canyon at Mile 41.3, with a trail leading into it. River parties stop to take showers under a convenient spring, and there are two picnic tables nearby. One is topped with planking from a wrecked boat. I had seen Bert Loper's boat, the one he was paddling when he died, on an earlier float trip through Marble Canyon, but now a river company boatman had to tell me where to look — about fifty yards upriver from the mouth of the canyon behind a dense growth of willows and tamarisks. The springs, ferns, and columbine make this little canyon a real attraction.

Buck Farm Canyon also met my expectations. There was a little rain water in pools, but no springs. I used obvious bypasses to get around some chockstones. Some delicate climbing was needed to get past a difficult narrows. A shelf high above the bed on the south side was the only way I could find to get around it. Where the canyon forks in the lower Redwall, I was finally stopped. There was a steel spike in the rock only twenty feet above in the north branch. Several good climbers have said that there might be a way to get up Buck Farm Canyon, and Ken Walters had made a serious attempt to come down from above. He found other spikes in the rock and even a wooden ladder. My guess is that some of the men who worked for months below Buck Farm Point testing the rock for a proposed dam may have rigged a way to get down through Buck Farm Canyon using ropes and ladders.

The second main objective of this trip was to get color slides of the Bridge of Poles. I paddled my inflatable downriver a ways, until I was offered a ride the rest of the way by a passing river party. They dropped me off at the vicinity of the 1,100 year old pole structure. There was a pathway in the clay leading up to it, but I found the crux move of the climb to be a real struggle for a man of sixty-nine. Hundreds of years of winds had shifted the flooring of light poles. After several attempts, Kenton Grua and Ellen Tibbetts succeeded in crossing here using a rope, which I thought was pretty courageous.

Buck Farm Canyon to Nankoweap

Walking the Redwall rim on the right bank from South Canyon to Buck Farm must be a fascinating trip, but its length and roughness make it a real challenge. Those who attempt it should choose a cool time of year shortly after a storm. Then, the water pockets would be full. Ron Mitchell, who went along the Supai rim, was used to carrying enough water to last for two or more days. He would hike ahead and bury plastic jugs of water at strategic places. Even today, there are signs that the Ancestral Puebloan used the area. When Euler was observing the region from a helicopter, he spotted a storage bin at the base of a Supai cliff facing south toward the river at Mile 45.4. He also saw a mescal pit on top of the Supai south of the main bed of Saddle Canyon and just west of a tributary.

After a college hiking club trek to Vasey's Paradise, a student hiker named Dan Gable was out on Buck Farm Point admiring the view. He noticed that there might be a way off the rim at the head of Buck Farm Canyon. Ron Mitchell and Dale Graham, a friend of Mitchell's, came back with him to try the descent. They rappelled a short distance to get off the rim and then found a ropeless walk through the Coconino. In the main bed at the top of the Supai they found a seep spring,which was still running when I went back with them in early May. After burying several gallons of water, they were able to find a way out without using a rope.

In May of 1974, I helped Mitchell and Graham with a car shuttle at the start of their four-day trip down to the Supai in Buck Farm Canyon and then around into Nankoweap. Ron left his car at the old hunting camp north of Saddle Mountain and we used my car to reach the rim of Buck Farm Canyon. After passing the former rappel site, we found a ropeless way down. Ron

commented that this way was different from his previous route
and was much easier. The route through the Coconino south of
here, was easy to find. I noticed a rock pile that seemed to have
been built by the Ancestral Puebloan to assist one at a four-foot
drop. The three of us went along the Supai rim northeast from the
seep spring to the Mitchell-Graham water cache. After an unsuccessful attempt to get down through the Supai nearby, Mitchell
and Graham started along the Supai rim toward Nankoweap.

Contouring around the top of the Supai under Buck Farm
Point, I attempted to locate a way down to the Redwall. In the
bay just north of the point, a slide covered all of the Supai. If one
were coming along the Redwall rim from South Canyon and
wanted to go out Buck Farm Canyon, he should come up here.

Four and a half years before Mitchell and Graham started at
Buck Farm Canyon and walked around Saddle Mountain, I had
done the same thing, starting at Saddle Canyon. My long walk
was not planned. Ever since Euler had seen the mescal pit and
the granary, I thought that there might be a more direct approach
than the distant route via South Canyon and Little Nankoweap.
Twice, I had come down into Saddle Canyon looking for prehistoric ruins and a way through the Coconino. To the southeast of
the fall, an ancient landslide had covered the Coconino cliff, but
floods had cut the clay and rubble into a vertical wall. It could be
used to go down about half the Coconino, but there would still be
an eighty-foot rappel. On the first visit, I didn't have a rope and
on the second, a young companion talked me out of the rappel.
Alone now, on the third visit, I would rappel with no one along
to object.

On the east side of the slide, bare rock formed a sheer drop
with trees to tie in to. The one hundred and twenty foot goldline
rope would reach with plenty to spare. I got my diaper sling in
place and started down. After the first twenty-five feet, I found
myself well away from the wall with rope turning me around
faster and faster. I shut my eyes and continued sliding the rope
through the carabiner. I was almost sick when I reached the bottom.

Harvey making an ascent using jumars.
(Photo: Joseph G. Hall)

I had left the car at 7:15am and was able to walk down the bed of Saddle Canyon and have lunch on the north side above the river on the Redwall rim.

I was back to the rappel by 2:30, expecting to jumar up the rope and get home that night. As soon as I got off the ground, the rope began to twist me around. Thinking that I could work the jumar clamps faster, I untied the waist band that holds the sling against the body. I was only a few yards up, when the inevitable happened. My feet flipped out and came up level with my head. I clung to the clamps as long as I could and then fell backwards. No one knew where I was and the jumar slings were fastened firmly around my feet. Except for several fortunate coincidences, I would have hung there until I froze. If I had been a foot lower, I would have bashed my head against a rock. If I had been a foot higher, I couldn't have touched the ground with my fingers. If the ground had been level where I hung, I couldn't have helped myself. As it was, I could claw my way up the steep bank until there was some slack in the rope. A stout shrub allowed me to hold myself with my left arm while I could just reach up and loosen my shoelaces with my right hand. After forty-five minutes of false moves and struggle, I was free to put on my shoes and leave. The shortest way I knew back to the car was down to the Redwall rim, downriver to Little Nankoweap, and clear around Saddle Mountain by the Nankoweap Trail.

My situation was still uncertain. I had no jacket to wear over my flannel shirt and I could feel the chill of the night air through my clothes. Fortunately, the evening was devoid of wind and I kept warm as long as I kept walking. I had only a little food left from my lunch, but I did find a spring where I could fill my canteen. This water, coming from the south down through the Supai, can be counted on during cool or wet times, since Mitchell and Graham reported finding it flowing well into May. I reached the Redwall to the south of Saddle Canyon about dark and walked the rim downriver as well as one can by starlight.

It was about ten o'clock and I was making slow but steady

progress. Unfortunately, hiking in the dark has its drawbacks. I missed seeing something that Mitchell and Graham saw on their four-day trek — a possible way to the rim north of the old park boundary. In the darkness, I also passed the route down to the river at Mile 49.9. When I finally entered Little Nankoweap Valley along the rim of the Redwall, I could tell that there might be a way down through the Redwall to the bed. If I could get to the valley floor I knew I could proceed up to the Nankoweap Trail on top of Tilted Mesa. Actually, a year and a half later, I discovered a simple deer trail connecting the bed of Little Nankoweap with the Redwall where I was walking that night in December. Instead of chancing a dead end detour near midnight, I continued along the Redwall rim around the north arm of Little Nankoweap. It was rough and slow, but I finally reached the trail at sunrise. I had been without water for hours when I came to a supply cached near Marion Point. With this I could eat the last of my food. I finally reached my car by 2:45pm, exhausted but glad to be alive.

The route I missed in the dark was just east of a gate at the lower end of the open valley of Little Nankoweap. Down the canyon east of here, the bed drops over impossible falls. There is no water in the upper section of Little Nankoweap, but there is a strange rumor about an Indian ruin near the upper end of the valley. It is supposed to hide a boat made of reeds.

Mitchell's tip about a possible descent from the ruin east of Saddle Mountain inspired my curiosity to see if there could be a direct route down to the Redwall break at Mile 49.9. One August day, I walked from the hunting camp via the Saddle Mountain Trail across the ravine, then east along the north slope of Saddle Mountain. When the trail gave out, I went up on Boundary Ridge to get the view. About noon, I was on the promontory where the old park boundary went down to the river. On the north side of the neck to this headland, I spotted a break in the Kaibab rim that looked promising. The day was hot and there wasn't enough time to do a good job of exploring the route, so I returned to the car.

In December, I went back with two friends to do a better job. Again, we followed the Saddle Mountain Trail. When it gave out, we headed east to the rim. In this pinyon-juniper forest we found an ancient ruin, and two additional ones when we returned. Mitchell's suggested route was in a bay farther north than the place I had considered possible in August, so we looked there first without scrutinizing our descent route off the rim. When we returned to the area I had liked, we tried the main ravine. We were stopped halfway through the Kaibab, where we found a cave with smoke stains and a bit of pottery. Then we descended via my proposed route, just beyond a striking mushroom-shaped rock tower. One place in the Kaibab nearly stopped us a second time. We continued north along the bench to where I thought there was a break through the Coconino, but I was wrong. Right below where we had come through the Kaibab was a better route. We could walk down a ravine through the Coconino. For a few yards we used the rope as a handline, but even here this was optional. A simple scramble took us through the rest of the Coconino. To get down the Supai, we went to the southeast until we came to the broken section on the right of a wash. A rock pile built up for a step at one place indicates that someone used this route. Darkness comes early in December, but I had time to get down to the Redwall and thus connected this route with the one from the river up at Mile 49.9.

Upriver from
President Harding Rapids

A great view of President Harding Rapids can be seen on the way down to it, by a short detour to the rim of the Redwall. A large rock splits the current into nearly equal channels. Prior to the building of Glen Canyon Dam, this rock was submerged in high water. The wooded beach upriver for a mile is quite wide and is a favorite stopping place for river parties.

Near one of the popular campsites, a path leads back to the base of the cliff. A ring of stones and some writing on the wall commemorates Peter Hansbrough, one of three men with the Brown-Stanton railroad survey party who drowned in July of 1889. His remains were found by the second survey party several months later and buried here. On a more recent river trip, a Boy Scout also died here and is buried nearby. In 1956, a veteran river runner died of a heart attack and was buried farther downriver.

If one walks upriver past the riffles above the main rapids, the platform built of driftwood poles can be seen on the opposite wall, at Mile 43.3. This is the structure that was first located by Gordon Denipah, a Navajo student at NAU and part-time surveyor's assistant. Gordon spotted the structure from a helicopter though thousands of river runners had passed beneath without ever noticing it. After hearing about it from Gordon, I wanted to see the platform at close range and this was the motivation behind my trip down Eminence Break. On my first visit, I crossed the river on an air mattress, but neglected to scout out the location of the platform from the opposite river bank prior to floating across the river. I climbed the talus and fissures in the rocks thinking that I would find it only when I was right on top of it. After an interesting climb, I did find a shallow cave with two sticks fitted from wall to wall near the ceiling. They were far above the highest driftwood and were probably put there by someone who wanted to hang things above the packrats and mice. A system of cracks above this cave might make it possible for a daring climber to go to the top, especially if he were to use some sort of artificial aid in the cracks. I was unable to find the platform and went home frustrated.

I ran into Gordon Denipah on campus and talked with him in depth about locating the structure. Gordon told me that the pilot had landed him on the bank below, and from there, he climbed to where he could have stepped onto the platform. He also said that I should locate it by sight from the opposite side of the river before crossing. The next time down there, I stood on the opposite bank and spotted the platform's exact location before crossing the river. Once on the other side of the river, I climbed directly to the platform. The last fifty feet up to the platform was a good scramble, but not too difficult for an active man. I marveled at the care with which the structure had been built. The logs had been cut to the right length and fitted in place with stone axes. A trapezoid of larger logs was still firmly in place, but a flooring of slender poles had been disturbed by canyon winds. One of these was lying on the talus sixty feet below. A natural ceiling above the platform protected it from all moisture except a very slanting rain. I assumed that this wooden platform would decay given enough time. I cut a chunk of the fallen pole and brought it out. R.C. Euler had this piece identified through Carbon-14 dating as cottonwood, obviously driftwood from the river. The laboratory study showed it to be 1,100 years old. This date puzzled Dr. Euler since it was 300 years older than the bulk of dwellings in the canyon. Why the ancient people went to so much trouble to build it here is another riddle. The immediate thought was that it was a bridge on a prehistoric trail to the top of the cliff, but this was rejected in view of the impossibility of further travel beyond the platform to the west.

At the base of the cliff across the river from the platform is a knoll formed by an old landslide. Just west of the knoll top against the base of the cliff, is a ruin. A veteran river runner told me where to look for it. Five of us from outfitter Ken Sleight's river party came up to see it. While I was locating the ruin, one of Ken's party, Michael Houck, a school teacher from Iowa, climbed the ledges above. When he got as far as he could, he urged us to come and see what he had found — five unbroken Ancestral Pueblan pots. Two were nested upside down on a shelf in plain sight and three more were wedged back in a crack. I called attention to the antiquities act which forbids the removal of artifacts and explained the importance of letting scientists study them in place. We photographed them and left them intact. At the end of the trip, I tried to get an archaeologist to come see the pots, but the staff at the Museum of Northern Arizona were otherwise engaged. After receiving instructions on how to take pictures of the find, I went down to recover them for science. I reached them on one of the hottest days of the summer, when it was ninety-six in Flagstaff. The two on the open shelf were easy to reach, but a rockfall had locked the other three in the crack. I couldn't get them without using some sort of tool. A piece was already broken out of one of the three, so I brought it along with the other two. Lex Lindsay of the museum staff said that the three types represented by the two bowls and the sherd had never been found together before. Months passed and the right authorities made no efforts to recover the other three pots, so I went back with a lug wrench. When I got there, I found that someone had already taken the three pots for his private collection.

One can walk a long way upriver. I stopped for lack of time opposite the Royal Arches, alcoves where ferns grow in the seeps and swallows build their nests. If one should cross the river, it would be possible to visit the Redwall gorge of Buck Farm Canyon, a real beauty spot. Near the mouth, above the high water mark, is Bert Loper's boat. Bert was known as the "Grand Old Man of the River," and when he was just short of his eightieth birthday, he was at the oars taking part in a traverse of Marble-Grand with a party of river runners. About twenty miles upriver from Buck Farm Canyon, his boat capsized. His passenger was able to stay afloat and was picked up by another boat. Some think that Loper collapsed with a heart attack, while others think that he just lost control and drowned. The boat was found and pulled out of the water at Mile 41, but Loper's body was never seen again. In 1975, a few of his bones were found at Mile 70.5.

Downriver from President Harding Rapids

John McComb and some friends combined a descent of the Eminence Break Route with a trip downriver to Nankoweap and beyond. I didn't try this until November 1974, but I immediately became an enthusiast for this part of the canyon. The riparian vegetation, the lofty walls, and the bright fall weather made a combination that is hard to beat. For most of the 2.5 miles down to a point opposite Triple Alcoves, I followed a big buck at close range. The trail alternated between going up on the dry slopes and then through thickets beside the river. I could average more than a mile an hour. Opposite Triple Alcoves, the trail became sketchy as it went higher and higher on a bench. At river level the bank ended at a cliff. I made my camp here.

Since Glen Canyon Dam was built, water comes through the generators from deep in the lake and is cold the year round. At that time, I no longer crossed on an air mattress but instead, brought a little inflatable boat that weighed only three and a half pounds. In the morning, I inflated it and paddled across while lying prone. I allowed for downstream drift and got to the other side without getting wet or cold.

The trail was just as good on the right bank where I watched another fine buck swim across the river. Leaving Triple Alcoves behind, I was soon passing the mouth of Saddle Canyon. Farther on, a spring trickled over a cliff and made a little stream into the river. At Mile 49.3 I passed a side canyon but proceeded to my goal, the canyon from the right at Mile 49.9. A prominent fault crosses the river here, and George Billingsley had told me that I should be able to climb clear through the Redwall in this canyon. Billinglsey was a geology major at NAU and was credited with discovering a previously unrecognized formation which was named the "Surprise Canyon Formation." Back in May 1973, I had

1923 USGS expedition camped on President Harding Rapids. (Photo: Grand Canyon Museum, 17070)

come up the bank from the mouth of Nankoweap Canyon and had tried to climb through the Redwall. For some reason my courage failed when I was almost to the top. A year later, on a fine bracing November day in 1974, I went up the place that had baffled me, got to the top of the Redwall and came down another way which I had previously examined and also rejected. The route down was a little easier. There was some exposure and one must be careful not to roll loose rocks. Still, I couldn't see why I had been too timid to finish the route the first time.

On the return upriver, I detoured into Mile 49.3 Canyon and turned back rather soon when I saw it choked with great fallen blocks beneath impossible cliffs. I allowed more time for a visit to the Redwall gorge in Saddle Canyon which had been highly recommended by Billingsley. I went into the high valley past the barrier falls on the north side and then discovered a real trail on the south slope. Above the steep slope through the shale is a gem of a glen. It is nearly level and wooded with junipers and redbud trees. A brook runs down the middle. At the upper end, the vale narrows to a cleft and the water flows over chutes in the bare rock. By wading and climbing, I could have gone farther, but I reluctantly turned away since I had already fallen behind my schedule for returning to my camp by daylight. With flowers blooming here in November, this glen charmed me as much as Elves Chasm.

For the river crossing I went far enough upstream to avoid being swept past my campsite. I landed my little ark well before dark. It had been a fine adventure on one of the most beautiful days I have ever spent in the Grand Canyon.

Nankoweap Basin

Ancestral Puebloan graineries in Nankoweap.
(Photo: Michael Quinn, Grand Canyon Museum Collection, 4893)

The north side of the river is certainly as interesting as the south, though less visited. Nankoweap Valley is becoming more popular, but as long as the access routes remain rugged, it will hardly be crowded. Drive to the north side of Saddle Mountain through House Rock Valley, or leave the car on the high plateau west of Saddle Mountain. Along either route, the walk to Saddle takes over an hour. The marvelous view from the top of Saddle Mountain can be reached by a trail up the northwest side. Although this summit is lower than the rim forest, the trees are more exposed and they show the effects of the timberline gales.

Nankoweap Creek and debris from recent flooding.
(Grand Canyon Museum Collection, 4892)

The Nankoweap Trail goes south over the Saddle and levels off below the top one hundred feet of Supai. It stays on this bench all the way to Tilted Mesa. On the southwest slope of this mesa, parts of the old trail are so badly weathered that I prefer a deer trail which starts farther down to the south. The trail isn't shown at all on the new map of the park and the old east-half map showed it ending at the bottom of the Redwall. It is true that a section of the trail is missing. Just below this bad place in the shale, a deer trail contours east. The old horse trail reappears as it breaks through the Tapeats. This is probably easier than scrambling down the ravine directly below the missing section.

Every arm of Nankoweap has its interesting features. The one between Marion and Seiber Points offers the possibility of climbing the break through Redwall on the south side. One can go on up through the Supai and follow the Hermit around to the regular trail. The branch north of Woolsey Point has a beautiful waterfall below a perennial spring. A number of ruins remind one of the time when this valley was home for quite a clan. There is at least one well-preserved cliff dwelling on the north side. The arm between Woolsey and Mt. Hayden almost hides the largest natural bridge of the Grand Canyon. All knowledge of this had been lost until Senator Barry Goldwater rediscovered it from the air.

There is another access route down into the arm between Kibbey Butte and Brady Peak. After getting through the Redwall via a ravine to the north, contour to the right around to the north side of Kibbey Butte. After this rather precarious and exposed footing, it is a relief to follow a deer trail up to the Kibbey Saddle and reach the rim north of the promontory. There are definite signs of trail construction in the Coconino and near the rim, so we can conclude that prospectors came this way.

A window through the fin projecting southeast from Alsap Butte is interesting to visit. Another good scramble is Nankoweap Butte, relatively low but still affording fine views. Nankoweap Mesa requires more climbing and care in route finding, but a deer trail goes to the top. One feels like Robinson Crusoe as he explores this extensive sky island. There are small springs spotted all throughout the basin of Nankoweap. Pottery fragments indicate that it was occupied about eight hundred years ago. Little Nankoweap does not go through to the river, but it is interesting both above and below the barrier falls at the lower end. One should be able to climb north at the lower end and get a view down on the river. Don't count on finding water in this valley.

Nankoweap Creek flows from the broad basin to the river at a gentle gradient and it is easy to reach the cliff dwellings just south of the mouth. River runners have beaten a path to them.

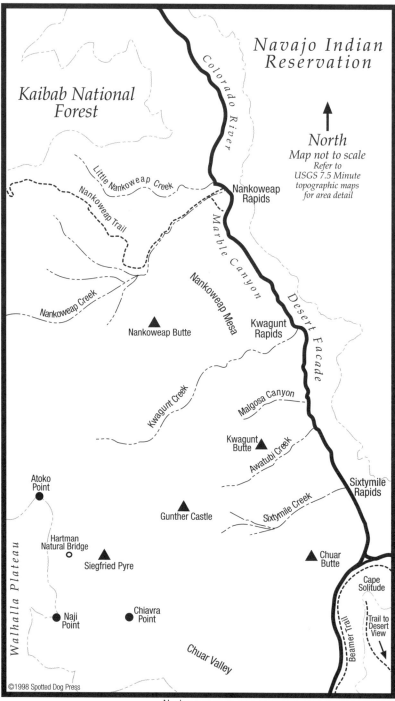

Navajo Indian
Reservation

Kaibab National
Forest

Colorado River

North
Map not to scale
Refer to
USGS 7.5 Minute
topographic maps
for area detail

Little Nankoweap Creek

Nankoweap Trail

Nankoweap
Rapids

Marble Canyon

Desert Facade

Nankoweap Mesa

Nankoweap Creek

▲
Nankoweap Butte

Kwagunt
Rapids

Kwagunt Creek

Malgosa Canyon

Kwagunt
Butte ▲

Awatubi Creek

Atoko
Point ●

Sixtymile
Rapids

▲
Gunther Castle

Sixtymile Creek

Hartman
Natural Bridge ○

▲
Siegfried Pyre

▲ Chuar
Butte

Cape
Solitude

Walhalla Plateau

● Naji
Point

● Chiavra
Point

Beamer Trail

Trail to
Desert
View

Chuar Valley

©1998 Spotted Dog Press

Nankoweap area

Kwagunt Canyon

This is a welcome watering place on the Horsethief Trail which connects the Tanner with the Nankoweap Trail. It is also another fine place to slow down and take a look around. The ranger scouting party of 1928 reported seeing a lost city of at least twenty-five rooms near here. Later, the man who claimed to have seen it, disclaimed his find. The city has never been rediscovered but a terrace on the south side of the stream and just west of the river narrows is said to have a number of room outlines on it. A walk through the Tapeats narrows of the upper bed is rewarded with a view of the jagged skyline of Coconino Sandstone. Just beyond, but out of view, are the Kaibab limestone towers called Tritle Peaks.

Just west of Banta Point, a steep arm comes down from the Kwagunt-Lava Creek Saddle. A break through the Tapeats wall east of the junction leads to a deer trail through the Redwall of this arm. The Supai section of this ravine is forested. One can turn to the right and go along the Hermit north of Atoko Point to a deer trail which can be followed to the rim east of the head of Kwagunt. At the bottom of the Coconino just west of this trail, and about a quarter mile east of the end of the main canyon, is a little spring. There is another small spring in the lower Redwall along this route. The spring that keeps water in Kwagunt at the Horsethief Trail crossing is surprisingly low near the Butte Fault. Water is certainly scantier in Kwagunt than in Nankoweap.

The Horsethief Trail is straightforward, but very strenuous. Map study hardly prepares one for the number of stiff climbs needed to cross the traverse valleys. Kwagunt forms an easy route to the river and hikers have also climbed down Malgosa. One can walk the riverbank from the park boundary at least as far south as the mouth of the Little Colorado.

Looking north across Awatubi, Kwagunt Butte on right. Horsethief Trail in valley on left. (Photo: Harvey Butchart)

It would also appear possible to go south out of Kwagunt valley west of Gunther Castle. The latter commands a terrific view from the top and it can be climbed through a Redwall ravine on the southwest side.

Chuar Valley

This broad drainage goes by the names of Chuar and Lava. The actual lava is all near the river with Chuar Lava Hill on one side of the creek and Lava Butte on the other. The latter challenges the climber with a vertical crack on the southwest side. There are some old mine shafts in these ancient basalt flows. The ore was mostly copper with a trace of silver. Harry McDonald began this mine around 1891, making him a contemporary of Ben Beamer who was at work at the mouth of the Little Colorado. During World War I, the McCormicks renewed this mining activity, taking the ore up the Tanner Trail. McDonald was also seen with his burros on the Walhalla Plateau. Otis "Dock" Marston, who suggested so many historical projects concerning the Grand Canyon, prompted me to find McDonald's old route off the rim.

This lead was responsible for my finding the deer trail west of Atoko Point. One can park a car off the rim road where the map shows the elevation of 8,353' and in a few minutes, be starting off the rim in the bay just east of the one at the very end of the main arm of Kwagunt. McDonald and his burros stayed high at the Kwagunt-Lava Saddle and passed along the west base of Siegfried Pyre. They would have broken through much of the Supai before rounding the corner toward Hubbell Butte. The route is along the west base of Hubbell and over the top of Poston Butte. The burro route follows the Redwall down northwest of Point Chiavria, and then turns right along the Tapeats rim to a break on the south side of Chiavria.

A person can also scramble directly down from the Kwagunt-Lava Saddle south into Lava. A Supai ledge near the top seems like a barrier, but there is a break to the west. The Redwall requires some study and the main bed drops over a sixty-foot cliff at the bottom, which can be bypassed on either side. To the west, one passes close to the second largest natural bridge in the park. To the east, one would go quite close to a shallow cave where Donald Davis, an expert ornithologist, climber and beekeeper from Parachute, Colorado, found seven unbroken pots in 1969.

The grandeur of the walls above this upper arm of Lava is enhanced by the beauty of the vegetation along the bed near some little springs. One can also get through the Redwall just west of Hubbell Butte, but this is harder than either of the other ways. Perhaps too hard for a burro is the route on the south side of the neck leading to Point Chiavria.

These routes almost converge on one of the most interesting Indian ruins in the whole park. It is under an overhang on the north side of the bed several hundred yards west of the junction of the main arm and the one from the west of Juno Temple. One room is almost intact and there are several low room outlines as well as some pictographs on the ceiling. It is a fine campsite during a storm, but bugs like it too. We once saw a scorpion near our bedrolls.

The south arm must be entered directly across from the ruin since there is an impassable barrier waterfall in the bed. To reach the saddle between Cape Final and Juno, we stayed to the west and caught the deer trail near the top. It continued down into the north arm of Unkar. We have climbed Juno and Jupiter and have found that the fastest way to get down into Lava is via a rope route on the north side of Cape Final. Here, in the biggest ravine, one has to rappel about fifty feet and a few yards ahead, a short rope is a comfort getting off the ledge. The route from Lava over the pass into Unkar continues to the river with no difficulty. A dry waterfall in the Tapeats has an obvious bypass.

One can also go from Chuar Valley over into Basalt Creek. The west arm of Basalt is blocked by a high waterfall, but the route through the east arm is easy. There are old cairns, presumably dating back to mining days, on the summit of Apollo, the Apollo-Venus Saddle, and in the east arm of Basalt. There are scattered remnants of old mining camps on both sides of the river at the mouth of Basalt.

Apollo, Venus and Jupiter, near head of Carbon Creek, Chuar Valley.
(Photo: Harvey Butchart)

Another trace of not-so-ancient human activity is the bootlegging site. It is near the bed of Lava Creek at the junction with the draw that comes east from the north end of Juno. The ranger party of 1928 estimated that it was older than the Volstead Act. Some barrel hoops and the rock base of the still were about all that was left. The bootlegger had cut down a cottonwood and had screwed the grinder to the stump. By the early sixties, four shoots had grown up surrounding the grinder and the new trunks were five or six inches in diameter. By now I thought that the old grinder would have been swept away by floods, but a hiker told me that it is still there. There is a nice little spring a few yards up the arm by the still.

Unkar Valley

One can walk from the ruin near the forks of Lava Canyon Pass to Unkar and then down to the Unkar Delta in about eight hours. Here, one of the most extensive ruined pueblos in the entire park was excavated under the direction of National Park archaeologist, Douglas Schwartz, during the summers of 1967 and 1968. Farming must have been possible on this expanse of sand and gravel. A little water surfaces at two or three places in the bed of lower Unkar and there is more assurance of permanent water at some cottonwoods below Angel's Window and in the Tapeats of the branch just west of the long main arm. One can climb through the Tapeats and the Redwall to the saddle between Freya and Vishnu Temples. From there, the Redwall rim west of Freya is followed and the Supai is climbed directly up to the notch between Cape Royal and Freya. The descent through the Redwall into Vishnu Creek here is actually easier than getting up through the Supai. From this notch, one can work one's way along the Hermit Shale to a break in the Coconino south of the elevation 7,994'. About one hundred yards west of this ravine, there is a dripping spring at the base of the Coconino. At two places near the bottom of this Coconino route, one needs a thirty-foot rope to pull up the pack. At the top of the sandstone, angle to the east and walk up through the limestone. Near the top, one passes Indian pictographs hidden under ledges. They include the usual mysterious designs. There is also an impression of a child's hand in red clay. It is only a few hundred yards to the parking lot where the exhibit describes the Indian occupation of the Walhalla Plateau. A path leads to an excavated ruin and to the east, there is a citadel ruin on an easily defended sky island.

From the Freya-Cape Royal Saddle, one can follow the shale to the southwest and eventually reach the break in the Coconino at the northeast end of Wotan's Throne. With patience, one can locate a safe route up through the sandstone, and a gate in the Toroweap, then along the north side of the Throne. Over near the west end, one can walk up through the woods. It takes an easy scramble of about eight feet to be out on top through the rim cliff. Surprisingly, there are ruins up there, including a crude shelter along the route through the Coconino.

Back at the Freya-Vishnu Saddle, one can continue southwest into Vishnu Creek. Near the bottom of the Redwall, it is necessary to contour around to the right to a talus slope. From the saddle, one can stay on the Redwall rim and climb Krishna Shrine. Vishnu Temple was climbed twice by Merrel Clubb and different companions. He also climbed Wotan at least three times.

Rama Shrine can be climbed far more safely than Vishnu Temple. There is an easily traversed ravine through the Redwall east of Rama drainage into Asbestos Canyon. I found evidence in the form of a flint knife that the Indians used this route. One can stay on the Tonto north of Sheba and The Tabernacle, and eventually get down to the bed of Unkar two miles from the river, or go east from Solomon down the wash to reach the river a mile southwest of the Unkar Delta. I have walked the slope below the Basalt Cliffs to go from Basalt Creek to Unkar, but if one has a way to cross the river safely, it is easier to proceed along the left bank of the Colorado.

Various routes are possible in and around Vishnu Canyon. It is a stiff six to eight hour waterless route to go along the Tonto to Clear Creek. There are springs in Vishnu Creek near the top of the granite, in the Tapeats narrows, and near some cottonwoods at the Tapeats-Bright Angel Shale contact. Getting down to the Archean bedrock from the west requires care in following a narrow ledge of travertine. It is impossible to go down the main bed to the river, but these falls can be bypassed by some rugged climbing over spurs east of the bed.

I have climbed Newberry, Sheba, and Solomon, all from their east sides. They all require some route finding. A chimney on the

Solomon route is a trap with an unstable chockstone ready to move at the top.

The asbestos mines were booming before 1900 and it is interesting to poke around the old camp trash. Coming from the west, one can enter the canyon along the ramp of red Dox Sandstone or along the broad slope north of a knoll. To connect with the former route, one needs to leave the Tonto back about halfway from Newberry Butte to Asbestos, and this trail winds so much that it is probably faster to keep to the more direct northern route. In fact, one can come down into the nameless ravine where the name "Asbestos" begins on the map. At this point, there is still a bit of the old trail connecting the lower valley with the upper. The main bed is blocked by an impassable waterfall. The map shows a spring in the upper valley, but the cartographers should move it about a third of a mile southeast of its current location on the map. It is high in a ravine which parallels the arm from the east side of Rama. There is also some water where the name "Asbestos" begins on the map, and the best spring of all is in the lower valley where the red Dox meets the black basalt. In wet seasons, this water persists above ground and drops over a high waterfall.

A good trail connects the mining camp with the river. It goes to the east near the brink of the high fall and turns upriver. Sloping down along the natural ramp, it meets the Colorado below Hance Rapids. The river is still quite swift and below the rapid, the ferry must have had safe passage only during periods of low flow on the river. One can go from the mining camp to the Tonto southwest of Sheba and directly up the ravine in that direction.

Comanche Point Route

I became interested in this part of the "Palisades of the Desert" when a young geologist told me that he had gone up Palisades Creek to within sixty feet of the top of the Redwall. If one could get down from the rim near Espejo Butte, a rope could be used to score another rim-to-river route. My four-wheel drive rig would be useful for the approach over the jeep road from north of Cedar Mountain.

After one preliminary inspection, I took Jim Ohlman to the rim northeast of Espejo Butte. Between us, we found a way down and up to the top of Espejo. We could see that the route was fairly easy down to the Redwall in Palisades Creek. Later, Bob Packard, an excellent climber and river guide, with Ken Walters, climbed Espejo later, using our report and completed the project by going down to the Redwall. They reported that the necessary rappel was more like an awesome two hundred feet instead of sixty!

While Ohlman and I were on Espejo, we were intrigued by the idea that the ravine on the north side of Comanche Point might be well worth investigating. Distant views are often deceptive, so I asked Ken to go with me to see what we could find in the ravine north of Comanche Point. On our approach we climbed Comanche Point and enjoyed perhaps the finest panorama of the entire Grand Canyon, a spectacular 360-degree view of the Painted Desert, Navajo Mountain, and all of the spires and temples in the eastern part of Grand Canyon National Park. Directly below to the southwest was the detached tower, that has only recently been summited by the most skillful of climbers. Ken and I had no problem in getting down this fault ravine through the Coconino, but at one place in the Supai, we had to leave the bed along a narrow, exposed ledge. On the return, we found a way to avoid this shelf with the low ceiling. The upper Redwall was also simple, but towards the lower half we came to a sheer fall with smooth walls.

Checking a landslide to the west of the bed, we walked down a minor ravine paralleling the main wash. Bighorn droppings led down the scree to a narrow ramp sloping down across the vertical face of the lower Redwall cliff. I was soon willing to concede that sheep will go were I won't, but Ken carefully went ahead and down. I kept in contact by shouting words of advice like "Don't get stuck – we don't have a rope." After about forty-five minutes, Ken rejoined me and urged me to come on down and see for myself. The sloping ledge we followed was the most spectacular route through the Redwall that I have ever done. It was narrow and even missing for a few feet, but there were some good finger grips at that point. This route is better-suited for skilled rock climbers.

The ramp ended at a rough-walled slot where one could descend ten to fifteen feet to another ledge which went back to the west and ended at a saddle in the clay of the lower landslide. We felt sure that we had another route to the river.

Several months later, Al Shauffler came with me down the Tanner Trail to follow the route Ken and I had taken upriver. Al was a veterinarian who had devised an unusual method to keep mice away from his pack at night in camp. He spread kernels of corn some distance away from his pack as a lure, and it worked. On the second day, we took daypacks up the winding bed of Comanche Creek. Getting out of the bed, we walked on the north side. When we came to the basalt, we either had to detour up and around or climb down precariously to the bed. Al took the adventuresome direct way while I detoured. While he was waiting for me, he had the thrill of watching two bighorns walk along a nearly invisible shelf on the face of the cliff. They went out of sight around a corner, but soon came back the same way. Evidently, they were only experimenting with a blind alley. We followed their tracks up our route. At the fork in the creek, we took the west arm. Seeing a barrier fall ahead, we climbed a steep clay slope, about the hardest part of the entire route. It was a simple walk up to the base of the Redwall and east to where Ken and I had been. This route is an adventure, but I would prefer to use the Tanner Trail as a way to reach the mouth of the Little Colorado.

Routes Away from the Tanner Trail

Earlier, I described the route over the saddle between Escalante and Cardenas Buttes from the Tanner Trail down to Unkar Rapids. Another interesting dayhike leaves the Tanner Trail at the head of Seventyfive Mile Canyon and goes to the end of the promontory west of Escalante Butte which forms the north wall of Seventyfive Mile Canyon. The view from the end is fantastic and the little nameless butte at the beginning of the ridge is a sporty rock climb.

A more challenging project was suggested by Al Doty, Jim Sears, and some of their friends who had tried coming down the ravine west of Lipan Point. It was a ropeless climb except for a sixty-foot rappel in the Coconino. They also found a tricky route through the Redwall. Sears interested me in going down the Tanner Trail to the head of Seventyfive Mile Canyon and then contouring to the west to his Redwall route down to Seventyfive Mile Canyon. Sears, Jan Jenson and Ellen Tibbetts went ahead of Eric Karlstrom and me, shouting directions as we approached along the Redwall rim. As we neared the ravine, we passed by a neat window in the limestone.

The route required study. The only hard place was a twelve-foot drop with some handholds. We used a rope to lower our packs. Tibbetts and I also used the rope as a handline. We were then on a slide that brought us to the Tapeats rim of Seventyfive Mile Canyon. If we had gone to the right, we would have found a break in the Tapeats much closer than the one we finally reached by difficult sidehill walking to the west.

Going down the bed to the river was routine, with a minor bypass or two. Eric found a fine overhang above smooth sand for our beds that night. Sears spent several hours making geological notes and then found a new route up Papago Canyon. I led Eric up the Tonto just west of lower Seventyfive Mile Canyon, and then up the east arm of Papago Canyon.

Tanner Trail

The original Tanner Trail left the rim west of Cedar Mountain across the bay from Desert View. All but the top hundred yards are gone. However, with careful route-finding, one can still follow the old trail. Below Desert View, the trail goes around to the west along the rim of the Redwall. It is also possible to intercept this old trail by leaving the rim just north of the Watch Tower. There is a rough scramble down a ravine to the west. It is interesting to note that in 1994, some tourists in the area around Desert View found a large, intact prehistoric pot, which measured nearly 2.5 feet in diameter. They went to an appraiser in Flagstaff to find out how much it was worth and if they could find a buyer. The appraiser promptly notified the authorities and the pot is now part of the Grand Canyon Museum's permanent collection.

The route was marked by some cairns and crossed the west arm of Tanner Canyon near the fall over the Redwall. In the bed is a large rain pocket that may be reliable as a water source. It was at this pool that George Wharton James and his companions met a well-armed group of men who were driving horses across the Canyon. James and his party had left their horses at the trailhead on the rim to travel on foot down to the rain pocket. They had heard rumors about a group of armed thieves who had stolen horses from nearby Kanab, Utah and were purported to be driving them down into the Canyon to alter their brands. They would then take the horses to Flagstaff to sell them. When James and his group encountered the rustlers face to face, they hid their suspicions and attempted to be friendly. The thieves accepted the proffered whiskey, but still took the horses that James and his party had left at the trailhead.

The present Tanner Trail is shown on the map. To get to the trailhead, we parked off the highway along the approach to Lipan

Point. The head of the trail is quite distinct and was marked with the sign, "Trail not maintained. Permit required." It descends sharply through the upper formations, but there are only a couple of places that would be difficult for a horse or mule to negotiate. Contouring below Escalante and Cardenas Buttes seems tedious, but it takes only about an hour to do this section. Their accessibility makes these buttes attractive climbs. The rain pocket would be quite a detour, so carry plenty of water for the estimated twelve miles to the river — at least two quarts during winter months. This walk is too long and hot to attempt between April and October. Another water source is still farther from the trail, a seep in the shale below the Redwall in the southeast arm. Coming back from the river on a hot day can be quite fatiguing and one should allow six hours or more with at least three to six quarts of water, depending on the time of year.

Without water, the heat of summer can be fatal, and tragedy has befallen many hikers who have neglected to carry enough water. I remember once incident in particular, when a man and two boys attempted to go to the river and back in one day, carrying only a bottle of water. They reached the river but were unable to reach the Redwall on the return before nightfall. They wandered around the lower valley most of the night trying to find their way out. By the middle of the morning, they decided to return to the river for more water, but by that point it was too late. The man, deranged by thirst, insisted on trying to climb down an eighty-foot waterfall. He soon lost his grip on the slick surface and cartwheeled to his death on the rocks. The boys, backing away, found a bypass to the bed below the waterfall. One was unable to go on and died from heat exhaustion no more than a forty-five minute walk from the river. The other reached the river and stayed there waiting for help. As time quietly passed, and the hope of a rescue faded, he wrapped himself around a driftwood log and attempted to float down the Colorado to Phantom Ranch. Almost drowning in Unkar Rapids, he continued as far as Hance Rapids. Ahead, he could see the river entering the granite

Beamer cabin. (Photo: Janet Balsom, Grand Canyon Museum Collection, 13712)

and realized that he would never survive the next twelve miles to Phantom Ranch. By this time, a helicopter search had begun in earnest for him back at the Tanner Trail. He attempted to hike and swim back upriver, building "S.O.S." signs on the sandbars out of rocks and driftwood. Just as the search was about to be abandoned, he was spotted from the air and rescued. He had been able to go back upriver a mile and a half.

There is an interesting prehistoric route going north from the Tanner Trail over the pass between Escalante and Cardenas Buttes. I found a bit of pottery on the north side of the pass.

One can angle to the right through the Supai and continue down an easy ravine through the Redwall. It is possible to continue north along the Tapeats to a break on the west side of the promontory. The basalt can be descended to the north and from here there are various ways to reach the river. This is the most direct route from the rim to an Indian ruin on the hill south of Unkar Rapids.

From the regular trail, at several places below the Redwall, one can see a natural bridge to the west. We followed the top of the Redwall around the bay and got down beneath the bridge. We were also able to get down the east side of the promontory just north of the bridge. The Tapeats is also broken on this side. We were unable to find a way through the basalt so we contoured east over to the regular trail. The lower part of the Tanner Trail through the red shale is narrow, but safe enough. It was never maintained by burros in this section of the park, and for some reason, even deer are rare and subsequently, so are their trails. The route has become increasingly popular over the years with hikers and because of this should remain fairly distinct.

There is no longer any definable trail upriver. It is easy to find a way behind the hills or just above the mesquite. About a third of the way to the mouth of the Little Colorado was a low water ford where horsemen crossed. Stay near the river to the mouth of Lava Canyon. One could go north along the Butte Fault west of Temple, Chuar, and Kwagunt Buttes. It is tiring but not

View from the Tanner Trail. (Photo: Andy Zdon)

otherwise difficult to cross Carbon, Sixty Mile, Awatubi, Malgosa, and Kwagunt Creeks before reaching the Nankoweap Trail. This was the cross-canyon route of the old horse thieves.

There are old copper mine workings between the Tanner Trail and the mouth of the Little Colorado at Palisades Creek. The miners lived in a cabin made of driftwood, and the usual mining camp relics — rusted cans, broken bits of purple and blue glass — are still there.

At Palisades Creek, one must decide whether to go high on a slope above the bluff or follow the narrow bench along the river. The latter pinches out about two-thirds of the way to the Little Colorado. When it is impossible to go any further, one is at the source of Hopi salt (Editor's note: the Hopi Salt Mines are sacred and closed to all visitation, except with special permission from the Hopi Nation).

Until about 1912, the Hopis came as pilgrims to this spot. It was a religious observance with many rituals. Entering the Little Colorado Canyon through Salt Canyon six and a half miles from the mouth, they had to use a rope for the last twenty feet to the bank of the Colorado. The salt is in the form of stalactites and stalagmites in shallow caves. I recognized this as the right place when I came down from above and found a peculiar knob of worn bedrock, where the Hopis would fasten their rope.

From Palisade Creek, the route to the Little Colorado goes along the bluff about two hundred feet above the river. Known as the Beamer Trail, it was improved by Ben Beamer, a prospector who built the rock cabin on the south bank of the Little Colorado, a short walk from the junction. He must have expected to stay some time and grow things on the terrace near his house because he brought a plowshare with him. In 1869, John Wesley Powell spent several days here, twenty-two years before Beamer. At that time, the site was covered by an Ancestral Puebloan ruin. From the pottery sherds found in the soil near the Beamer cabin, one can infer that he knocked down the ruin to build his place.

The Little Colorado at Cameron is dry about half the year. At these times, the entire flow at the mouth is from clear blue springs. This permanent water source starts twenty-one miles up from the river, but by far the largest spring is 13.5 miles from the mouth. This mineral water is fit to drink but the taste test is not appealing. It covers the bed with a filmy white cream. Even the shallow pools seem to be pale blue and the deep lagoon at the mouth is a much deeper blue than the sky. It would be wise to filter or treat the water before sampling it.

When the Little Colorado is not flooding, it is simple to walk up the bed. One can ford the stream when the walking seems easier on the other side. About 1.6 miles upstream, there is a break in the north wall. Don't use the bed of the gorge as it is blocked. Go up the shale on the west and around a corner into a ravine through the Redwall. Going north up the steep valley is right, but near the top one turns into a narrow slot. The top three hundred feet is high second-class and requires the use of the hands for balance. An Indian told an acquaintance of mine about this route and he predicted that white men wouldn't like it. Powell wrote in 1869 that his brother, Walter, spent a day going to the top and back. This may have been the route to which Powell was referring.

About 4.5 miles up the Little Colorado from the mouth is a travertine cone formed from the minerals of a little bubbling spring. This is the original Hopi Sipapu, the reputed route from which the progenitors of the human race issued from the underworld. At 6.5 miles from the mouth on the north side is Salt Trail Canyon. The trail is now marked by many cairns and is an easier way to reach the rim than the Walter Powell route.

Melvin McCormick, who helped his father mine copper at Palisades Creek and occasionally look for the fabulous lost gold mine of John D. Lee, said that they used to swim the horses across the Colorado north of the mouth of the Little Colorado. From there, a person on foot can go along the bank and climb out at Malgosa Canyon. Or, he can continue along the bank to the easy creek beds of Kwagunt and Nankoweap. There are ruins all through this eastern part of the park, particularly in Nankoweap, Kwagunt, and Lava Canyons. The occupation was mostly from 1,050 to 1,200 A.D. and the dwellings were only well-preserved if they were built under overhangs. By now, most of them are only faint outlines of rocks with some pottery sherds scattered about.

Papago Canyon Route

Many years ago, I was shown some prehistoric ruins along the rim east of Zuni Point. I took pictures of several including a couple which had rock walls as breastworks facing the rim. These narrow promontories seem to have been citadels where the local Indians could take refuge during raids. There were room outlines back from the rim and some granaries in niches below the rim. Back in civilization, I saw photographs of a grid design in charcoal on the ceiling of an overhang, which I had missed on my first visit. On later trips, I returned to all of the sites to take my own pictures, and was able to locate everything with the one exception of the elusive charcoal grid drawing.

I have always been skeptical about the stories of vanished mines and the prospectors who lose them, but I finally did give up trying to locate that charcoal-decorated ceiling. While trying to find it, I noticed that the rim to the east of the head of the east arm of Papago Creek is broken into ledges. Slow and cautious scouting got me down to a blunt little tower at the head of a ravine through the Coconino. One goes down to the west of this landmark. The lower half of the Coconino requires a switch to a parallel rift to the left.

The lowest part of the Coconino seemed so precarious at first sight that I left my canteen and camera above while I checked out a descent route. It required the use of my hands and feet, but on a later trip, we came up here without removing our packs. A log wedged in for a step indicated that prehistoric people used this route. The Hermit Shale led northeast to a slide that covered all of the Supai. At the Redwall, I continued north and found a place where I could walk to the Tonto. Several trips were necessary to put this entire route together.

After several years, I talked Ken Walters into going with me to find the way to the bed of Papago Canyon near the river. Ken was the first person to hike from the top of Humphreys Peak (12,633'), the highest point in Arizona to the Colorado River via the Kaibab Trail in less than twenty-four hours. From the Tonto, we could get through the Tapeats where Jim Sears had found a way, but I couldn't see how his group of three good climbers had come up the Shimuno Quartzite in the east fork of lower Papago. Continuing northeast on the Tonto, Ken and I tried again closer to the river. Just when we were about to descend a steep ravine, we noticed a large cairn. When we came to the actual rim of the final gorge, I thought we were stuck! Ken gingerly maneuvered down about thirty feet to a ledge and, just around the corner, found a continuation. From this point, it was a routine scramble to the bed where I had once been before, coming up from the river. On that occasion, it seemed that my descent from the Tonto would require a long rappel. There are other technical routes in addition to this one, which expert climbers could use if they were to go out either fork farther south.

New Hance Trail

This trail is shown on the map, but finding a parking spot is not that easy. About a mile southwest of the turnoff to Moran Point, a faint car track goes through the juniper forest to the trailhead, but is usually blocked by a scatter of trees. If you walk along this track and go to the left down the first draw, you will come to a cairn marking the start of the trail. If this takes more than six or seven minutes, you have overshot the mark. Since the Old Trail isn't well-known, and was destroyed by a storm in 1895, this trail is usually called the Hance Trail. All confusion would be avoided by calling it the "Red Canyon Trail." On it, Hance guided his tourists by horse and mule all the way down to the Colorado River. The miners also used the trail to get to the asbestos mines.

The trail is still quite clear down to the base of Coronado Butte, but don't panic if you lose the trail temporarily in the Supai Formation. Even though hikers have put up more and more cairns in recent years, the route is still difficult to follow. It is still worse along the rim of the Redwall where it has to head several ravines. Consulting a topo map is a real help in this area.

Park ranger, Dan Davis and a companion, spent a couple of hours trying to locate the right place for the Redwall descent. Although he had been over the trail three years earlier, he gave up the search and went down the Redwall by a deer trail which was closer to the head of the gorge. Once, we had several close encounters with a bighorn ram until it went down this route. There is water in the bed at the base of this descent, certainly an advantage not shared by the regular trail.

The place where the horse trail starts down is marked by cairns and some old lettering painted on the side of a big rock. In the talus below, there are several ravines and a net of wild burro trails. Once again, the topo is useful. After the trail crosses a tributary from

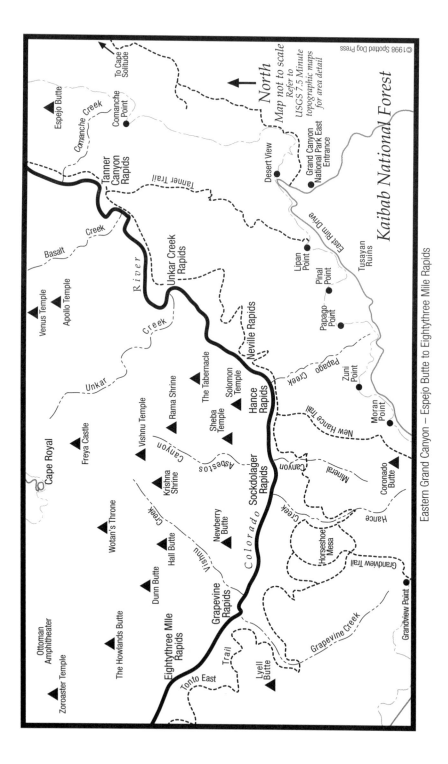

North

Map not to scale
Refer to
USGS 7.5 Minute
topographic maps
for area detail

Kaibab National Forest

To Cape
Solitude

Espejo Butte

Comanche Creek

Comanche
Point

Tanner
Canyon
Rapids

Tanner Trail

Desert View

Grand Canyon
National Park East
Entrance

Basalt Creek

River

Unkar Creek
Rapids

East Rim Drive

Lipan
Point

Venus Temple

Apollo Temple

Pinal
Point

Tusayan
Ruins

Unkar Creek

Papago
Point

Neville Rapids

Rama Shrine

The Tabernacle

Solomon
Temple

Papago Creek

Zuni
Point

Cape Royal

Freya Castle

Vishnu Temple

Sheba
Temple

Hance
Rapids

Moran
Point

Krishna
Shrine

Asbestos Canyon

Sockdolager
Rapids

New Hance Trail

Mineral Canyon

Coronado
Butte

Wotan's Throne

Vishnu Creek

Newberry
Butte

Colorado

Hance Creek

Horseshoe
Mesa

Dunn Butte

Hall Butte

Grandview Trail

Ottoman
Amphitheater

The Howlands Butte

Grapevine
Rapids

Zoroaster Temple

Eightythree Mile
Rapids

Tonto East Trail

Lyell
Butte

Grapevine Creek

Grandview Point

Eastern Grand Canyon – Espejo Butte to Eightythree Mile Rapids below Moran Point, it slopes down into a bed of Red Canyon and stays there.

Hidden in the mesquite east of the wash and about seventy-five yards from the river is an old camp. The clutter of trash suggests that it must have been used for some time. It was an overnight stop for the miners who were bringing asbestos from across the river up to the South Rim. There was also a three-day trip for tourists with stops on Horseshoe Mesa and at the mouth of Red Canyon. The Grandview, Tonto, and Hance Trails were all in good shape for riders and accommodations were available on Horseshoe Mesa and at Hance Rapids. Since 1910, the wilderness has reclaimed its own.

The crossing to the asbestos mines was made by boat below the rapids. During the early summer, the current ran swift and high. The ferry must have operated only at low water. The trail on the north side slants up along a ramp made by an ancient intrusion of lava. From Hance Rapids, one can see the tailings pile in front of a large mine working high on the slope. The trail goes below this tunnel, around Asbestos Canyon. If one has a way to cross the river, it is interesting to visit the ruins of the miners camp — the shacks with buckets and other debris scattered about. The trail continues from the camp to the mines high above the river and to the west. I tried to go up the main bed but was stopped by a high, dry waterfall. Some students found an old trail to the west of the dry waterfall going into the upper valley. They also found a spring about a half mile away from the location shown on their map. I have entered Asbestos Canyon from both east and west and have found that the steep ravine southwest of Sheba Temple is a reliable access route.

Hance Trail

John Hance and William Wallace Bass were outstanding Grand Canyon prospectors who came to the canyon about 1882 and spent the rest of their lives in or near the Grand Canyon. They built trails and operated mines, but eventually both found the tourist business more profitable. John Hance chose the scenically superb eastern part of the canyon while Bass developed a section far west of the present village.

Hance first built the "old trail" down the east arm of Hance Canyon, by merely improving an Indian route. It is not shown on the Trails Illustrated map, but its head is at the first viewpoint with off-road parking east of the paved picnic area where the map shows Buggeln Hill. The Hance Ranch buildings and the old Buggeln Hotel, now torn down, were in the woods to the south. The top fifty yards of the old trail are still in good shape. Below this trail, use your own judgment. Washouts and rockslides have taken a severe toll. In general, keep to the west side of the ravine until you are through the Coconino and then cross east and descend through a juniper-covered slope. Cut trees and vestigial retaining walls mark the trail as you near the Redwall. It goes into a wash just east of a big cairn set on a prominent rock. Just before this wash meets another from the west, leave the bed and skirt the base of an impressive pinnacle of limestone. The trail soon leads back into the bed at the base of the Redwall. There are no further obstacles until one is deep in the Archean rock.

In a ravine on the right below the Redwall is a fairly reliable seep spring. Near this, under some cottonwood trees, Hance built a rock cabin. The trees and the cabin are long gone, presumably taken out by a flood, with only a picture in an old book to remember the place. Nearby, on higher ground are rock walls, all that remain of an old corral. Hance would take his clients to

Scouting Hance Rapids during the Kolb Expedition, circa 1911.
(Photo: Emery Kolb, Grand Canyon Museum Collection, 17164)

this cabin the night before their big trip to the river and back. Fast hikers can cover more ground than this in a day. Without the help of a maintained trail, Allyn Cureton and I went down the route to the river, returned to the rim via the Grandview Trail, and then walked back to the car at the head of the old trail in one day.

At the first outcrop of Tapeats Sandstone on the west side of the wash, there is an overhang where the wall is coated with hard clay. Between 1885 and 1895, visitors carved their names and dates in this clay. Tourists also wrote their remarks and names in the guest book at the Hance Ranch. Bucky O'Neill recorded his visit with sentiment:

"God made the Canyon and John Hance made the trails. Neither would be complete without the other."

Deep in the Tapeats, is a small but permanent stream, and an alcove which used to be called the "Temple of Set." Down in the granite, before the bed plunges over the first waterfall, there are routes to the Tonto both to the east and the west. Wild burros used to be numerous in this section and subsequently, the trails were padded smooth as a result of the burros walking on them. Hance could lead his tourists down past the waterfalls using fixed ropes and ladders. One now has to bypass these barriers by going over spurs that project from the canyon walls. My system takes me out of the bed three times, alternately to the east, the west, and then the east. These are rather rugged scrambles and one needs to be psychologically as well as physically prepared. The reward at the end is a fine view of Sockdolager Rapids.

There are the usual detours away from the old trail. From the rim, one can go over to the Sinking Ship. A trail loops around its base and one may note some well-preserved ruins just north of the middle of the east side of the Sinking Ship, on ledges above the trail. Routes to the three southern summits of the Sinking Ship are hard enough to be interesting. The lower north summit requires technical climbing hardware. One can get down through the Supai on the east side of the Sinking Ship and follow the old trail to the junction of the two arms of Hance Canyon. One can return to the rim via the west arm and the ravine leading to the saddle south of the Sinking Ship.

From where the old trail meets the Redwall, one can go up to the saddle south of Coronado Butte. Some Grand Canyon buffs prefer this route to the regular old trail. Coronado Butte has been climbed, but it is more difficult than the Sinking Ship. One can walk along the east base of Coronado, but the west face is sheer.

Some hikers along the Tonto Trail, east from Hance Canyon, have been far down Mineral Canyon. This is difficult and the usual route stays above the inner gorge. The Tonto Trail slopes down to the beach at Hance Rapids. If you meet a man who claims to have walked through the canyon from the Little Colorado to Supai, you might ask him if he stayed in the Tonto Trail all the way. If he has even studied the map, he would know that this long trail starts at Hance Rapids and ends at Garnet Canyon, far short of Supai. Rock-studded Hance Rapids is far more difficult to run by boat than Sockdolager.

Coronado Butte. (Photo: Michael Quinn, Grand Canyon Museum Collection, IM5559)

Grapevine Canyon Routes

Most of the routes in Grapevine Canyon require comfort with exposure and some technical rock climbing ability. Good climbers have been down the south arm of Grapevine that starts near Thor's Hammer. A fine set of ancient pictographs are located on the wall just below the rim about a mile to the west. Chad Gibson, a seasonal ranger at the South Rim, and I made it down a crack at the base of the Coconino. It seemed to be wider near the bottom and I felt it would be difficult to get back up if it became necessary to do so.

Jim Ohlman, the first person to climb all but five of the one hundred and thirty-eight named summits in the Grand Canyon, led a small group of climbers down there, where they found all of the right moves for getting through the Supai and the Redwall, to the Tonto. I was told that the Supai is even more difficult to get through than the Coconino where I had stopped on a previous trip, and one must be clever at finding the right combination of ravines to bypass big drops. Going down here and coming back up the east arm of Grapevine would make a very challenging loop-trip for the very experienced technical rock climber. However, one should be prepared to do some rock climbing and back-tracking if the route seems to dangerous.

If I had a good climbing companion and the assurance of a rope, I would undertake this. According to Jim Ohlman, two cliffs in the Supai are bypassed to the east. At the impossible drop at the Redwall rim, one should go to the second ravine to the east. This leads via a ramp back to the original slot below the barrier fall. There is an obvious detour through the upper Tapeats to the Tonto Trail. Twenty or thirty yards west of where the trail crosses the wash south of Lyell Butte, a small overhang protects an interesting inscription. Bob Dye and others told me to keep an eye out for this. I finally found the words "Hotel de Willow Creek" and the names of two well-known prospectors who were here before 1900.

Shoshone Point Route

I have explored routes east from the Kaibab Trail along the Redwall and up in the Hermit Shale. When Alan Doty used my route and made a first ascent of Lyell Butte, he noticed that the Coconino below Shoshone Point forms a sloping promontory and that it just might offer a short cut to Lyell, Newton and Pattie Buttes.

Scouting the rim for a descent, he found that a shallow bay on the east side seemed to offer the best chance. Several hundred feet below the rim, a ten-foot wall formed a barrier clear across the bay, but a log was leaning against the wall at the easiest place. Alan found that he could scale this small cliff without even touching this log, but I was willing to accept this aid. We worked our way north and down to the Coconino. The route left at the very point and seemed safe except for a steep slab of sandstone. Moki steps cut by the prehistoric inhabitants indicate that this was once an ancient route.

Toward the bottom we doubled back to the south on the east side of the promontory. This is not a route for a person with a fear of exposure, though it was easy to get down the Supai and the Redwall west of Newton. One might continue on from there to the river via Lonetree Canyon.

Clear Creek Trail. (Photo: Harvey Butchart)

Clear Creek Trail

This trail leaves the Kaibab Trail approximately 0.3 mile north of Phantom Ranch. It is 8.7 miles over to Clear Creek, the first sure water supply. This trek takes fast hikers less than four hours but heavily loaded backpackers have taken as much as eight (camping is no longer permitted in the Clear Creek area). The first section of the trail leading from Bright Angel Creek to the top of the Tonto Plateau is well-preserved. The whole trail has been used more in recent years and there is little chance of losing it. The only water that is sometimes found along this trail is in rain pockets in the wash between Sumner Point and Zoroaster Temple, but this is too near the beginning of the trail to be of much importance. It would be a good place to camp before attempting ascents of Sumner, Brahma, or Zoroaster. The ravine through the Redwall at the base of the ridge leading to Sumner Point can be climbed. The assault on Zoroaster is a technical rock climb which requires the appropriate climbing hardware. An old cairn on Sumner suggests that it was climbed long ago. Brahma was first climbed after Zoroaster.

If the Clear Creek Trail seems long and tedious, remember the Kolb brothers and the three rangers who came over here in 1928 without any trail. The Kolbs were interested in photographing Cheyava Falls on the east side of the longest arm. Twice Emery Kolb, with different companions, made his way upriver to Clear Creek, and once Emery and Ellsworth Kolb came overland.

In the early days of Canyon exploration, the park rangers seemed to have had more time for discovery trips than they do now. In 1928, the three rangers reported that the stream was permanent and would support fish. They also found ancient ruins high on a ledge south of Cheyava Falls and others against the cliff west of the junction of the long arm, the one containing the most water. They were young and lighthearted. One of the three, Glen Sturdevant, wrote in a humorous vein concerning their failure at cooking mescal and keeping warm at night. Tragically, Sturdevant and another ranger drowned within the year trying to pass Horn Creek Rapids with a light boat.

On my first trip to Clear Creek, I was surprised to see how far the trail stays on the Tonto level before it finally goes down to the bed. It passes Zoroaster and most of Brahma before it comes to the right break. Here, one can leave the trail for an interesting detour. A deer trail goes over the ridge and down into a valley whose head is the saddle between Brahma and Deva. After I had been stopped by the Redwall in the southwest arm, I ignored a better chance in favor of the upper end of the valley. I found at least two possibilities, but chose the narrow ravine going up to the south toward Brahma. At one place, two or three huge chockstones form a twenty-five foot overhang, but I was able to wriggle through a narrow hole behind them. Al Doty, once a student at NAU who now sells art objects in Sedona, got up there without finding the hole on a day hike from Clear Creek to the top of Deva and then to Bright Angel Campground via the Redwall rim west of Brahma. This is a route to the prehistoric ruins and spring in the middle of the Supai Formation on the southwest side of Deva.

Many other fine side trips are possible. Hiking down to the Colorado is one. There is an eight-foot seasonal waterfall at a chockstone barrier, but it can be bypassed on a sloping ledge of polished granite. There are no handholds so rubber-soled shoes are the key. Walking is easy along the gently sloping gravel, but don't be caught by a flood. The walls go up nearly straight for quite a distance. As in so many of the Grand Canyon tributaries, the lower bed through the hard Archean rock is more meandering than it is in the higher valley. I have also seen several instances of another anomaly — a streambed which has been going straight along a fault line between the hard Redwall on one side and the Supai Sandstone on the other, then suddenly takes a short plunge into the hard rock. After a short meander through

Cheyava Falls (Photo: Harvey Butchart)

an awesome narrows it emerges and continues in the logical bed. Clear Creek at the very end becomes quite straight. Parallel fins of schist project into the river causing turbulence and making it almost impossible to moor a boat here.

An interesting return from the river can be via the Tonto Plateau east of Clear Creek. One can follow the rough rocks along the bank upriver for a few hundred yards to a beach where the early river parties camped. Then scramble up the steep granite into a ravine to the east and out on top of the Tonto. Either side of Howland's Butte is all right. A deer trail goes down the bed of the ravine heading northwest from between Howland's Butte and Angel's Gate. Before reaching Clear Creek, we came to a tributary from south of Cape Royal. It has another spooky narrows through the quartzite and Tapeats. Merrel Clubb, a professor of Old English Literature from the University of Kansas who spent many vacations hiking in the Canyon, told me to watch for a ruin on a high ledge on the south side in the quartzite. I have looked for it several times without success. The valley above, hemmed in by Wotan, Cape Royal and Thor Temple, is the most inspiring. The Redwall is the absolute barrier. I wish I had more time to explore the area just north of Thor Temple.

As one crosses the terrace just north of the junction of this canyon with Clear Creek, watch for the mescal pit. This is a low mound of small rocks about twenty-feet across and hollow in the center where Indians used to roast century plants. They last for hundreds of years and sometimes one can find bits of charcoal in them.

If one has just come down the Clear Creek Trail, the usual impulse is to go upstream rather than down. Most visitors would like to see Cheyava Falls, the highest in the entire Grand Canyon. In the long northeast arm, it comes from a cave about one-fifth of the way down the Redwall cliff. Very rarely is there a good flow. Most of the time, the fall is just a wet streak down the wall. Ellsworth Kolb entered this cave twice. He and his brother Emery came down from the rim by a very rugged route. At one place, they even lassoed a tree and used the rope to get over and climb down the tree. At the rim of the Redwall, they built a windlass and Emery let his much heavier brother down the wall. Interrupted by a terrific storm, Emery tied the rope securely and sought shelter while his brother had to endure it. When it was over, the ropes were so badly twisted that Ellsworth couldn't be raised or lowered. Neither could he touch the wall of the overhang, so Emery lowered him a pole to push against the wall and get untangled. After discovering a wall in the cave, Ellsworth came back with a ladder. A little farther on he was stopped by a deep pool. Three parties of cavers have repeated this exploit, but they all used modern methods of rappelling.

In 1928, when the rangers found the dwellings south of Cheyava Falls, they leaned a log against the cliff and climbed up to inspect them. Later climbers have used a rope to rappel down from above. It is interesting to see the rest of the canyon up to its head in the Redwall. In the spring while the snow was melting, we found a 400-foot free fall at an overhang in the Redwall. There was a fine detached pinnacle and a couple of barriers in the bed with adequate bypasses. Using a bit of agility at a chockstone, one can scramble on to the top of the Redwall. Bob Dye climbed up through the Redwall here to the top of the Walhalla Plateau and found a spring near the rim of the Redwall at the east side. Later, he came down from the plateau above and a little to the north where he found a good route through the Supai.

Returning to the junction of the long northeast arm and the north arm, one should look for some more prehistoric ruins. They are strung along the base of the west wall opposite the Cheyava Falls arm. At the best of these is a sheet metal tag with the inscription "Surface Collection by Gila Pueblo." Nearby is a fine overhang that would protect several sleepers on a rainy night. Packrats like to bring cactus spines into such places, so check well before putting down your air mattress.

A walk up the wet arm of the creek, past the cascades and fern-bordered pools is a must. Pushing through thickets is slow, but we finally came to a thirty-foot fall in the shale, which can be

Mel Simons downclimbing a steep route through the Redwall in Clear Creek.
(Photo: Harvey Butchart)

bypassed to the west. Watch for a cave near the base of the Redwall to the west. It is accessible, but the route takes a bit of study. In the 1930's, a young man working for the Civilian Conservation Corps found split twig figurines. They have been dated back to over 3,000 years old by Carbon-14. Cavers have traced Clear Creek to its source, but have found no other cave.

Another interesting day can be spent going out of Clear Creek up the tributary that comes down from north of Deva. When we saw the Redwall ahead we felt so sure that we would be turned back that we put down our lunches and canteens. When we went on just to say we had slapped the wall at the last handhold, we were surprised that we could continue on right up through the Supai. Merrel Clubb and "Kit" Wing, a World War II vet who later became Superintendent of Petrified Forest National Park, had already found a way down from the rim through Obi Canyon to the Deva Saddle. I found quite a variety of petroglyphs and pic-tographs at the bottom of the Coconino just west of Obi Canyon.

Clear Creek is worth seeing even if one has only a day to come over from Bright Angel Creek and return. Still it would be far better if one had a week here to check the attractions. There is water in all the main arms below the Tapeats, but for day-long trips at higher elevations, water should be carried. During the cool season, one can go along the Tonto Platform from Clear Creek to Vishnu Creek and beyond. This is incredibly strenuous and requires carrying several gallons of water during the summer.

According to a legal notice in the archives of the Flagstaff courthouse, John Hance was planning to build a trail from the mines in Asbestos Canyon to Clear Creek, but after eighty years, only a small portion of the trail is evident.

Redwall Routes In Kwangunt, Vishnu and Clear Creek Canyons

Bob Dye and Ed Anderson, students at NAU, had expected to leave the eastern valleys via my route up from Kwangunt Canyon to the Atoko-Siegfried Saddle, but they passed the break in the Tapeats north of Banta Point without noticing it. When they came to the head of the gorge, they found a complicated, technically difficult route through the Redwall and Supai to the known deer trail through the Coconino. Jim Ohlman gave me a move-by-move description of this route.

Many years ago, Doc Ellis, a geologist who worked for the USGS, found a deer trail up from the bed of Vishnu Canyon through the Redwall and used it for a first ascent of Hall Butte. It is a few hundred yards north of the butte.

Ohlman and others checked out another Redwall route directly west of this one, which descends on the other side of the promontory. The expert climbers who scored a first ascent of Angel's Gate discovered a Redwall route coming up to the Wotan-Angel's Gate Saddle from the north. The climb is not too difficult, but a few yards, are very exposed. When Scott Baxter and I came up here to climb Hawkins Butte, we noticed a possible route through the Redwall across the Cape Royal arm of Clear Creek. A year later, Mel Simons, a geologist from California, and I checked it out and found that it goes. We climbed east through the Tapeats in the bed of the creek and then doubled back to the west beyond the ravine, and up to the saddle west of the butte at elevation 6,057'.

The route is in a minor ravine caused by a fault. One might come up here for the view or to climb Thor Temple. Thor was first climbed by Alan Doty, who used a rope to get down from the Walhalla Plateau. Ohlman and Kirschvink later climbed it via a Redwall route up from the Cheyava Falls Arm of Clear Creek.

Hermit Trail

This formerly popular trail leaves the rim at the end of a service road behind Hermits Rest. It was built for the tourist trade by Fred Harvey and was maintained by the Park Service until 1931. Accommodations were available at Hermit Camp during the main tourist season, less than an hour's walk from the river. Just off the Hermit Trail, at the foot of the Coconino is Santa Maria Spring which is fairly reliable. Dripping Springs keeps its basin full, but this is a mile and a half to the west of the Hermit Trail. Especially during the spring of the year, this is a beauty spot and a bird lover's paradise. As shown on the topo, the trail continues past Dripping Springs and goes up the Coconino to the northeast. Then it swings to the south and reaches a road end.

Watch for fossil footprints beside the Hermit Trail at a certain depth in the Coconino Sandstone. Found at many places in the Grand Canyon, in the same formation, they were first studied by scientists here. These footprints, of reptiles and amphibians, were formed about 300 million years ago. Unfortunately, no fossils of the entire animals are ever found. The prints range in size from tiny insect tracks to large tracks measuring some eight inches long. They are not to be confused with dinosaur tracks in the Painted Desert left some 60 million years ago.

Just north of the junction with Dripping Springs Trail the head of Hermit Gorge is reached — a sheer drop for hundreds of feet. The trail turns to the right and descends slowly through the Supai. Santa Maria Spring, with its ivy covered shelter, is a good rest stop. Don't waste time looking for Four Mile Spring. Still shown on the map, it is either dry or covered by a rock slide. In fact, slides have obliterated the trail at several places making it impossible for pack animals to use. These places might bother a person at night if he couldn't see the continuation ahead. Cope

Butte is visible to the right on the route down through the Redwall at Cathedral Stairs. There is an exposed, third class route up Cope Butte which requires skill on rock and comfort with exposure. A rope may be used for a belay. We did climb it and found an old cairn on the summit. Though it has a great view from the summit of the inner gorge, it should be only attempted by skilled climbers who are comfortable with exposure.

At the base of Cope Butte, on the Tonto, is a fork in the trail. The right branch goes to Indian Gardens. In the old days, this formed a popular loop trip for guided horse parties. On the first day they would take the left branch at the fork to see Hermit Rapids before spending the night at Hermit Camp. The next day, they would return to the rim via the Tonto and Bright Angel Trails. The old iron cots under an overhang at Monument Creek indicate that occasionally they stopped overnight here. Modern backpackers also find this loop attractive. I have walked from Indian Gardens along the Tonto Trail to Hermit Creek, up to Hermits Rest and about half the rim drive — then walked down to Indian Gardens in one long day. Family groups can enjoy a week in the same area. Monument Creek nearly always has enough water for camping and it is also easy to walk down to the river there.

Granite Falls at the end of Monument Canyon is a fine example of a rapid where huge boulders from the side canyon have pushed the full force of the river against the cliff on the far side. This is the locale of the most commonly copied illustration, "Running a Rapid" from Powell's book, *The Exploration of the Colorado and It's Canyons*. The quiet pool and stark skyline complete the setting.

Hikers are increasing their use of the Tonto Trail, but routes from the plateau down to the river are far from being crowded. A chockstone in the bed of Salt Creek stopped me, but when the bed was dry, an agile climber was able to make it down. The rest of the bed to the Colorado is easy. I succeeded in getting down the broken wall on the east side. George Wharton James wrote an account of his futile attempt at recovering a boat that a prospector had left at the mouth of the second canyon west of the Bright Angel Trail. He and his two companions were not sure whether the man meant Salt Creek or the nameless canyon between Salt and Horn. After some fumbles, I succeeded in going down both canyons. Burros used to be common here and I once saw a bighorn ewe in the nameless canyon east of Salt. I call it "Epsom Canyon" from the bitter deposit of a most unpalatable seep. There are lots of ticks here during springtime.

Horn Creek is another challenge. There is a trace of an old trail along the west side below the Tapeats cliff. West of a pinnacle dominating the mouth of Horn, a ravine goes down to the river. This easy scramble brings one to the foot of Horn Creek Rapids. The trail continues along the base of the Tapeats and then, if one can find it, goes to the river across from Ninetyone Mile Creek.

Following a tip from Emery Kolb, I went up Ninetyone Mile Creek into the Trinity Creek Basin. One can walk up the Redwall between Isis and Shiva to reach the North Rim at the departure point for Shiva. Allow two days to cover this route from the South Rim to the campground on the North Rim. West of Horn Creek, high above the river, the Kolbs found a fully clothed skeleton.

When you try to reach the river down the bed of Horn, you come to a forty-foot waterfall. A number of people have given up here, but Allyn Cureton tried an exposed third-class bypass to the east, trusting the friction of his soles on the smooth rock. Beyond this friction pitch there are breaks in the cliff. With care, an experienced climber, comfortable on third class, can bypass a second waterfall in the bed to the west, and reach the beach. Horn Creek Rapids looks wild in pictures, but the best are taken from the north bank where the fury of the current is defied by a projecting rock. This is where Ranger Glen Sturdevant and one of two companions drowned in 1928. They planned to carry their light boat around the rapid, but lost control and were swept away from the landing. The other escaped to the north shore and found a way to get out of the inner gorge and over to Phantom Ranch. We have repeated this route and have slept beside the roaring rapids.

An alcove on the Hermit Trail. (Photo: Andy Zdon)

Back now to the fork in the trail below Cope Butte — it would be about a mile to the camp beside Hermit Creek. In the old days before 1903, a tent village complete with piped water was located here. There was an aerial tram which brought supplies down from Pima Point, and a Model T Ford which must have been the only motor car in this section of the Grand Canyon. Cottonwood trees were started with the irrigation water. George Wharton James was writing about the Grand Canyon when the Hermit Trail was being built, and he called this the scenic heart of the canyon. When Phantom Ranch was developed along the cross-canyon route, Hermit Camp was abandoned.

A trail goes from the camp down to the river. When I saw Hermit Rapids I realized for the first time what a Grand Canyon rapid should look like. People drown in the riffles at Bright Angel and Pipe Creeks, but for fury and power, they are not in the same league with Horn, Monument, or Hermit Rapids.

There is no trail up Hermit Creek, yet the little stream has great charm. Much of the trail to the river has been washed out, but it is easy to go in either direction. One passes little falls and finally comes to a shady pool bordered with flowers. Above this source of Hermit Creek there is no vegetation to fight.

Across the creek from Hermit Camp, the trail continues to Boucher Canyon. The name commemorates a hermit named Louis Boucher, who lived here for over fifteen years. Alone, he irrigated a garden and grew fruit trees. He built a trail to his secluded world from Dripping Springs and pushed a mine shaft into the black rock. The Boucher Trail was omitted from maps of the area for some time as it was deemed unsafe. It has been finally included once again on newer maps. The enthusiasm of hikers who made the loop trip down the Boucher Trail and back along the Hermit Trail was primarily responsible for the trail being renovated and included on recent maps of the area. The Boucher Trail is not maintained and rockslides and washouts have left their marks.

If one leaves the Dripping Springs Trail about 0.5 mile from the end and goes north along the top of the Supai Formation, it remains as distinct as a good deer trail around the point to a break near the head of Travertine Canyon. The place is marked with a couple of small cairns. Steel rods still show at a difficult spot in the sandstone. The trail is so thrashed here that a horse or mule can no longer get by. Getting down to the Redwall is a challenge and one must keep a good eye out for the trail. The route is more defined in the ravine at the base of Whites Butte. It joins the Tonto Trail where the latter is starting through the Tapeats.

The ruins of Boucher's old rock cabin is south of the trail just before one reaches the bed of Boucher Creek. It takes twenty-five or thirty minutes to walk to the river from here. The ruins of another small rock structure southwest of the cabin may have been a chicken coop. There is an old mine tunnel on the right side of the wash about a hundred yards north of the cabin. The tunnel is probably best viewed from the outside looking in because of the danger of a potential cave-in.

Louis Boucher must have been quite a character. Unable to wrangle dudes like Bass and Hance, he did befriend ship-wrecked river runners and once entertained a geologist and his wife. As southwest writer Edwin Corle once said, "He wore a white beard, rode a white mule, and told only white lies."

Where the trail meets the bed, Boucher Creek may be dry, but there is water both upstream and on the way down to the river. The walk up the canyon is fine for the scenery. The stroll to the river is a still greater attraction. Boucher Rapids doesn't seem overpowering like Hermit Rapids, but it is lively and long.

The trail goes down the bed as far as the junction with Topaz, the west arm of Boucher, and then climbs back to the Tonto. Some go up just to get a close view of Scylla Butte, a neat little tower of Bright Angel Shale. Neighboring Slate Canyon is large with many points of interest. We found a trace of a trail well to the north of an obvious break through the Tapeats. Once you are in the bed, walking to the river is easy. Slate Creek at its mouth has no beach where one can land above the rapids. Crystal Creek,

Louis Boucher and Silver Bell, circa 1912. (Grand Canyon Museum Collection, 5972)

across the river, has piled boulders in the riverbed above the mouth of Slate so that the current roars past. Crystal Rapids was regarded as rather mild until the winter of 1966. The great flood came down from the north rim and rolled more boulders into the channel.

In Slate Canyon, above the Tonto Trail, one can almost surely find water throughout the year. There are some minor obstructions which are bypassed by deer trails and one can walk on up through the last of the Redwall. There are several caves in the region. At least one is both accessible and deep. It doubles back to a window in the sheer cliff face. Above the Redwall, one can proceed up to the rim by going either east to the Diana Temple Saddle or west to the notch north of Jicarilla Point. Both of these routes require some climbing ability and strength. I prefer having a fixed rope both in the Coconino west of Diana Temple Saddle and in the Kaibab a hundred and fifty yards to the west. The way up near Jicarilla Point is only a little easier. The route through the Kaibab is southwest of the point just beyond a natural bridge right at the rim. Strong young climbers do this freehand, but I use a leaning log.

There are ruins and fine petroglyphs near the Jicarilla notch on the east side of the spur and a few more designs around to the west of the notch. One can go north along the top of the spur and get down to the saddle south of Pollux Temple as well as getting down the slot on the east side of the notch. There are two big mescal pits on this saddle, and Pollux Temple can be climbed from here.

One of these difficult routes must have been used by rivermen Leslie Clement and August Tadje when their boat got jammed against a rock in the river. Their companion, Charles Russell, a traveling promoter, went back to the Boucher Trail and finally got to Bass Camp. Meanwhile, Clement and Tadje made one of the most hair-raising unroped ascents out of the Canyon through the Coconino Sandstone. When Clement and Tadje told W.W. Bass that they had come from the river to the rim between the Boucher and Bass Trails, he could hardly believe the story. Incidentally, Diana and Vesta have both been climbed. On the west side of Diana, a faint game trail goes to the top.

The Tonto Trail west of Slate Canyon leads on mile after mile. Progress is slow as the trail contours around the side canyons. Views into the inner gorge alternate with closeups of the towering cliffs of the south rim. Geikie Peak is a splendid background for spring cactus flowers. There is seasonal water in potholes, but if one needs to get to the river, there are routes west of Turquoise, almost surely in Ruby, and certainly in Serpentine, as well as the nameless canyon east of the latter. Serpentine to Bass is possible along the river, but it is easier to stay on the Tonto Trail.

Upper Boucher Creek

A loop trip down Boucher Trail and back to Hermit Rest via the Tonto and Hermit Trails has become fairly popular. As an alternate route, it is possible to go up Boucher Creek, then through the Redwall and even the Supai.

Years ago, I went up on a casual inspection, but did not have enough time to give it a good try. Royce Fletcher, a climber from Albuquerque with whom I exchanged route information over the years, told me that the Redwall goes. He had followed a couple of bighorn sheep. There are two barriers that require bypasses. One of these is a real challenge. Near the top of the Redwall, one has to enter a very narrow curving slot where he would expect to be stopped by a fall. Walking ahead, one comes into the open at the bottom of a conical pit. A broken slope on the east side gets one above all of the Redwall. Scramble to the right into the main bed and go up most of the Supai. Bob Packard has found a way through the top of Supai cliff.

When I attempted to follow Fletcher's directions, I was intrigued by two bighorn ewes ahead of me. I was only minutes behind them when I rounded a corner and entered the final bay where I discovered that they had vanished. I couldn't understand how they had disappeared unless they had gone up an almost perpendicular wall on the west side. My nerve failed when I used some very meager handholds for about fifteen feet. Later, I came back with Paul Schafer, a friend from the Sun City newspaper. With him below to spot me, I was able to climb the crucial forty feet. From here, I could see how Packard had gone along the bench to the west, then up and back to the middle of the bay and out on top of the Supai. I would surely have enjoyed watching those bighorns go up those steep forty feet. A few years later, Paul was backpacking down West Clear Creek through Camp Verde. He was transporting his backpack across a deep pool when something went terribly wrong. He disappeared beneath the surface of the pool and never came back up.

One might find it easier to climb Vesta Temple from Boucher Camp than from Mescalero Point. There is a route off the Kaibab rim a short distance west of Mescalero. A hundred-foot handline is a real help here because of the verticality and exposure. Then one can go along the west side of Diana Temple and follow a deer trail to the top or go down to the east from the saddle along the south side of Diana. Good rock-climbers have found ropeless routes through the Coconino here, but again a rope with a safe belay is a help. Below the route, along the Hermit to the south and east reaching Vesta Temple, lies a room-sized chunk of Coconino that has a fine display of fossil footprints.

Alan Doty showed me how to go along the east side of Vesta and reach the top via the north ridge. I found this a long hard day for me and Lee Dexter, one of the best rock climbers at NAU at the time. We were still looking for our car at 10:30pm that night. There was a deer trail through the break in the Kaibab at the head of Boucher Bay and I used this to go to the saddle south of Diana when I climbed it. One can follow a sketchy trail along this bench for miles. Routes for good climbers connect with the rim west of Mescalero Point and also southwest of Jicarilla Point. Student hikers found a way through the Coconino ravine east of Jicarilla and Doty discovered that he could get down through the Coconino on the west side near the end. I needed a roped belay to get down a steep slab, but the others climbed without aid.

There are mescal pits on the flat saddle south of Pollux. Doty made a first ascent of Pollux and, on another trip, he and Donald Davis went west to climb Castor Temple. Doty rediscovered a route off the rim and down through the Coconino at Walapai Point, finding Moki steps cut in the sandstone on this route. Doty also found some possible routes for going down the Supai. Jim Ohlman even descended the Redwall in Ruby Canyon.

Bass Trail

When William Wallace Bass came to Arizona, he soon visited the village of Supai. From the local Indians he learned about the canyon, including the location of "Trail Canyon," the early name for the present Bass Canyon. An Indian trail went from the rim to Mystic Spring which was north of Mt. Huethawali. According to Edwin D. McKee, Mystic Spring had been dry for years, which resulted in its being deleted from most recent maps. Actually, Mystic and several other seeps in the general area of Spencer Terrace are seasonal, and run for several months of the year. William Wallace Bass, Jr. gave me a location photo for the spring. George Billingsley went right to it after viewing the picture. The spring is actually twenty feet below the surface of the Esplanade just south of the ravine near the second "e" in the name Spencer on the Grand Canyon Map. I proved its authenticity by matching the picture with that of the one in the book The Grand Canyon of Arizona by George Wharton James. The spring is a full mile north of the location on the Matthes-Evans map. Old mining camp trash was still there beneath a protective overhang. The seep spring at the base of the Coconino south of Chemehuevi Point is, however, still dripping.

For some reason the Bass Trail has withstood the years better than the Hance Trail. The only place where one might need to consult the map would be on the juniper-covered Esplanade. It is very distinct through the Kaibab and Coconino. Just east of the break through the latter formation several Indian ruins can be seen. The map shows how the trail skirts the east base of Mt. Huethawali and then doubles back through the Supai to the head of the gorge in the Redwall. One can take a climber's short cut down directly from the saddle between Garnet and Bass. There is a juniper log to help at the hardest place.

Where the Redwall gorge begins to widen there is a cave on the west side. Hikers who have climbed into it report nothing of interest. North of the Redwall section one can see sky through a hole a hundred feet or so below the crest of the ridge to the east.

About six hundred feet above the river, Bass had a campsite that was called Bedrock Tanks. Tools and buckets beneath an overhang mark the place and one can see how Bass hoped to get water by driving a pipe into a crack. It is no longer a trustworthy water source.

Some hikers have panicked when they came to the dry waterfall where the bed drops sheer to the river, and started back up the trail with empty canteens. They could have followed the trail west out of the bed down to the riverbank.

Near where Bass used to cross the river still lies the metal boat "Ross Wheeler." Canyon river guide Bert Loper built it in 1914 at Green River, Utah, and it was abandoned in 1915 by Russell, Clement, and Tadje on the latter's daring climb through the Coconino.

Across the river, where the map shows BM 2,477', Bass had a small farm irrigated with water from Shinumo Creek. Prehistoric Indians also irrigation-farmed the same area by diverting water from Shinumo Creek and others. Their dwellings are scattered throughout the Shinumo Basin.

One of the more fantastic suggestions about modifying the Grand Canyon was to build a railroad through it. Robert Brewster Stanton, the engineer in charge of survey, thought that the open terrace just north of Bass Rapids would be a good place for a switchyard.

West of the ferry site, the trail continues along the south side of the river to the old cable car which Bass used during high flows on the Colorado River. The cable has now been cut for fear it might be a hazard to canyon tour boats. The same fate has befallen the other tram three miles down river which was used to reach the asbestos mines in Hakatai Canyon.

To leave the Bass Trail, the map shows two routes, both heading west along the Tonto. It omits the spur trail down to the copper

W.W. Bass, Joe the burro and Shep. (Photo: Grand Canyon Museum Collection, 833)

mine Bass operated in Copper Canyon. The trail doesn't become clear until one has found an obscure break in the Tapeats well to the north of the Tonto Trail. On the way to the mine, one fork contours north above the camp. Later, it starts down steeply, apparently in the direction of another shaft, but we were able to continue below the Tapeats and reach the river opposite the mouth of Shinumo Creek.

When Bass ceased operating the mine, he stored some of his duffel in the tunnel. Farther in, the horizontal tunnel is cut by a vertical shaft. This holds rainwater that comes through a hole in the ceiling. Drinking this water may be a risky venture because of its close proximity to the mine and the potential for contamination. During wet spells, there is often some water in the bed of the wash. The only drawback for using this as a stop for the night is that it is not even a full day's walk from the rim.

It is quite easy to go from camp west up to the Tonto Trail

again. I didn't locate the trail down to the Hakatai tram, but the slope to the river west of Copper Canyon all looks rather easy. From the Tonto, one can see the mines where Bass mined asbestos across the river in Hakatai Canyon. There may have been a trail on the north side of the river connecting the camp on Shinumo Creek with the mines. The Matthes-Evans map used to show the trail extending as far as Burro Canyon. Cliffs bar this approach.

Farther west along the Tonto one can look down on the black rocks in the river at Walthenberg Rapids and downstream. The crags projecting from Powell Plateau are impressive. Near some Indian ruins at the last big ravine before Garnet Canyon one can find water in rain pockets, but this source would give out in the hot season. There are deep waterholes in Garnet and at times, there is a trickle in the lower bed. To reach it one should leave the clear trail which goes east above the bed and look for the descent route. This route was used by prospectors and the burros although it was never shown on a map. The water in Garnet is slightly salty. One can continue out of Garnet along a vague trail below the Tapeats to camp beside the Colorado.

The vestige of a trail helps for a third of the way from Garnet to Elves Chasm. Scrambling over the blocks beside the river is slow and a mile an hour is fairly good progress. Strong hikers should go from Copper Canyon to Elves in an easy day. Every river party seems to stop here for glamorous pictures of the falls and the shady pools. This is a logical destination for a four day round-trip from the head of the Bass Trail.

One can continue downriver, however the going is slow and rough, especially in Stephen Aisle. Ancient deposits of travertine, cut by many ravines, create formidable barriers. The going is best close to the river as far as this route is possible. Where the granite is bent down to the west and disappears beneath the river, one must climb and continue on top of the bluff. Carry plenty of water because you will be away from the river for at least four hours. Rain pockets are few and unreliable. In Conquistador Aisle, the walking becomes faster. Even this area was used by the

Camped above the water near Royal Arch Creek
(Photo: Jorgen Visbak)

Ancestral Puebloan, suggested by the location of a rock shelter at the mouth of Fossil Canyon.

A Supai Indian told R.C. Euler that the Indians used to farm the delta at Fossil Creek. When he was a boy, his father had taken him there but he couldn't remember the route. I have been off the rim into Fossil Bay at a break near the head and I was also able to get to the rim of the Redwall on both sides of the gorge. Aerial views suggest the possibility of getting through the Redwall about halfway from Fossil to Forster. The clincher is that there is a rockpile to serve as a step at the bottom of this presumed route.

Esplanade West of the Bass Trail

At Garnet Canyon, the Tonto Platform finally gives out, but a new terrace has already become the dominant plateau between the rim and the river. This terrace is called the Esplanade and it is at the top of the Supai Sandstone. Captain Burro, the father of Euler's informant, Walin Burro, started to build a trail which would go from the Bass Trail to his home at Supai. It is still recognizable all the way to Forster Canyon, but this was far short of his goal. There is also a connecting trail off the rim at Apache Point.

Below Toltec Point, you are in the Royal Arch Creek basin. From the rim above, one can see the fine fortification on the promontory at Toltec. Royal Arch Creek is one of the most interesting canyons in the park. There are several ways to get down to the Redwall rim, but only the bed of the wash will take one through this formation. One of the more interesting routes is to drive out on the Topacoba Hilltop Road to the sign indicating the park boundary. From there, take a compass bearing and follow it through the junipers to Apache Point to the east. A clear trail descends from just west of the point as the map still shows. Across the deep notch on the very top of the pinnacle north of the trail is a fine example of a prehistoric ruin. The trail loops below the pinnacle and then descends to the Esplanade on the east side. If the Indians wanted to go west along the Esplanande, they could get through a similar break on that side. The map shows a natural arch near the lower end of the bed of Royal Arch Creek. The promontory pointing to this arch is the way down through the Supai from the west. The route is followed down the middle until stopped by a cliff. Then go northwest along the rim to a break behind a detached block of sandstone. Follow the rim of the Redwall gorge until the burro trail drops into the bed. This is also bighorn country, and we saw six of these beautiful animals near some water halfway through the gorge.

There is a spring in the lower Redwall large enough to keep water on the surface and link flower-bordered pools. Progress beside the little cascades is easy, although at one place it is necessary for the inexpert climber to wade through foot-deep water. Eventually coming around a bend, you find the Royal Arch for which the creek was named. It is about sixty feet up to the ceiling with a similar span. It escaped detection from the air because it is about forty feet through. Though not the largest natural bridge in the Grand Canyon, it is the only one with a permanent stream through it. About fifty yards north of the bridge, the stream comes to a high waterfall. There is no way to go directly down to Elves Chasm.

A fragile-looking column nearby seems about ready to topple into the void. One can climb to the flat-topped buttress east of the arch. It was here that a helicopter picked me up when I broke my heel with a foolhardy jump. The level ledges under the bridge furnish a fine campsite out of the sun and rain.

The only way from here down to the river is a bighorn trail that goes along a bench east of the bed. Climb to it about three-fourths of a mile south of the bridge. It leads to the terrace east of Elves Chasm. The old maps showed a benchmark. At the time of this writing, a seven-foot cairn marked the spot shown as a benchmark on the old maps. Nearby is the trace of a prehistoric dwelling. There is much travertine on this terrace and the springs may have been active as recently as the Ancestral Puebloan occupation. Toward the east of the terrace one can climb down to a shelf in the travertine. Only twenty feet of rappelling gets one down to where it's a quick walk to the river. A rock, perhaps cemented to the shelf, makes a safe anchor for the rope. This should only be attempted by experienced climbers who are comfortable using a rope.

There are several routes through the Supai east of Royal Arch Creek and another from the west where the creek starts through the Redwall. The valley going north just west of Toltec Point has some Indian ruins in it. It is all splendid wilderness with very few visitors as of yet.

Point Huitzil Route

When Gary Stiles was working on fire control, he noticed a possible route off the rim and down the Coconino south of Point Huitzil. Following an aerial observation, he went there on foot, and descended without a hitch.

He gave me a good description of the Coconino section, which included a tree trunk ladder, some petroglyphs and Moki steps. However, he failed to describe a good location for the beginning of the Coconino route. Stiles said it was at Point Huitzil, but finding it continued to elude me on numerous trips. It is easy to drive a mile west of Pasture Wash Ranger Station and then follow the old phone line for about fifteen minutes. North through the junipers, one soon comes to the right side of the bed of clay above the Coconino and sheep trails can be followed for miles along this bench.

Early on, during my attempts to find the "Stiles Route," I recognized twin flat-topped towers of unusually yellow Toroweap rock just south of Point Huitzil. I did a little rappelling north of these towers, but the route just wouldn't go. The distant view of the section below Montezuma Point seemed promising. I found a vertical crack at the lower end of a scramble. With a forty-foot rappel in the crack, I made it down through the Coconino. Packard also did this and then went north along the base of the Coconino. About one hundred yards away, he found a most interesting free climb through that formation. This involved passing through a large hole beneath a fallen rock. Much farther north, at Chemehuevi Point, Packard, Ohlman and Walters found another route through the Coconino.

I remembered that Stiles had said that his route could be seen better from below. Scott Thybony came with me to look for it. First, we rappelled down my route at Montezuma Point and looked at the Packard route. Beneath an overhang in the Supai below, was evidence of prehistoric use. Then we went along the base of the Coconino south of Point Huitzil. Scott climbed fifty or more feet up into the Coconino at one place before giving up.

A real possibility was a little shelf that took us into an angle above a fifteen-foot drop in the Hermit Shale. Starting up the sloping sandstone, we soon found Moki steps cut in the rock. Moki or "Moqui" is the Hopi word for dead and is another reference to prehistoric ancestors. At the top of the slope, we could go left and climb up and above the next barrier at the end of a bench.

On the next level, the route turned to the right and passed petroglyphs on a wall. In the upper part of the Coconino, we entered a tunnel capped by a big block and found logs in place for a ladder. Before the final scramble to the open sandstone platform, we found a prospector's steel drill. The bare, gently sloping Coconino platform at the top of the route was walled on the north by the base of one of the Toroweap blunt towers and was decorated with petroglyphs. The name "Point Huitzil Route" is not entirely appropriate since it is much closer to the wash between Huitzil and Centeotl than it is to the former point.

When one is going along the bench near the bottom of the Toroweap, the bare Coconino platform seems to lead only to a big drop, but when you go near the outer edge, it is only a few feet down to the route which leads to a tunnel containing the ladder. What surprised me most was that I could walk the sheep trail above the Coconino around and under Point Centeotl, then look back at the right place without recognizing that it was a perfectly safe way down. It is about the most interesting way through the Coconino I know. It was also the most direct way down to the Royal Arch and a rappel to the river east of Elves Chasm. Gary Stiles was able to climb up the wall to a shelf leading to the terrace east of Elves without the fixed rope which I had considered to be absolutely necessary.

Enfilade Point Route

The rediscovery of this route gave me more satisfaction than any other in the canyon, perhaps because I had been looking for it for ten years. Archaeologist R.C. Euler told of a Supai Indian named Walin Burro, who said that the Indians used to farm near the mouth of Fossil Bay. I found Burro taking a steam bath near the creek at Supai and he graciously stopped in the middle of his routine to answer my questions.

He put on his glasses and studied the map that I had brought, but said he couldn't remember how his father had taken him to that area on the east side of Great Thumb Mesa. He gave the impression that there should be a shorter way to reach the river at Fossil Bay than the obvious one down the Bass Trail and along the Tonto, then along the river — more than a two day walk for a good hiker. On flights with a friend, I became interested in a broken part of the Redwall between Forster Canyon and Fossil. I could also see a good way through the Supai on the south side of a ridge that forms the south wall of Fossil Gorge near the river. It would have saved a lot of time if I had also studied the rim and the Coconino from the air.

During a period of about ten years, I took trip after trip before I got it all together. One time, I came along the river from the Bass Trail, then walked up a scree-filled ravine through the Muav and into the Redwall. I became discouraged when I failed to follow a steep slope around the south into a ravine that goes through the rest of the Redwall. However, the key discovery was made with Donald Davis, the beekeeper from Parachute, who came down from Colorado to help me investigate the possibilities. We drove out to Great Thumb along a road to Topacoba Hilltop and hiked along the rim well to the north of Enfilade Point. We looked for a break in the Kaibab that would let us down to a possible route through the Coconino which I remembered from a former trip along the Esplanade.

When we failed to find a break, we went south to the area around Enfilade Point. About of a quarter of a mile north of the point and a few hundred yards south of where the jeep road comes to the rim, we went down to a rockslide behind a projecting fin of limestone. We then hiked north along the top of Toroweap, but there was just no way down. Davis, on the return, spotted a potential route to get through the Coconino. Directly below our route down from the rim, we checked a possible break in the Toroweap. Davis was leading and found a few rocks piled up as a step. He called my attention to the charcoal decorations on the ceiling of an overhang nearby.

A four-inch wide sheep trail went north in the steep clay bank and, when we were above the Coconino break, we found we could climb down an eight-foot wall with handholds. This was the hardest place on the route. We ran out of time, but when Davis returned the next day without me, he found the Coconino break on a walk, locating two rain pools and prehistoric ruins near the bottom on the Esplanade. He also walked out to the head of my suggested route through the Supai and reported that it was all right. I was teaching while he did this, but the next weekend I came with an overnight pack to investigate the entire route. Davis had warned me that the four-inch sheep trail along the crumbly clay slope might be difficult if I were burdened with a pack, but I stepped carefully.

Getting down the eight-foot wall in the lower Toroweap seemed to be the hardest part. The Coconino was a walk-down. I found water pockets and a mescal pit or two, but not the ruins Davis had seen in the time I had. The Supai descent just south of the mouth was also easy. I knew the Redwall ravine I needed was not in the bay right at the foot of the Supai route, so I checked the slot at the top of the Redwall, finding a good water pocket. I planned to camp here if I didn't reach the river. It was also possible to get down through much of the Redwall immediately to the south of the ravine. I recalled from aerial views, that the lower part would probably be impossible. The right ravine is over a half-mile south of the Supai descent, almost directly east of Enfilade Point. It forms a minor drainage north of the next big bay beyond Enfilade Point on the south.

Near the very head of this ravine, it narrows with a big chockstone blocking the way. This place startled me and I left my pack on the top. Unencumbered, I was soon deep in the Redwall, finding another chockstone. It was much smaller than the first one and I could lower myself beside it to find a footing. A little farther comes a big fall in the bed, but here one can go out of the ravine to the north on the bench, getting down to the head of the slope that I had been up before.

There was a sequel to this discovery trip. Later, four of us carried full packs down here without feeling heroic. Below the last cliff above the river where I had seen the prehistoric step in the form of a rock pile, was an Ancestral Puebloan ruin. The Enfilade Point Route ranks among one of the most interesting ways to get from the rim to the river.

Another improbable route off Great Thumb Mesa is down Matkatamiba Canyon. Connecting the entire route would also be the culmination of a long effort. P.T. Reilly had suggested a possible route through the Redwall in a ravine about a half-mile west of the mouth of Matkatamiba.

On a solo trip, I camped at a spring in the fault east of Mt. Sinyala near the top of the Redwall in Sinyala Canyon. I spent a day going up the fault ravine and down to the Redwall rim of Matkatamiba. I followed the Redwall rim out and along the river and back into Sinyala Canyon. At Mile 148.5 Canyon I soon saw that barrier falls blocked the way down, but not to be discouraged, I experimented and found a viable bypass through the Supai to the Esplanade here. On another trip with Jorgen Visbak and Bob Dye, we camped at the Sinyala Spring. While Jorgen nursed a sore knee, Bob and I went over to the Redwall rim of Matkat and turned south.

Very soon we had to cross a minor drainage with a water pocket and, in about ten more minutes, came to a break where a slide let us get down to the bed of Matkat. We had set a time for turning back, but sensing victory, we extended our deadline and got to the river via one of the most spectacular narrows. Later, I learned that only a year or so before, some river runners had found a way to get up this canyon and on to the top of the Redwall. Indians had told Jacob Hamblin that they used to go down Kanab Canyon and cross the river to trade with the Supai Indians. Going up Matkat and down into the Supai from the Esplanade would seem to be, by far, the best way.

This discovery made me want to find a more direct approach than that of the parking lot at Hualapai Hilltop. I recalled vaguely a route off the rim in the vicinity of Paya Point that Cureton and I had once seen from the Esplanade. When I came out on Great Thumb Mesa in search of it, I stayed on the rim looking down into Matkatamiba Bay. Later, I learned from Jim Ohlman that hikers had found this break east of Paya Point and had used it to reach and climb Mt. Akaba. Nothing promising on the east side of the bay below, but on the other side, about halfway between the head of the canyon and Towago Point, was a real possibility.

Immediately to the north of the elevation marked 6,010' on the map, I could go down the Kaibab. It took some scouting, but I found a way through the Toroweap and then down a little to the east, where the Coconino is covered by an old slide. When I told Billingsley about this route off the rim to the Esplanade, he took two companions and they went down and found a way through the Supai in Matkat, the most interesting part of the entire route. It is easy to start down at the head, but there is a sportier shortcut from the west. Deep in the gorge is an Indian ruin under an overhang on the right. One twenty-foot fall has an obvious bypass, but toward the bottom, there is an awesome 120+ foot sheer fall.

One can climb down a crack just west of the fall and reach a dirt-covered shelf going to the east below the lip of this fall. I know of two hikers who looked at the exposure with the bad footing and quickly retreated. Another man wouldn't cross until I carried his pack for him. Beyond this ledge, one drops into a charming oasis of cottonwoods and mimulae surrounding a pool fed by seep springs. I found a second way to reach the bottom of the Redwall gorge on the west side and a way to walk out on the east side too. It is a pity that the Supai Indians who legally control the top of Great Thumb Mesa don't want hikers to enjoy this fine area.

For a still more challenging climber's route to the river, it is possible to drop down to the Esplanade in Fossil Bay and then almost directly down the main bed through the Supai and Redwall. I have been through the Supai via an easy way south of Stanton Point. Gary Stiles got me through the spooky Redwall gorge up from the river. I made it past a smooth chute unaided, but Gary helped me past two chockstones. The scramble up the last fifty feet of limestone on the north side was not too hard. A few hikers, principally Jim Ohlman, have told me that there is a spring in the lower Supai, and by clever scouting, they were able to get through all the Supai without detouring very far away from the main drainage. At one place one has to go along a shelf beneath a large rock.

Aerial views made me wonder about going down from the Esplanade in Specter Chasm. Once I started to scout it on foot coming down through the Supai in Fossil Creek. Turning back, I tripped and broke a rib. Much later, I came down the Enfilade Point Route and went up the talus-filled wash of Specter from below. Near the top of the Redwall, the bed was in smooth bare rock and I had to give up. The Supai in the southwest side of Specter also seems somewhat broken so one may come down here with a rope to get past the difficult top of the Redwall. Lower Specter took us rather easily to a picturesque section of the river.

Colonnade Route

While collecting first ascents, Alan Doty discovered that one can descend directly to the saddle between Colonnade and the North Rim. To reach this place, we drove a fire road that ends in the woods northwest of Widforss Point. A deer trail leaves the rim a few yards northwest of the end of the point closest to the Colonnade. A potsherd on the saddle indicates that the Ancestral Puebloans came here.

It is just a good scramble from here to the top of the Colonnade, but what has intrigued me is the idea of going along the Hermit Shale east of the bay below Widforss Point. Distant views indicate the feasibility of getting down the Supai to the head of the Redwall gorge of Haunted Canyon. Walking up the bed of Haunted Canyon I thought that a sixty-foot handline should get one down the steep, though not completely vertical headwall. With a rope in place, one could get water at Haunted Canyon Spring and come back above the Redwall to camp. From this base camp, an experienced rock climber might climb Manu Temple and likewise Shellbach Butte. However, they are both very exposed and require a rope for a safe belay. Buddha Temple is for the experts with complete climbing hardware.

There is also the possibility of going down the easy break through the Redwall in the ravine immediately west of Sturdevant Point. Good climbers have been through the Supai above this route, but this way seems too hard for me. Connecting the Colonnade Saddle with the bed of Haunted Canyon or the Redwall route down Sturdevant Canyon might still be a "first" for someone. At least, I have only been down a little farther than the saddle.

Trinity Creek

My own explorations of Trinity Creek have led me to conclude that some very wonderful hikes are possible. One can come up on the Tonto from Bright Angel Campground as if on the way to Phantom Canyon. There is a deeper trail down through the Tapeats across the valley east of Cheops Pyramid.

We have also climbed into this valley from the river where the telephone line crosses from the north to the south side. On another occasion, we stayed on top of the Tapeats south and west around the base of Cheops, but this was the slowest way to Trinity. East of Trinity is a safe route to the river down Ninetyone Mile Canyon. Emery Kolb told me about taking a light boat down from the end of the Bright Angel Trail and carrying it around Horn Creek Rapids. He and a companion came up Ninetyone Mile Canyon and went over to Trinity. They could go up the Redwall to the Shiva-Isis Saddle and then up past Shiva to the North Rim. Their return was via Bright Angel Creek.

I followed his example except that I used an air mattress to go from Pipe Creek to the head of Horn Creek Rapids. Between trying to avoid being carried down through Horn Creek Rapids and being pushed back upstream into the back eddy next to the cliff, I had little room for error. When I asked Emery Kolb what he had done about the boat at Ninetyone Mile Canyon, he couldn't remember. He was sure that they hadn't abandoned it.

When I had gone a little way up Ninetyone Mile Canyon, I took what I thought was a short way to Trinity Creek, up a slide to the base of the Tapeats and around to the west above lower Trinity. Just before my shelf gave out, I found a low rock wall which some prospector might have built for a windbreak on a chilly night.

The way down to the bed of Trinity seemed too dangerous so I backed up and went out to the Tonto in Ninetyone Mile Canyon, camping at a rain pool near the top of the Tapeats in the bed of Trinity. On my second day, I got through the Redwall to the Shiva-Isis Saddle and experienced only a minor problem in route-finding through the Supai to Shiva Saddle. I went up the main ravine east of Shiva until the last hundred feet of Supai barred my way. A shelf around to the north led to an easy route. I was able to walk through the North Rim forest to the campground before dinner that night.

On another trip, Allyn Cureton and I investigated the escape route used by Chief Ranger Brooks in 1928 after Rangers Sturdevant and Johnson were drowned in Horn Creek Rapids. They had attempted to do what the Kolbs had done, carry a boat past Horn Creek Rapids and launch it from above. Before they could get into the back eddy, they were swept into the rapid and two of the three men were drowned. Brooks found a way out on the north side of the river and reached Phantom Ranch where he recuperated before hiking out.

In checking his route, Cureton and I went along the base of the Tapeats above Ninetyone Mile Canyon and then went east above the Colorado until we reached a chute where we could descend. Our ledge along the base pinched out east of the head of this chute, so we figured that we had found the only possible way to the north bank at Horn Creek Rapids. When I talked to Emery Kolb about this area, he said that he had gone up a similar chute on the north side of the river farther east than Horn Creek Rapids.

When Allyn Cureton and I climbed Cheops Pyramid, Allyn went back to Bright Angel Camp and waited for me to investigate the yellow chute that Emery had climbed. I reached the river too soon to camp on the north side. Inflating my mattress, I paddled upriver between projecting rockslides where the water was still. Walking over the slides, I went far enough upriver to be east of the cliffs along the south side that drops directly into the water. Sleeping that night on some sand on the south side of the river, it was an easy walk east to the River Trail the next day. It was a much easier way back to Phantom Ranch than if I had retraced my steps and followed the route of the previous day.

One of my last trips to Trinity had a different objective. Gerrit Degelicke and I wanted to travel along the Tonto west of Trinity. We were hampered by rainy weather but had a fine, dry overhang for a camp at the foot of the Tapeats on the east side above the bed. A seep spring was in the bed below and an Indian ruin was only yards away from where we slept. We did hike the Tonto west almost to the rim above Ninetyfour Mile Canyon. What puzzled us was to find an old rectangular five gallon kerosene can lying on the Tonto. I spotted a natural bridge through the Redwall rim southwest of the little butte at elevation 5,290'. The ravine between this butte and the Tower of Set looked like a possible route, and we later learned that it was.

Before Gerrit and I left Trinity, we went down the bed into the schist of the Inner Gorge. We were soon stopped by a steep, impassable waterfall in the narrow slot. Just before this dead end, I found that I could scale the east side slope up to the base of the Tapeats where I had found the prospector's windbreak before turning back to Ninetyone Mile Canyon.

We learned later that this route and the kerosene can are inextricably connected to each other and to a wild project. In 1919, a promoter named Davol convinced Secretary of Interior Lane and National Park Supervisor Horace Albright that it would be in the best interest of tourism to have the South Rim and the North Rim connected by a scenic tramway. Davol hired surveyors and a supporting crew who worked here for several months, but for various reasons, the tram project was eventually abandoned. When I was about to cross the river and go up on the Redwall near the Tower of Set, Ranger Tim Manns showed me a long letter he had received from one of the men who had been on the survey crew of 1919. They had crossed the river on a raft constructed from empty kerosene cans and had established a camp near the natural bridge.

From Trinity Creek, Allyn Cureton and I came up to the Shiva-Isis Saddle and then continued west along the Redwall rim south of Shiva. We went far enough to look at the possibility of climbing the Redwall up to the Ra-Osiris Saddle. I concluded incorrectly that this would be hopeless. We also looked at the southwest side of Shiva and figured that this might be a way that deer get to the summit. Climbing Claude Birdseye Point also seemed possible from this side. If we had known that we would find a good stream coming off Shiva from melting snow on this southwest side, we could have carried our packs with us that day and would have had time for something interesting.

As it was, we went back to a dry camp above the Redwall at the west end of Phantom Canyon. In the morning, we got down a very sporty third-class Redwall route to the bed of Phantom. We really should have lowered our packs by a rope at the worst spot. We did not go down the slot ravine clear to where it makes a drop. Instead, we followed a shelf out to the face and turned right. At the end of this shelf, we had to face in and use our hands and toes for nearly twenty vertical feet.

Following Stanton in 1890

During their 1889-1990 expedition through the Grand Canyon, Stanton's party stopped at the mouth of Crystal Creek. Harry McDonald, disenchanted and feeling that the services he offered to the project were not sufficiently recognized, decided to leave the party at this point and head out of the Canyon alone. It was sometime in February, the very dead of winter.

We don't know his route to the rim except for the fact it was so severe a climb that he left his blanket behind! He found two feet of snow on the Kaibab Plateau and was forced to break into a building at the unmanned VT Ranch to keep from freezing. He had crossed the highest part of the plateau and was just able to stagger to safety at an occupied ranch in House Rock Valley. Perhaps to give McDonald time to change his mind, the river party stayed at the mouth of the Crystal Creek while Stanton, Hislop and Kane took a hazardous thirty-hour hike.

Dock Marston furnished me with Stanton's field notes and photographs taken by the three men on their trek up to the Tonto, and then up around the Tower of Ra. After studying the pictures and field notes and seeing the whole area from a plane, I felt that we had a good idea where their route might have gone.

Donald Davis came with me down to the Tonto level in Dragon Creek via the Shiva Saddle and the easy Redwall ravine on the north side of Shiva. We wanted to identify Stanton's route by duplicating two of his pictures. I first led Davis from our base camp at the junction of Dragon Creek and Crystal up to the base of the Redwall on the north side of the Ra-Osiris Saddle. I figured that they had gone up the Redwall at the north end of the promontory going north from Ra.

Stanton described this route in his book, *Down the Colorado*, as being extremely dangerous, and I agree that none but the most

Robert Brewster Stanton sitting in a chair his party found floating down the river, circa 1897. (Grand Canyon Museum Collection, 5578)

expert climbers should attempt this route. As we studied their easier return route from above, I decided that obstacles at one point would eventually prevent me from moving forward. Davis decided to give it a real try solo while I backtracked the "Stanton Route" to their river camp. Soon after getting onto the Tonto, I located the camera position for a picture they had taken. They used a Tapeats break only a short way into Crystal from the river, then walked out to the point to photograph Crystal Rapids and the skyline across to the south. Davis and I came up from Dragon Creek by the same route that the Stanton party used to return and later, I went down to the bed of Crystal by the way they had started out.

Davis carried out a much more exciting project. With careful route study, combined with his skill and strength in climbing, he succeeded in making it up the Redwall to the Ra-Osiris Saddle. Just below the saddle he checked out a cave and found a pot with some corncobs. Going along the Redwall rim on the east side of the north-tending promontory, he also duplicated the location of a Stanton photo with great accuracy. We figured that the 1890 climbers had been on the top of this promontory, so Davis walked up and circled the Tower of Ra.

He came down the difficult part of the Redwall just as it was getting dark. I became intensely worried until he finally walked into camp around 9:30pm, aided by his caver's light. Going back the next day, he took pictures of the pot cave and I tried, without success, to follow him. He could use a handgrip that was three inches too far for my shorter reach.

Hindu Amphitheater

The Hindu Amphitheater in the Crystal Creek Basin is one of the seldom visited sections of the park. No horse trail has ever penetrated this bay, but there are at least five ways to enter it, the easiest way being from the river. A ruin can be found on the terrace to the west of the mouth of Crystal Creek.

In the good old days, one could walk down the Hermit Trail to the river then float down the river on an air mattress, being careful to walk around Boucher Rapids. The river is calm except for this rapid and it is easy to land on the right above the mouth of Crystal. Today, this method of river transport is highly discouraged by the Park Service for a multitude of obvious reasons — personal safety being one.

When the R.B. Stanton railroad survey party camped at the mouth of Crystal in February of 1890, Harry McDonald, who later went on to mine in the canyon, quit and succeeded in walking out of the canyon and across the rim through deep snow to the VT Ranch, which was deserted in the winter. From the ranch, he walked to another ranch in House Rock Valley. How he reached the rim remains a mystery. The main party delayed their departure while Stanton, Hislop, and Kane took a noteworthy overnight climb. They went to the Tonto on the east, just inside the side canyon, then around to the north side of the Tower of Ra where they made a heroic Redwall ascent over to the west side of the north face. After a cold night with only a small fire for warmth, they succeeded in coming down a daring route northwest of the saddle between Ra and Osiris. At the water pocket down in this tributary, they had their first drink in over twenty-four hours. Then they returned to the river along the creekbed. While they were gone, others of the party found a way to the Tonto west of the bed.

An obvious, but very laborious way to reach Crystal Creek is along the Tonto from Bright Angel Creek. Probably the easiest dry land route is to drive to within a mile of Tiyo Point and walk to the rim as if going to Shiva Temple. This is across the bay north and west of Tiyo. One can follow a deer trail down a ravine and then west to the ridge going south.

There is an easy way to go through the Coconino at the south end of this promontory. From the saddle, we walked down the arm of Dragon Creek just north of Shiva. Indian relics such as mescal pits, chips of flint, and pottery fragments have been found on Shiva Saddle. There were ruins on a terrace near Dragon Creek. One of these nine hundred year-old relics was swept away by the great flood of 1966. Other routes up the Redwall can be found at the heads of both arms of Dragon Creek and also below the northwest side of Shiva.

Just south of the large mescal pit on the Shiva Saddle lie several very large rocks. On their broad surfaces, large pits hold a surprising amount of water after the rains. Other rain pockets are down in the ravines both east and west of the saddle. At the heads of both arms of Dragon Creek, fir forests hide little springs. In the east arm there is an impressive limestone tower shaped like a blockhouse. A small natural bridge is located in the Redwall rim nearby. The main Dragon Creek Spring is located down canyon from the Tapeats dry fall.

For some reason, the 1966 flood didn't tear out the trees in Crystal above the junction with Dragon. Crystal Spring is found in a grove of cottonwoods midway between the Tapeats narrows and the Redwall gorge. This gorge cannot be climbed at the end, but as the canyon narrows, a fault provides a route to the west rim. A careful study of the route shows a way north to the Kaibab Plateau.

It is possible to walk the bank of the river from Crystal west to Tuna Creek. There may be no barrier fall in Tuna and it is certainly possible to walk along the Tonto from Crystal to Tuna. There is usually a seep to provide water in the lower Tapeats and one can usually find some in potholes at the base of the Redwall.

South of a hill on the Tonto west of Tuna, there are still some signs of a temporary camp. In 1944, when the pilot of a bomber feared that the plane he was flying was about to crash, he ordered his three companions to parachute into the Canyon at night. They were found the next day and were supplied with provisions by air drop until they could be guided out to Point Sublime ten days later. R.E. Lawes and Alan McRae were credited with finding the crewmen's route, but they did not record it. I rediscovered the route to their camp off the rim west of Point Sublime to the pass between Flint Creek and Tuna. The way down through the Redwall in this arm of Tuna requires some route finding. A burro trail goes south to the vicinity of the camp and a break in the Tapeats close to Tuna. The river side leads down to a boat landing at a sandy beach.

Merrel Clubb, who talked to men present during this search, thought that the Lawes-McRae route was down below Grama Point into the east arm of Tuna. It would be interesting to check the feasibility of this and also of the passage through lower Tuna to the river.

Rescuing the Parachutists in 1944

When the newspapers reported on the rescue of the three crewmen who parachuted to the Tonto, just west of lower Tuna Creek in the middle of the night, they omitted all details about the route used to get them out of the Canyon. I was determined to find their route and satisfy my own curiosity.

Based on my own observations made first from the air, then later on the ground, I believed that they came up through the Redwall to the pass between Tuna and Flint Creeks, and from there on to the plateau west of Point Sublime. When I later learned that I was mistaken, I realized that I needed to find Alan McRae, the one man who could straighten this out once and for all.

Then, one day, I happened to be standing at the railing at Lipan Point when a woman, only two yards away, remarked to her husband that Colin Fletcher must have logged more miles in the vista below than anyone else. I couldn't resist mentioning that Fletcher's forty-two day walk from Supai to Nankoweap didn't put him ahead of a number of others and cited Alan McRae as one example.

It was purely coincidental that they had just attended a slide show given by Alan McRae only two weeks prior. They gave me their address and passed on to Dr. McRae a letter I wrote to him. He responded to my letter with a full account of how R.E. Lawes and he had gone down from Grama Point following the directions of the crewmen. At the Redwall rim, they first went down along the east rim of Tuna Creek. Arriving at the place where talus covers more than half of the Redwall, they wouldn't consider going down the sheer wall above that talus. To the west, across this arm, they could see a possible seep spring. They reached it in time to camp there that night.

In the morning they located a fine Redwall route down through the entire formation on the west side. Soon they contacted the parachutists and brought them up to Grama Point. Jim Ohlman and I repeated this route. When I stopped by to visit with Dr. and Mrs. McRae, they were very interested in seeing the pictures I took of our ascent.

Shinumo Amphitheater

There are a number of ways to get down into this area. The old North Bass or Shinumo Trail is the best known. The route down from Swamp Point to the saddle and on to the top of Powell Plateau must have been rebuilt during the thirties. A frame building just west of the saddle perhaps served as a dormitory during this construction work. It takes only ten minutes to reach a good spring at the bottom of the Coconino east of the saddle. The trail beyond the spring, as shown on the map, is badly overgrown with brush and it is easier to scramble down a rockslide or bare ravine below the spring. Below this steep talus, one stays in the dry creek bed to the Redwall. There is water, however, in a tributary from the east and also in the main bed near the top of the Redwall.

The faint trail, marked on occasion by plastic ribbons, veers out of the bed and goes through the junipers west of the bed. Close to the start of the Redwall gorge, on the east wall, one can see a natural bridge where a cave collapsed. To ensure locating the route down the Redwall, one should have the 7.5 minute topo, as with all of the routes below the rim and away from the Bright Angel or Kaibab Trails. One needs to go down the last of several parallel ravines to a ledge running south beneath a bare wall. It seems like an improbable route, but more switchbacks take you to the bed below the Redwall. A little farther there is more water flowing along the bare shale. The map shows the trail going down through the Tapeats in a wide swing to the southwest. This stretch is hardly recognizable at present and it is both more direct and easier to follow a burro trail down just east of the benchmark at elevation 3,150'.

A distinctly different alternative is to stay on the east side of

White Creek almost to its junction with Redwall Canyon. We walked down to the bed below the Tapeats through a ravine. To the north there is a deep, narrow fissure found in the Tapeats, perhaps, the deepest and most narrow in the entire park. At the time of this writing, a huge boulder was lodged between the walls eighty-feet up, just as it was when the Kolbs photographed it sixty or more years ago. One can walk down White Creek to Shinumo Creek and see signs of trail construction suggesting that Bass brought his tourists here.

The main trail crosses Shinumo Creek to reach the site of the old Bass Camp. The terrace across on the right bank is surprisingly broad and free of rocks. Irrigated by both the prehistoric Indians and William Bass, it was a fine garden site, much more suited to this purpose than the tract used by Louis Boucher.

Instead of continuing along the creek for the last mile to the river, the trail goes up to the south over a ridge. The open terrace below was where Stanton planned to build a switchyard for the railroad that was never built. Bass had two ways to cross the Colorado — a boat above the rapid and an aerial tram for use during high water.

Most of the new maps omit some trails that were shown on the old Matthes-Evans West Half map. A trail built by Bass west into Burro Canyon is still recognizable and so is his trail rising along the south wall of Shinumo Creek east of its junction with White Creek. The latter doesn't go far enough to do much good and the hiker still needs to make his way along the creek bed.

Back where the main trail encounters the Tapeats in White Canyon, there is yet another choice. Stay above the Tapeats past the mouth of Redwall Canyon and follow a good burro trail along the east rim of White Canyon. This continues as a fast and clear trail around to Merlin and Modred Abysses. One can move fast, while admiring fine views of the entire area. Just north of the junction of Merlin and Modred, one can cross to the other side. The burro trail continues for a short distance north along the east side of Merlin, but then progress becomes difficult through the

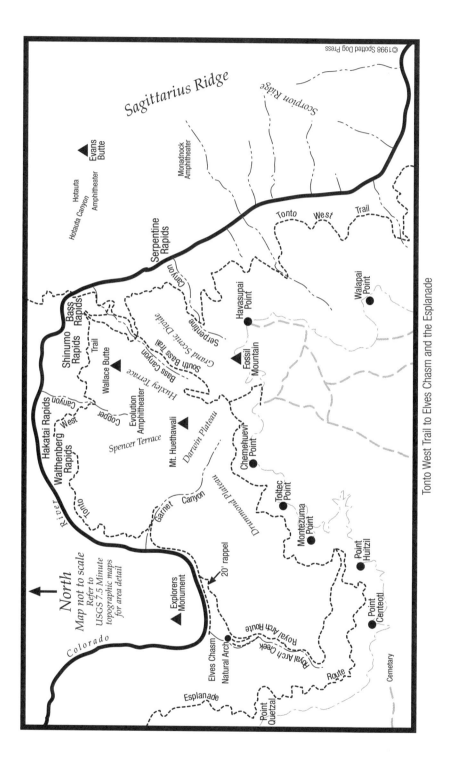

Tonto West Trail to Elves Chasm and the Esplanade

Sagittarius Ridge

Scorpion Ridge

Evans Butte

Hotauta Canyon

Hotauta Amphitheater

Monadnock Amphitheater

Serpentine Rapids

Tonto West Trail

Canyon

Serpentine

Havasupai Point

Walapai Point

Bass Rapids

Shinumo Rapids

Trail

Grand Scenic Divide

Wallace Butte

South Bass Trail

Bass Canyon

Fossil Mountain

Huxley Terrace

Hakatai Rapids

West Canyon

Copper

Evolution Amphitheater

Spencer Terrace

Mt. Huethawali

Darwin Plateau

Chemehuevi Point

Walthenberg Rapids

Tonto

River

Garnet Canyon

Drummond Plateau

Toltec Point

Montezuma Point

Point Huitzil

20' rappel

North

Map not to scale
Refer to
USGS 7.5 Minute
topographic maps
for area detail

Colorado

Explorers Monument

Elves Chasm

Natural Arch

Royal Arch Creek

Royal Arch Route

Point Centeotl

Route

Cemetery

Esplanade

Point Quetzal

dense vegetation along the stream. The dry bed above the main spring is easy again and the bed remains clear even when the small flow from South Big Spring appears on the surface. A team of expert rock climbers got up through the Redwall in Merlin Abyss, but those hiking or backpacking would turn east into Shinumo Creek, really the main canyon. Just before this becomes impossible, there is a transverse fault cutting a route through the Redwall both to the south and north. Merrel Clubb found the route down here from the Elaine Saddle. It is a sporty rock scramble and a solo hiker would need to pull up his pack with a rope at one place. Near the top of the Supai, the route turns away from the ravine to the east.

Above the Supai, there is another choice. Fight through the brush to the bed below South Big Spring, go through a break in the Coconino north of the bed, and on to the road. Or go south at the top of the Supai and get to the forest on Lancelot Point near the end of the point or farther east along the south side.

Elaine Castle can be climbed from the south side. Beneath the Toroweap caprock are a number of rooms built by the Anasazi. The break through the Toroweap is on the north side. One can also go down southeast from Elaine Saddle directly to Modred Abyss. There are more additional ruins in Modred and caves that attract spelunkers. An expert climber can get out of Modred to the east and southeast, but the brush is bad above the Redwall. Modred has a fine stream coming out of the Abyss Cave and here one can experience the feeling of perfect and total wilderness. Through the whole Shinumo Basin, the creeks have cut deep without removing the great mass of rock — quite a contrast to the open valleys of Nankoweap and Unkar.

Along the Tonto Trail on the left side below the junction of Merlin and Modred, wild burros established another fine trail. This is the easy way from Modred to Flint. On the south side of Flint, opposite the mouth of Gawin Abyss, there is a very adventurous route up the Redwall. I flew over it more than once, but I had to try it before I felt sure it would go. A good rock climber would do it handily but when I tackled it alone, it almost stopped me. By this time, I had accepted the challenge of completing a route below the North Rim from one corner of the park to the other. To fill in one of the gaps, I walked over to the top of this Redwall climb from the Flint-Tuna Pass. I found an old cairn pointing away from the pass toward my Redwall descent.

No discussion of the Shinumo area should omit the Powell Plateau. It forms the western skyline for the viewpoints along the south rim scenic drive. The trail from Swamp Point continues through the fine Ponderosa forest. Magnificent views of the river and the canyon are obtained from any point on the rim. This sky island slopes gently down to the south and is divided about equally between Ponderosa Pines, junipers, and sage. On one of Powell's two river trips, he was guided to what must have been Swamp Point. When he left, he claimed that he had seen the finest panorama from Wyoming to Mexico.

Powell Plateau

This area merits special attention. Although there is no water source on top of the plateau, R.C. Euler found the top covered with prehistoric ruins. To get water from the spring below the Coconino south of Swamp Point would mean a round-trip of over an hour. In July, after a summer rain shower, I found a trickling stream at the Toroweap level near the head of the north arm of Bedrock Canyon. Donald Davis found several ways to get down to the Esplanade on the west side and in late May, there are numerous rain pools and a few springs. Not too surprisingly, he found a scattering of ruins on this side.

Davis also discovered a route, good enough for a burro, through the Coconino on the east side of Dutton Canyon. There was enough water for several hikers in the gravel of the bed right at the base of the Coconino in Dutton Canyon. I came down here by a route farther east and went up another way. Between the two routes, under an overhang at the bottom of the Coconino, I inspected an inadequate set of drips from the ceiling. Down where Dutton Canyon reaches the Supai rim, Davis found another spring and a miner's pick nearby. He walked out on the Alarcon Terrace on the west side and to Marcos Terrace on the east side. The pick and one mescal pit were the only signs that anyone had preceded him in this area.

More recently, Lester Olin, a doctor from Yuma, and a friend of mine came down to the Esplanade off the west side on the plateau and walked around below Wheeler Point and up near Dutton Canyon. Alan Doty used two routes through the Coconino covering a loop east of Dutton Canyon to climb King Crest. Along the ridge north of King Crest, Doty found a ruin. He also scored a first ascent of Masonic Temple by going down the

North Bass Trail to the Redwall rim and then up to the Temple. To the ordinary scrambler, some of the most challenging and successful climbs in the Shinumo basin seem incredible and virtually impossible, especially Holy Grail, Dox Castle and Excalibur.

I would have supposed it impossible until Jim Ohlman and Jim Kirschvink crossed the river above Elves Chasm and climbed up to the top of Explorer's Monument. Amazingly, they found an Indian ruin near the top. They also climbed Fan Island. A long hike, rather than a difficult climb, was our first ascent of Steamboat Mountain. We were soaked by a sudden rainstorm, then spent an unplanned night by a fire rather than try to return to Swamp Point by flashlight.

In earlier notes, I mentioned the old trail from Shinumo Creek into Burro Canyon. Following the example of Donald Maddox, a hiker from Albuquerque, and his friends, Bob Packard and I hiked this trail to the rim above Hakatai Canyon.

We found a cairn in the ravine that leads down to the Bass asbestos mines, but the drop seemed formidable without a rope. Bob and I soon found a good trail that goes down the Tapeats near the north end of this lower canyon. The mine shafts are about halfway from here to the river, near the contact with the Archean rock. Barrier falls in the bed forced us to continue to the river over the broken slope to the west. Strangely enough, there seemed to be no distinct trail down here to where the Hakatai Cable was anchored. W.W. Bass had used a cable car to take his asbestos ore across to the south side. While I rested at our beds by the river, Bob used the last two hours of the day to go up and follow the trail to the rim of the Tapeats west of Hakatai Canyon.

He spotted an Indian ruin near where the trail reaches the top of the Tapeats. Maddox wrote to me and told me that their party found that the trail continued to the bed of Walthenberg Canyon. They went to the river, but were unable to find a trail going farther west. Later, George Steck and his friends went on below all of Powell Plateau on the Tonto level when they walked the north side of the river from Lee's Ferry to the Grand Wash Cliffs.

Tapeats and Deer Creeks

This is the region made famous by the Thunder River, perhaps the only river that is the minor tributary of a creek, and
almost surely the shortest river in the world. This river bursts
forth from two openings in a cliff. Below the initial hundred foot
fall, it foams down over cascades and more falls for about a half-
mile to join Tapeats Creek.

This wonderful stream is usually reached from the Indian
Hollow Campground at the head of the horse trail. There is no
hint of anything unusual where one parks the car, but the whole
new world of the Grand Canyon appears with startling abrupt-
ness at the top of the next rise. At the top, the trail goes to the
west and shouldn't be hard to follow. After threading its way
through grotesque rock forms, the trail descends the Supai and
Redwall by many short switchbacks. Surprise Valley below may
have received its name from its unusual bowl shape and the nearly
hidden outlet through Bonito Creek. The trail leaves the bowl at
the northeast rim and one immediately sees and hears the thunder of the spring, the most dramatic beginning imaginable for a
stream. The trail continues down to Tapeats Creek affording
more glimpses of other falls and cascades.

There is a shorter route which is safe enough for Boy Scouts
although too rugged for horses. A little southeast of Big Saddle
Hunting Camp, a fireroad branches toward the rim from the main
road. When close to the rim, take the fork paralleling the rim to
the west. Park at the depression where the rim bends toward
Monument Point. Walk the jeep trail along the east side of the
promontory and leave the top on the east just short of the point.
A deer trail goes down through the Kaibab Formation and it continues below the point to the west at this level. After walking

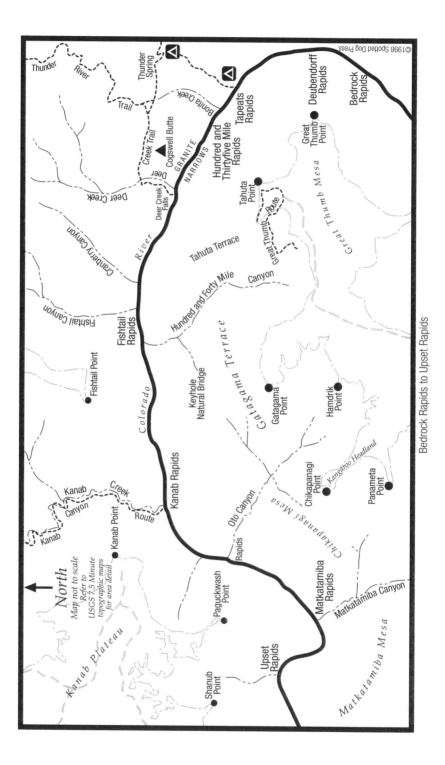

Bedrock Rapids to Upset Rapids

Thunder River

Thunder Spring

Trail

Bonita Creek

Creek Trail

Cogswell Butte

GRANITE

Deer Creek Trail

Deer Creek Falls

Deer Creek

NARROWS

River

Cranberry Canyon

Tahuta Point

Tapeats Rapids

Hundred and Thirtyfive Mile Rapids

Deubendorff Rapids

Bedrock Rapids

Great Thumb Point

Great Thumb Mesa

Great Thumb Route

Tahuta Terrace

Hundred and Forty Mile Canyon

Fishtail Canyon

Fishtail Rapids

Colorado

Fishtail Point

Keyhole Natural Bridge

Gatagama Terrace

Gatagama Point

Hamdrik Point

Kanab Rapids

Kangaroo Headland

Panameta Point

Kanab Creek

Canyon

Kanab Route

Oto Canyon

Chikapanagi Point

Chikapanagi Mesa

Kanab

Kanab Point

Rapids

Matkatamiba Rapids

North

Map not to scale
Refer to
USGS 7.5 Minute
topographic maps
for area detail

Kanab Plateau

Paguckwash Point

Matkatamiba Canyon

Matkatamiba Mesa

Upset Rapids

Shanub Point

about ten minutes northwest from the point, one reaches a break through the Toroweap and Coconino Formations. One can go almost straight down to the regular horse trail and thus save an hour of walking.

The popular route from the end of the trail to the river is along the east side of the creek, although the high water of early June makes fording dangerous. Here, in the open valley, one will see some pot-hunted ruins. Where the creek drops into the narrow lower gorge, cross again and follow a rising ramp. Near the river there is an easy descent through a ravine.

The interesting and more remote Stone and Galloway Canyons can be reached by staying on the east rim of the lower gorge of Tapeats Canyon. Proceed upriver at this level. Stone Canyon has a permanent flow of water, prehistoric ruins, and a superb headwall formed by Steamboat Mountain. Deer or bighorn trails lead to the river and also up the east wall of Stone Canyon. One can enter Galloway along the beach or above the Tonto.

Some adventurers also go from the foot of the Thunder River Trail up the bed of Tapeats Creek. This trip through the striking narrows may be impossible near the first of June when the water is both high and cold. For a short distance, the water fills the bed from wall to wall and several crossings are necessary. A bit more than a mile upstream from the trail, a tributary from the north contributes almost all the water. At the head of this V-shaped valley beneath the Redwall are the springs. Above and to the east, is a cave which can be followed to where the entire flow is in one large corridor. At the highest stage, the cave serves as a spillway.

If one continues east beyond the cave tributary, it is possible to go up the Redwall and on to the Kaibab Plateau by two different routes. The first is a short distance into Crazy Jug Canyon along the west wall. Upon reaching the Esplanade go west to a horse trail that reaches the rim between Monument Point and Crazy Jug Point, or east across Crazy Jug Canyon. Another trail connects with the rim at Big Saddle.

The second way through the Redwall leads to the South Rim

of Saddle Canyon. This is more of a climb and requires a rope to pull up the pack. The route to Muav Saddle and Swamp Point is longer and harder to follow.

Deer Creek, a real gem among the Grand Canyon tributaries, is reached by going west from the Thunder River Trail in Surprise Valley. In 1882, the geologist Clarence Dutton took horses down a newly constructed prospectors trail to what he called Tapeats Creek. His description fits perfectly with the route going down to the river at Deer Creek Falls. Only a little of the old trail construction still shows. South of the trail at the bottom of the Redwall, a spring spills from the cliff. Cavers have rigged a scaffold and explored the hole, but the depth wasn't comparable to the caves behind Thunder Spring and the Tapeats Creek source, approximately 3,000 feet and 6,000 feet respectively.

Ancient ruins are to be found in at least three distinct parts of Deer Creek Valley, close to the bottom of the trail, on the west side of the stream a quarter of a mile north of the final gorge, and east of the stream about the same distance from the Colorado. Thickets of cane on the level floor indicate that Indians may have irrigated the valley and raised crops. Perhaps this swamp explains the prevalence of little flies that nearly drove us crazy when we camped here in early June.

The upper arms of Deer Creek have been found to be rough going. The arms north of Vaughn Springs are impossible without climbing hardware and ropes, but the northeast arm has been traversed without a rope by skilled climbers. Perhaps the most interesting excursions relate to the lower end of the valley. The most photographed route penetrates the narrow gorge where the stream cuts deeper and deeper below a narrow ledge.

Out of sight in the curving slot, the stream makes a final one hundred foot plunge to the river level. At the end of the gorge, one can follow a trail down to the river and come back beneath the fall. A good scramble along a route east of the fall brings one up on the ridge separating the valley from the river. It is not hard to follow the bench east beyond Granite Narrows and then to go

Near mouth of Kanab Canyon taken during the Kolb brothers first trip down the Colorado River in 1911. (Grand Canyon Museum Collection, 17174)

down to the riverbank. This way, to reach the mouth of Tapeats Creek is much faster than the trail through Surprise Valley. A still more ambitious project is to follow the river down to the mouth of Kanab Creek. This area is second to none in possibilities for wilderness adventure.

Deer Creek to Kanab Canyon

Fishtail Mesa is a scenic destination. To reach it, we left Indian Hollow Campground with enough water for thirty-six hours, about six to eight quarts apiece. We followed the horse trail down to the Esplanade and then walked west. After going over the saddle between Fishtail and the mainland, we walked up the talus on the north side of Fishtail. Park Service experts have studied the plants on Fishtail Mesa which represents an area that has never been grazed by cattle. Brought in by helicopter with supplies for a week, they were able to lay out plots and count plant species. They also found a blowhole that was, perhaps, an orifice leading down to a cavern.

I walked to the south end and had a fine view by the last light of day. It was well that my partner, Donald Finicum, a teacher from Page, had a campfire to guide me back to my pack. One could combine this ascent of Fishtail with another interesting trek, and avoid carrying so much water. There is a constructed trail down to a spring in the east arm of Fishtail Canyon. The spring is located in the lowest part of the Supai. This is the country where the legendary part-time hermit and guide, Hualapai Johnny, used to hang out.

A few have gone around Fishtail Mesa along the Esplanade. George Billingsley reported finding some prehistoric ruins and a fantastic region of mushroom towers. Both Billingsley and Bob Dye called my attention to a peculiar picture in white clay on an east-facing wall about a mile south and a little west of where the horse trail comes through the Coconino from Indian Hollow Campground. The picture represents two larger than life human figures, each with three spikes or feathers standing upright on top of their heads. Billingsley has called the huge block of sandstone "Ghost Rock." About 200 yards before coming to Ghost Rock, there is an overhang where someone camped in 1905 and wrote the date in charcoal on the rock.

Ghost Rock is a good landmark for the starting part of one of the most interesting routes down to the Colorado. On a flight from South Rim Village to Toroweap in 1963, I spotted two possible breaks in the Redwall. I checked out one of these near the junction of Crazy Jug Canyon with Tapeats Creek, but accepted a discouraging report from some other fliers that the alternate route, halfway from Deer Creek to Fishtail Canyon, would be impossible. David Mortenson saw this same route himself and tried it with a friend. These two went there on Thanksgiving Day and wanted to call this nameless canyon just east of Fishtail Canyon, "Cranberry Canyon" in honor of the day. Cranberry Canyon lines up with a number of short canyons that were formed where the fault from Mt. Sinyala fractured the rock.

To reach the Mortenson Route, we went down a shallow drainage southeast from Ghost Rock and then away from Deer Creek southwest down the Cranberry Canyon drainage through the rest of the Supai. We followed the Redwall rim on the east side of Cranberry Canyon, then turned east above the river for a half mile to the break. The first place we tried didn't work, but a smaller ravine open to the east was the key. I believe I would have needed to lower a full pack with a rope for ten feet.

Mortenson and his friend went down to the river and crossed on air mattresses, then went up Hundred and Forty Mile Canyon to look at the Keyhole Bridge. Our party had only enough time to get down through the Redwall before returning to our camp by the spring in the east arm of Fishtail Canyon.

Several side canyons from lower Kanab Canyon are interesting to climb for a few hundred yards. One, however, is outstanding. It drains the big bay east of the headland of elevation 5,748', the main bay north of Kanab Point promontory. This side canyon is unique for a permanent stream coming from the spring. Opposite the mouth, a five hundred-foot spire of limestone catches everyone's eye. There is a prehistoric ruin on the right bank of Kanab Creek, a few hundred yards from the mouth of the side canyon. The main attraction of this tributary is that it provides a faint route up through the Redwall and Supai.

I stripped to my underwear and carried my shoes through a pool, using my hands and toes to get past a little fall. Then, when I was almost through the Redwall, I came to a chockstone that stopped me. With a boost from a companion, I could have continued. On separate trips, hikers from Albuquerque and Bob Dye, on his own, have gone up this way and have also made it through the Supai, which they considered harder than the Redwall. The Esplanade, north of Fishtail Mesa to Kwagunt Hollow, is very interesting. I came south from the Kwagunt Hollow Trail to the north side of Fishtail when I wanted to climb Racetrack Knoll. There was some water in one of the ravines, but a better spring is in the upper Supai in Indian Hollow Canyon.

Instead of heading the entire network of canyons between Sowats Point and Racetrack Knoll, I might have been able to shorten the route as well as to see more by going down into the canyons. The few hikers who enter this wilderness will feel that they are breaking new ground. Very few have already gone up Indian Hollow Canyon from the bed of Jumpup to the Esplanade and out.

There is also a world of good hiking on the Esplanade west of Kanab Canyon to Toroweap. An easy way from the bed of Kanab Canyon to the Esplanade is through Chamberlain Canyon, a tributary about three miles south of Hack Canyon. Years ago, three of us mistakenly went up here when we were looking for a way out of Hack Canyon at the end of our trek, which started at Big Saddle.

I know the route from here to Toroweap only from hearsay, but trips down into Hundred and Fifty Mile Canyon to the Redwall, down Tuckup Canyon to the river and down Stairway Canyon seem the most glamorous. The latter two require some skilled climbing with ropes for safety belays.

Western Grand Canyon

Mt. Sinyala (Photo: Harvey Butchart)

The original Grand Canyon National Park boundary ended on the north side of the Colorado at Thunder River and just west of Havasu Canyon on the south. This is the western Grand Canyon and its fine scenery is still relatively unknown. The approach roads across the Hualapai Reservation from the south and through the Arizona Strip on the north are fair only during dry weather. Contact the Grand Canyon Back Country office or the Hualapai and Havasu Tribal offices for information concerning driving conditions and accessibility to trailheads on tribal lands. Keeping a careful eye out for storms, hikers can experience a real wilderness adventure in this seldom visited section of the Grand Canyon.

Downriver from the mouth of Matkatamiba. (Photo: Harvey Butchart)

Great Thumb to Supai

One can drive a jeep or truck from the Topacoba Hilltop Road up on Great Thumb Mesa. One of the principal attractions is the defensive ruin on the detached promontory at Enfilade Point. Blocks of limestone form a parapet on the side that faces the mainland. It is hard enough to climb to the top without facing the rocks and arrows of the ancient warriors.

One of several routes down from the east side of the Great Thumb Mesa leaves the rim just north of where the map puts the check point called "Cave." It is a rugged bighorn trail. The sheep seem to have the Esplanade from Forster Canyon to Tahuta Point to themselves. I have had the thrill of three sightings of bighorn sheep during my brief visits. Burros and wild horses don't care to cross the steep shale guarding this territory.

Shallow depressions in the bare rocks catch plenty of water during the rains but the water sources are far apart during the dry season. Where the main bed of Fossil starts cutting into the Supai there is a deep pothole that should be reliable. There is also a seep beneath the Coconino at the head of Fossil.

A better-known spring, which has been omitted from some maps, is located at the lower end of the Great Thumb Trail in the bay of Hundred and Forty Mile Canyon. Even it went dry one year in October. This spring can be reached more directly from the south rim of Hundred and Forty Mile Canyon via a deer trail. There is a more reliable spring at the base of the Coconino due south of the one with the cottonwood grove.

Keyhole Natural Bridge is an interesting objective. One can leave the rim where the jeep trail first meets it and go down to the bridge from the southwest along a fault valley. The bridge forms one rim of a deep pit which would require a rappel to go down and through the bridge. A steep smooth incline below the bridge would probably require more rope. Luckily for the backpackers, there is a spring just west of the bridge and this may have drawn the prehistoric builders of a peculiar little cairn. The route below the bridge to the river has been checked by at least two river parties including that of the discoverer of the bridge, river runner Plez "P.T." Reilly. Reilly, who was once a boatman for Norman Nevills before running his own trips, along with environmentalist and newspaper reporter Martin Litton, reintroduced the old-style cataract boats on the Colorado River in the 1950's. Reilly had also written a detailed account of historical events at Lee's Ferry and had compiled a list of all the known deaths in the Grand Canyon and adjoining canyons. He discovered this bridge while studying a picture he had taken from the air. Reilly took more pictures of the Grand Canyon from the air than anyone else. When he wasn't leading river parties down the Colorado, he was usually flying with a friend in a small plane through the Grand Canyon.

A little study of the map shows that the same fault which controls the route to Keyhole Natural Bridge continues far to the southwest. It provides access to the Redwall rims in Olo, Matkatamiba, and Sinyala Canyons. The fault even lines up with Beaver Canyon on the west side of Havasu Canyon. I have followed it from the base of Mt. Sinyala northeast across the canyon of that name and then down into Matkatamiba. There is a seep spring near the top of the Redwall in Sinyala Canyon and another near the bottom of the Supai in the fault ravine into Matkatamiba. It would be interesting to try following this fault across Matkatamiba and Olo. Detours to head the canyons or even to go out above the river along the Redwall rim would be no more tedious than those of the usual route along the Esplanade.

There must be other ways to get off the plateau down to the Esplanade. Allyn Cureton and I found one in the bay between Gatagama and Hamidrik Points. From a distance, I thought I saw a route east of Paya Point. Two other routes lie on either side of Manakacha Point, but they both require ropes. About a half mile east of the point, on the north side is the upper end of the Apache

War Trail. Some route study was needed to find the way off the rim and also to get through the Toroweap and Coconino cliffs. About halfway through the latter, Jay Hunt, a professor who had the reputation of doing things that gave him a 50% chance of survival, drove a spike into a crack to serve as a rappel rope anchor. Jay once paddled a small two-man inflatable from Havasu to Pearce Ferry, without portaging, turning over nearly four times. From Jay's spike and only ten or twelve feet on the rope, we proceeded down a narrow, steep ramp which we followed all the way to the village.

Another better known route, called the "Rope Trail," is south of Manakacha Point and even south of where the old telephone line went down to Supai. We parked at the end of the south fork of the Manakacha Point Road and descended the valley south of the road. When we looked for this trail we had general directions from Earl Paya, a Supai Indian. Still, we walked right by the slot in the Toroweap where we should have started down. A rope about one hundred feet down this ravine is a convenience rather than a necessity, but there is another fixed rope below where a freehand climb is possible only for the expert. The route lies to the south of a little butte in the shale on the Esplanade. The final descent to the village is mapped and mentioned in the book on *Havasu Canyon* by Joseph Wampler. He recommends a guide, but if you remember that you should get down to the north of a big deposit of travertine, you shouldn't be long delayed. The Indians use this route very little and they warn you that the ropes may be getting rotten.

Routes to Havasu Canyon

Few tourists have ever heard of more than two trails to Supai and the vast majority of visitors use the Hualapai Trail at the end of the road from near Peach Springs. The longer Topacoba Trail which starts after thirty-six miles of rough road from Grand Canyon Village is little used today. Topacoba Spring is south of the switchbacks through the Coconino. There is a seep spring and some rain pockets east of where Lee Canyon meets Havasu Canyon, but one should carry plenty of water for the hot twelve miles from the beginning of Havasu Creek to the trailhead.

On the right wall of Havasu Canyon about fifty yards south of the junction with Lee Canyon, there is a fine display of petroglyphs and pictographs pecked into and painted on the rock. The pictographs look rather fresh as if they had been done with schoolroom chalk, but the petroglyphs seem very ancient. Some of the animal representations look more like the ibex than the bighorn, but the ibex never were in North America.

South of the Topacoba Trail, the next access is via Moqui Trail Canyon about six miles south of the park boundary. According to Earl Paya, there is another ropeless route down the north side of Havataguitch Canyon. One can drive much closer to the trailhead than the map indicates. There are some rough places, but a truck can reach Chikapanagi Tank. The route through the Coconino is a place of wild beauty, meandering in and around huge rocks in the defile. In the spring, numerous redbud trees are in bloom, and the birds love it. This was the way the Hopis came to trade with the Supais. There is a good spring just south of where the trail gets through the Coconino. This is on the map of the entire park, but the next routes to the south could only be studied from the 1:250 000 Williams map. The Kirby Trail is reached by driving southwest from the ranch just below the north

Havasu Falls. (Photo: Wynne Benti)

edge of the map at the designation R. 1 W. (Range One West). I had to ask directions at the ranch. One can also walk down the main arm of Havasu or Cataract Creek. There is usually some water standing in the Coconino potholes, and the old-timer Kirby had a spring near the foot of his trail.

About 2.5 miles northeast of the nearest road at Platinum Tanks is an old historic route called either the Kla-La-Pa or the Highwall Spring Trail. General James Crook was supposed to have come this way in 1882. There are prehistoric ruins on each side of the bed west from the lower end of the trail. Highwall Spring is at the end of a short spur. It is a trickle in the bed of the wash, and the Indians have left shovels nearby to dig it out.

Following the main streambed farther downstream, one comes to Black Tank Wash, a tributary from the south. In 1882, W.W. Bass and a chance acquaintance named McKinney came down the main bed to visit Supai. McKinney went on ahead to scout the route and didn't return to camp. Bass led a search party from Williams, but McKinney was already out of the canyon, having gone up to Black Tank Wash. The route through the Coconino is rather rugged with juniper logs wedged into some cracks. Another route is at the head of Driftwood Canyon. One enters the wash from Section 11 (R.4.W.) on the updated 1962 version of the Grand Canyon National Park and Vicinity map. There isn't a trail, but the climbing is easy.

West of the Hualapai Trail there is a rather rugged access route from the northwest side of Wescogame Point. At the top of the Coconino, walk around below the end of the point and down a ravine to the right. On the Esplanade, head north to the next tributary which is called the Horse Trail Canyon. There is a well-constructed trail and scenic route through this canyon, the trailhead of which could be found using the old National Canyon 15 minute topo now divided into four separate 7.5 minute maps: National Canyon SW, Gateway Rapids, Vulcan's Throne and Vulcan's Throne SE.

The same map shows how to drive to the head of the Beaver Canyon Trail. We left the main Supai Road 2.1 miles beyond the well-graded road which is marked with the sign "Camp 16." It is about twenty miles of fair to bad dirt road. The top of the trail is obscure, but going north to the rim and looking down to the right, the trail becomes visible. It is often steep, yet quite distinct to the bottom of the Coconino. From here on through the Supai gorge, we stayed in the bed. A couple of springs deep in the Supai seem to be reliable, and there is also a little spring at the top of the Redwall right in the bed. The trail stays at the top of the Redwall and eventually reaches the village at this level.

There are two ways to get off the Redwall down to Havasu Falls and they both involve a bit of hand and toe climbing. One is via Ghost Canyon which is a ravine north of Havasu Falls, and the other is a shorter scramble south of the falls.

For real adventure, one can try going down the bed of Little Coyote Canyon. Soon a barrier fall is reached at a big chockstone. It looks worse than it is to get down, but the inexpert climber has to struggle to get back up. A solo climber would have to lower his pack on a thirty-foot rope. There are no other serious obstructions all the way to Havasu Creek. There is a fine spring about halfway through the gorge, and the entire Redwall passage is fantastically beautiful. If one should also count as access routes the Redwall rims from upriver and down as well as the walk up Havasu Creek from a boat, there are at least sixteen routes to Supai. Perhaps an approach by helicopter could be counted as the seventeenth.

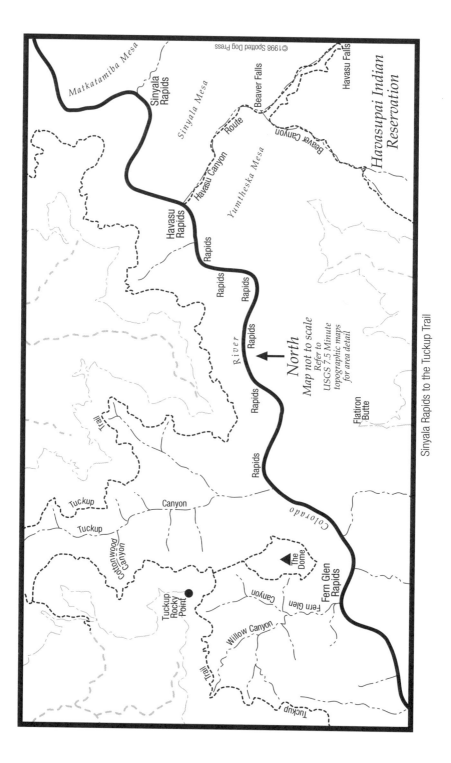

Sinyala Rapids to the Tuckup Trail

© 1998 Spotted Dog Press

Matkatamiba Mesa
Sinyala Rapids
Sinyala Mesa
Beaver Falls
Havasu Falls
Havasupai Indian Reservation
Route
Havasu Canyon
Beaver Canyon
Havasu Rapids
Yumtheska Mesa
Rapids
Rapids
Rapids
River
North
Map not to scale
Refer to
USGS 7.5 Minute
topographic maps
for area detail
Rapids
Rapids
Flatiron Butte
Rapids
Trail
Rapids
Tuckup
Canyon
Tuckup
Colorado
Cottonwood Canyon
The Dome
Tuckup Rocky Point
Fern Glen Rapids
Canyon
Fern Glen
Willow Canyon
Trail
Tuckup

Kanab Creek

The usual access is via Hacks Canyon. One can drive to the rim of Hacks Canyon southwest of Fredonia and find a trail to its bed only a few miles west of its junction with Kanab Canyon. This side canyon is an open valley and seasonal water can be found in pockets of rocks along the side or at a developed spring west of where the trail comes down. One can also get into Hacks Canyon at its upper end. The road that once led to a copper and uranium mine is only suitable for walking now.

The next tributary from the west, Chamberlain Canyon, has a spring with a trail going up it. There is more water in other side canyons, usually in plunge pools below the falls. Water flows all year from springs near the river. The Redwall Formation is deeper in the western Grand Canyon, and hikers down Kanab agree that this is tops for scenic grandeur. One can walk the bank, with a bit of a detour above a bluff, and reach Deer Creek with the option of going out the Thunder River Trail. This section of the inner gorge, a great trench in the Redwall rather than through the dark schist, impresses many people even more so than Granite Gorge.

A very interesting route from the river up through the Redwall lies about two-fifths of the way from Fishtail Canyon to Deer Creek. It has been used by the discoverers, David Mortenson and a friend at least twice. Starting from the top, they took the Thunder River Trail from Indian Hollow Campground. Below the Coconino, they left the trail and walked west, watching for an east facing wall below a terrace. On this slightly overhanging wall are painted white effigies of two persons, larger than life and higher than an artist can reach without a ladder. Both figures have three white spikes going straight up from the head. We call this place "Ghost Rock." They walked down the draw from Ghost Rock into the Deer Creek drainage and then cut over a saddle to the west into a nameless canyon which lines up with the fault coming all the way from Mt. Sinyala. Mortenson first came here on Thanksgiving and he wanted to name this fault tributary Cranberry Canyon. They followed the Redwall rim on the left side and turned east when they saw the river. The route down is a bit more than a half mile east of Cranberry Canyon. Lowering the packs with a rope for about ten feet was helpful. Once, I noticed this place from the air, and asked two friends who were flying the canyon to check it out for me. They took pictures and gave me their opinion, which was that it would be impossible on foot. Thus, it remained for David Mortenson to take the honors.

Other ways into Kanab Canyon start from upper Jumpup Canyon and from Sowats Point. The latter place has a trail down its south flank into Kwagunt Hollow. There is water at the bottom of the Hermit and also in the Supai gorge. The horse trail goes north below Sowats Point and a few cairns guide one to where you can get down to the bed of Sowats Canyon. As shown on the Jumpup Canyon 7.5 minute topo, there is a good spring in lower Sowats Canyon. It is shorter and more scenic to scramble down through the Supai in the Kwagunt Hollow gorge.

Below the junction of Kwagunt Hollow Canyon and Jumpup, the latter becomes a spectacularly narrow slit through the Redwall. Indian Hollow Canyon comes in from the southeast. At least one party of good climbers has passed the chockstone barrier and gone up to the Esplanade from here. A rope is needed for the packs.

The walk through lower Jumpup to Kanab Canyon is level and easy. There is a plunge pool of permanent water below a fall on the right. Kanab Canyon has a gently sloping gravel and boulder bed. Still I was amazed when I saw tire tracks down as far as the mouth of Jumpup Canyon. There was permanent, but stagnant water below a fall in the next tributary from the left. Once in May, I found cleaner looking water in the bed of the main canyon about two miles below the mouth of Jumpup. With the map in my hand, I could keep track of the big bends of Kanab Canyon, but Jumpup is so narrow that I lost count of the bends.

Toroweap Area

The McCombs have hiked along the Esplanade from Hacks Canyon to Tuckup. John McComb once worked for the southwestern field office of the Sierra Club in Arizona and had a reputation as a fast canyon hiker. He and his wife got down to the river and followed it to the Lava Trail at Toroweap where they climbed out. The map shows springs, but it would be well advised to go at a time when rain has filled the water pockets. Intriguing detours lead out to viewpoints and down into places like Hundred and Fifty Mile Canyon. Billingsley has been down Tuckup numerous times when he was mapping the area geologically. He located several natural bridges in the Tuckup Basin and found an old camp in Hundred and Fifty Mile Canyon. An expert can get down Tuckup to the river without a rope, but Billinglsey found that fastening ropes in two places was a help.

Downriver from Tuckup, several side canyons offer interesting detours. Fern Glen is as beautiful as the name. If you know just where to stand, you can look up through a hole in a fin of the Redwall called "Alamo Window." Further downriver is Stairway Canyon. A few years ago, three young people, contrary to the opinion of a man who had observed Stairway from the air, proved that Stairway can be climbed without a rope. It was routine scrambling until they came to the top of the Redwall. Jim Sears was able to get up the difficult place and then assisted the others with a rope. Cove Canyon, about three miles upriver from the Lava Trail, is also interesting. The lowest fall can be bypassed, but the next one is impossible.

A half mile downriver from Cove Canyon, the Redwall is covered by a landslide. This can be reached by going east from Toroweap Lookout about three miles on an old road to the head of a trail. This starts down into the Cove Canyon drainage and

Colorado River from Toroweap Point.
((Photo: R.S. Leding, Grand Canyon Museum Collection, 2361)

then hooks to the west below the top Supai cliff. The original trail, now about gone, went to a mine. Pat Bunday, a rancher on the Arizona Strip, has gone from the old copper mine to the river. It is possible to proceed farther east then this.

To go down the Lava Trail, leave the Toroweap Viewpoint Road and go around Vulcan's Throne to the west. There is a lake bed to cross, usually dry, but the last mile of the road is rough on tires. Walking it might be preferable. Be ready for some rough scrambling, but most of the way is well marked with cairns. Ranger John Riffey has said that the ordinary hiker should take two hours to get down and four to get back. These times allow for the worst. One warm August day, it took me sixty-seven minutes to get down and one hour and twenty minutes to return.

The Toroweap Viewpoint is famous for seeming to be directly above the river and 3,000 vertical feet up. The principal attraction at the bottom of the Lava Trail is the sight of Lava Falls Rapids (also known as Vulcan Rapids), reputed to be the wildest ride for boaters on the entire river. The river drops over huge chunks of lava which are the residue of a five hundred foot high dam formed over a million years ago when great rivers of melted rock flowed down from the mountains into the river of melted snow. The boaters have to avoid the center hole below the great rocks and then dodge the barn-sized rocks projecting from the bank. Sometimes the big rubber boats capsize in that maelstrom, but the people always manage to get a breath when they need it, thanks to their life jackets.

The second time I went down this Lava Trail, I crossed the river far above the rapid on my air mattress. I had heard about three ways to climb up Prospect Canyon. When Elwyn Blake, a boatman on the 1923 USGS party, and Emery Kolb went up the middle of the wash over a long rockslide, they felt hundreds of tons of rock begin to move beneath them. I still thought that this would be the easiest way, and had no trouble with the sliding rock. With a bit of route finding and some use of my hands, I got out into the open valley on top where there is a jeep road. I had carried an overnight pack down to the north bank of the river, but got back so early, that I returned to the car before nightfall.

Whitmore Wash and Parashant Canyon Area

When you drive down to the overlook at Toroweap you reach the Supai rim, yet coming down into Tuweap Valley is so gradual that it's hard to believe that it's in a canyon. Coming south from St. George through the crossroads of Bundyville, you know exactly when you are starting down into the canyon. The road is only slightly steep and winding, but not too difficult for an ordinary car. For twenty miles below the rim, the road goes through a green valley almost unique in the Grand Canyon. Lava spilled through gaps in the eastern rim of the former canyon and formed a dam. Soil has washed in behind the dam to form a level floor and enough earth covers the lava at the lower end to form the base for vegetation. Glaciers of black magma are frozen to the steep eastern side of the lower valley. The road goes down over this broad ramp to within 920 vertical feet of the Colorado. A good horse trail completes the route to the river. Among Grand Canyon trails, this route is distinctive for passing a "Devil's Postpile" display of lava which is cooled in a polygonal column design. This is where some of the river trips end with the passengers being brought up on horseback and flown out when they reach an airstrip.

More points of interest await the hiker who takes the road forking to the west about five miles north of the end of the main road. This goes to the west of the cinder cone in the middle of the valley and then crosses some deep ravines to reach the saddle south of Whitmore Point. It bends north and eventually ends on the Supai rim above Parashant Canyon. North of this road end, on big sandstone blocks are big, deep rain pools. There is also a developed water catchment just north of the road south of Whitmore Point.

To the northwest, across Parashant Canyon, one can see the road that comes down Andrus Canyon to the Esplanade. It goes past an airstrip to an abandoned copper mine. A number of faults through this region make it possible to climb down to the beds of Parashant and Andrus Canyons. South of Parashant Canyon, the Whitmore Point 7.5 minute topo indicates where a trail goes down the ravine east of the road through the Supai to Frog Spring. This is a rather muddy seep, but campers have used it. From here, one can go along the top of the Redwall to the biggest fault of all, where the throw is hundreds of feet. It is easy to scramble down the fault ravine to a constructed trail leading to the bed of Parashant. At the narrowest place, ranchers have installed a wire gate to keep the wild burros from competing with the cattle for grasses.

Another, though longer way to reach the same gate by an established trail, is to leave the road before it turns north, near the southern edge of the Whitmore Point Quad map. Jim Sears has found the trail down this draw through the Supai of the fault escarpment. The faint trail follows the fault valley northwest over the pass and down near Cedar Spring. From here we followed the Redwall to the northeast along the trail going down to the gate. Although there was no trail up the fault on the opposite side of Parashant Canyon, it was an easy scramble to get out on the north side.

From this point in the bed, it was an easy walk up Parashant through some very spooky narrows. Eventually, one can get out on either side. The bed downstream to the southwest was also spectacularly narrow in places. If one goes up Andrus Canyon far enough, it is a fairly easy climb out to the mine road. There was pothole water in the canyon below Cedar Spring, and also in the next canyon to the right, just past the mouth of Andrus. With the exception of one place where big barrier boulders make a bypass necessary, the bed of Parashant was an easy walk clear to the river.

Downriver from the mouth of Parashant, a broad beach makes walking easy for several hundred yards, but then the bank becomes rocky and choked with brush. A burro trail avoids the mesquite by generally following the base of the river cliff. With some interruptions, this trail, probably built by prospectors and most recently maintained by wild burros, goes along for about forty river miles. About three miles downriver from the mouth of Parashant, while I was seeking shelter from a storm, I found a group of pictographs beneath a substantial overhang. This place is back from the river on the north side of a stream bed. There was a mescal pit out where the trail goes down to cross the wash.

Upriver from the mouth of the Parashant, the walking is much more difficult. There were no more signs of burros, but the deer have established short and sketchy trails. About two miles upriver, the cliff ahead drops straight down into deep water. However, there is a convenient ravine where one can climb above this river cliff. We followed the bench to the east at the first chance and descended to the broad sandy area beyond. The ravine we climbed up was quite straight, since it was formed where a dike of molten rock split the sedimentary rock all the way to the top of the plateau. Billingsley discovered this route to the top of the Esplanade. It was the quickest way to get from a car down to the mouth of Parashant.

It is possible, but tedious, to follow the river clear to the foot of the Whitmore Trail. Much of the way is along precarious slopes above the river cliffs, and the routes up and down from the beaches are often difficult. At Mile 193, a steep ridge of loose cinders covers the lower cliff. Instead of going up the nose, one should go up a dry stream bed west of the ridge and cross at the upper or north end of the ridge. Across the north end, I found a way to get through the lava cliff to camp by the river. To avoid another place where there is no travel below the cliff, I had to go back up in the morning and proceed upriver there.

Just when I was most worried that the precarious route up there would pinch out, I found evidence of a constructed trail

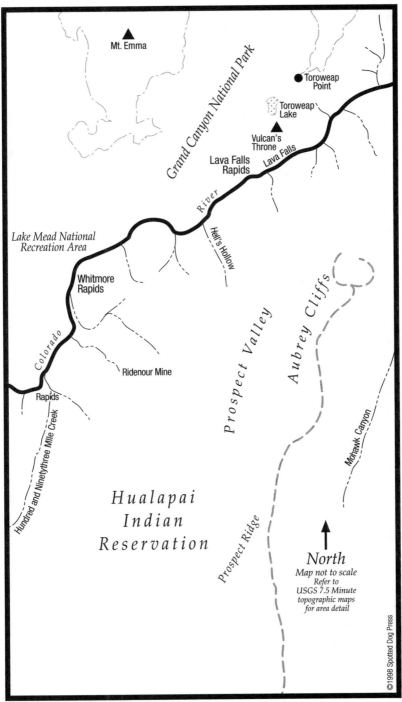

Mt. Emma

Grand Canyon National Park

Toroweap
Point

Toroweap
Lake

Vulcan's
Throne

Lava Falls
Rapids   Lava Falls

River

Hell's Hollow

Lake Mead National
Recreation Area

Whitmore
Rapids

Colorado

Ridenour Mine

Prospect Valley

Aubrey Cliffs

Mohawk Canyon

Rapids

Hundred and Ninetythree Mile Creek

Hualapai
Indian
Reservation

Prospect Ridge

North
Map not to scale
Refer to
USGS 7.5 Minute
topographic maps
for area detail

© 1998 Spotted Dog Press

Toroweap to Hundred and Ninetythree Mile Creek

which I followed for some time. I lost this trail in the broad open area downriver from Whitmore Canyon, but the last mile and a half to the horse trail was easy to follow.

Billingsley has pointed out another route for hikers. The road west of the volcano splits and the east fork goes down into the west arm of Whitmore Wash. On the Whitmore Rapid 7.5 minute topo map, a trail is shown going to Cane Spring. Billingsley sketched a route down the bed of the west arm and then showed me how to keep to the west of the bowl and eventually go south to the river.

Whitmore Wash
to the Shivwits Plateau

When I went from the volcano in Whitmore to Lone Mountain and then turned south to check Billingsley's dike route to the river, I got into the wrong dike and was stopped in the lower Redwall. After talking with Billingsley, I went back and found the right dike ravine.

One gets off the Supai rim a little to the east of the western boundary of the section labeled '6' on the Whitmore Point SE 7.5 minute topo. South and a little west of this break is the wrong dike ravine. The right one is about 200 yards to the east. Only down near the river is there a spot where one may wish to remove his pack, reaching back for it after a five-foot drop.

Armed with information from Jorgen Visbak and George Billingsley about a loop hike down Two Hundred and Nine Mile Canyon and up Two Hundred and Fourteen Mile Canyon, Scott Baxter and I undertook this prime trek. I was willing to risk taking my four-wheeler more than two miles south of Shanley Tanks. The road seemed more like a tank trap than a jeep road!

Scott and I wanted to walk the old road to a wash downhill from Rodger Tank, but the map puts this cattle tank in the forest out of sight of the road. We were afraid that we were going too far south and started down a draw into the Two Hundred and Nine Mile drainage. Coming out to a full view of the Grand Canyon, our wash dropped over an impossible fall, but we found a talus slide for a bypass to the south. We concluded that we should have left the road in the next draw to the south. There was only one more sheer drop in the bed, in the lower Supai. Again, there was a bypass around to the south. For a few yards, on this bypass, we recognized trail construction. It is a long way to the river, especially when we had to walk for nearly two hours on the road, so we camped by a rain pool in the lower Redwall.

By noon the next day, we were at the river. The day was hot and we were glad to relax in a few inches of cold river water. As we started walking the five miles of riverbank, it began to rain. Stopping beneath an overhang, we watched a river party float by in several boats. We signaled to the last boat and asked for ride. The operator even invited us to a fine steak dinner with his party for the last night that they would be out. Fortunately, they had been planning to camp near the mouth of Two Hundred and Fourteen Mile Canyon.

We were on our way up Two Hundred and Fourteen Mile Canyon early the next morning, since we knew it would be hot. When we arrived at the base of the Redwall, we headed for what seemed like the only possible break. Just as Billingsley had said, we found a well-preserved trail.

Even though the summer thunderstorm season had just ended, there was not as much standing water in the Redwall pockets as we had seen in Two Hundred and Nine Mile Canyon after the summer rain seasons of the past. No trail showed above the Redwall and we wasted little effort in reaching the Snyder Mine. The seventy degree temperature inside the mine shaft was a real help, as I was beginning to feel ill from the heat. It was only a little past noon, but we loafed at the mine for several hours and then went down to get water at Shanley Spring. Ten years before, I had found this fine spring without a map. Scott and I walked down to where I knew it would be. There is a fall in a bed of this arm of Trail Canyon near the top of the Redwall. I vaguely recalled getting below this fall on a meager trail to the right of the bed.

I noticed a trail going down to the left of the fall, so we walked down on that side. As I recalled, there was a pool back in the cave, but we couldn't find it this time. I should have backed-tracked and tried going down the other side of the fall, but I more or less panicked and talked about going back to the rain pool in Two Hundred and Fourteen Mile Canyon over an hour from Snyder Mine. Scott told me not to worry, but to rest at the mine while he looked for water. Going a little farther down, then turning up a little ways into another fork of the canyon, he found an adequate supply.

In the morning he returned to the rain pool and brought more water than he would need, as well as the two quarts I had been carrying when we started for the end of the jeep road east of Kelly Tanks.

Getting up the steep talus to the rim seemed unusually hard for me and I was soon ready for a long rest under the shade of a juniper. I had to take more and more frequent rest stops during the nine-mile walk along the jeep road to the car. I believed that it would be one of the last times that I would try anything as ambitious.

It is my opinion, that the mappers should have called Two Hundred and Fourteen Mile Canyon, "Trail Canyon," in view of the fact that the trail is a fine route, complete with constructed support walls in parts. Instead, Two Hundred and Nineteen Mile Canyon is called "Trail Canyon," while the trail found there is nothing more than a bighorn track. In fact, how to get through it was quite a mystery to us for some time. The horsemen who aided in the 1928 search for lost Glen and Bessie Hyde, preferred the Snyder Mine Trail to the Price Point Trail. The former must have been the trail in Two Hundred and Fourteen Mile Canyon.

When Scott and I were driving north on the Kelly Point Road, we met and chatted with Buster Esplin, one of the most knowledgeable ranchers in this entire region. Several years ago, he told me just where to leave the rim to go down the Price Point and Snyder Mine Trails. Now, he answered all my questions about trails to Amos Spring and Twin Spring in the Surprise Canyon basin. He noted that there was a second spring and a ruined shack in the Amos Spring tributary.

Shivwits Plateau

A four-wheel drive vehicle was standard equipment for this interesting area. Using a good map, we followed the road heading directly south from St. George about fifty miles to a fork. The left branch went to Bundyville and the Whitmore Trail; the right fork, according to the sign, went to Parashant and Mt. Dellenbaugh. We followed the right fork to where it forked again and turned left. The road out to the end of the Shivwits Plateau (the left fork) goes to the east of Mt. Dellenbaugh and becomes very rough. At Shanley Tanks, about ten miles south of Mount Dellenbaugh, the road was blocked by a huge pine tree that had been shattered by a storm. A cabin at that spot is a comfort on rainy nights. Henry Hall, a graduate student at NAU, and I first walked down Price Canyon looking for a water source called "Price Pocket." We found it and another larger hole where the upper ravine drops abruptly to the Esplanade. We then walked east through the junipers to Price Point, a volcanic rise in the rim. Henry was startled at the fine view of so much of the western Grand Canyon.

I had previously come up from Mile 205 Rapid to the Esplanade on an old horse trail, and had been told that the Price Point Trail leaves the rim on the south side of the point. My current project was to complete my previous route by connecting it with the rim. I found a place where it appeared I could start down, but if this was ever a horse trail, it was that no longer. I had trouble keeping my footing on the loose lava rock slide. At the bottom of this slope, I went to the left and kept on the high ground between Spring Canyon and Two Hundred and Seven Mile Canyon until I had connected with my former route. Before I turned back, I found a small prehistoric ruin and a bit of trail construction.

About six miles south of Shanley Tanks, near Kelly Tanks, a spur road goes to the east rim of the plateau. Here, a trail starts

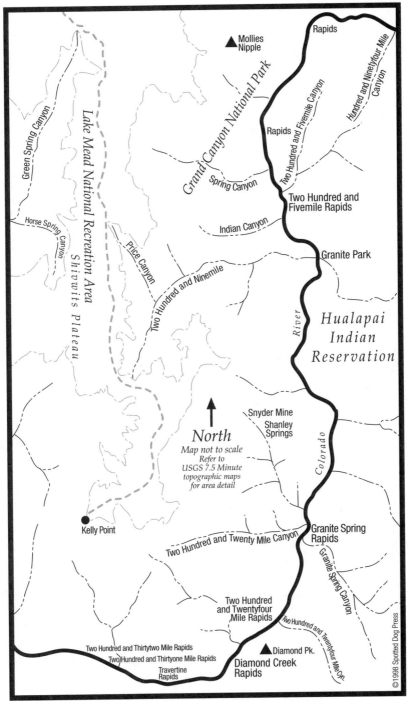

Shivwits Plateau Area – Hundred and Ninetyfour Mile Canyon
to Two Hundred and Thirtytwo Mile Rapids

down to the Snyder Mine. The ore was copper and the depth of the tunnel shows a lot of work. It is on the Esplanade in the drainage of Trail Canyon or Two Hundred and Nineteen Mile Canyon. We visited the area several times before we found the trail up to the mine from the river. We reached this area by driving down the Peach Springs Wash Road, and crossing the river in a boat. Travel was quite easy along an old burro trail.

In Trail Canyon, we walked up the north fork but were stopped by a fall. Finally, we discovered that we should have gone up to a bench higher than the fall at the steep slope between the two forks. A route up here, better for bighorns than for horses, brought us into the bed above the fall. We used the bed and then the slope on the northeast side and came to Shanley Spring. Shanley Spring is a small pool set back in a cave beneath the fall in the upper Redwall. A recognizable trail goes from the spring up to the mine. In 1928, the newlyweds Glen and Bessie Hyde, drowned downriver from this area. During the ensuing search, horses were brought up and down this Snyder Mine Trail.

Before I realized that Trail Canyon would go, I found a way to climb the Redwall at Mile 217. A great section of the rim had slumped. Jorgen Visbak and I decided that one or two places were too difficult even for the wild burros. I had met Jorgen through Dock Marston and hiked with him for many years. He was originally from Hillerup, Denmark just outside of Copenhagen, but now worked as a potash chemist in Las Vegas.

On one trek, Jorgen and I continued upriver to Mile 205 where we found many interesting side canyons. I entered Two Hundred and Twenty Mile Canyon and concluded that there is no way to get up the Redwall there. Jorgen told me how he and two friends had come down Two Hundred and Nine Mile Canyon from the top of the plateau. At Two Hundred and Seven Mile Canyon, Jorgen and I succeeded in getting up the Redwall just south of the mouth of the canyon, but we couldn't make it up the bed itself.

I found another neat route up the Redwall and on to the top of the Shivwits Plateau just across the river from Diamond Peak. About half a mile northeast of the crossing above Diamond Creek, I climbed up a ravine to the west of a big promontory. To one side of the route near the top of the Redwall was a smoke-stained cave, and through the rim nearby was a large window. I was able to float across the river on an air mattress, get up there, find my way across the Esplanade, and up to the top in time to camp at Kelly Tanks, all in one late November day. The next day, I got down Separation Canyon to the Colorado. The Supai gave me the most trouble in route finding, but I should have come down on the north side of the Kelly Tanks arm of Separation Canyon. There are no barriers in the bed of Separation except for those with obvious bypasses. At the river, I spent the evening and forenoon with the Marston party who were remounting a bronze plaque honoring the three men of the Powell Party who walked away from the river. I was then ferried across the river by a passing boater and walked back along the Tonto Platform past Bridge Canyon to Diamond Creek.

Green Spring Canyon

Green Spring Canyon originates at Green Spring on the Shivwits Plateau in Lake Mead National Recreation Area and is shown on the 1:100 000 scale Mt. Trumbull and Peach Springs USGS metric topo maps.

As it winds south, Green Springs merges into Surprise Canyon before crossing the Sanup Plateau. Billingsley conducted a group hike through this canyon from south of Mount Dellenbaugh to Lake Mead. He reported that there were some problems in route finding. The longest detour was to the east out of the canyon bottom. In the Redwall, the only difficulty was the necessity to wade or swim through pools of water. The bottom of the canyon is long and the party required four days to reach the river where they were picked up by a commercial boat party.

Surprise Canyon

Surprise is the next big canyon on the north side of the
Colorado River in the lower Granite Gorge area, and west of
Separation Canyon. I guess that it got its name from the very
large area that drains into such a narrow and inconspicuous slot
through the granite at the river. This creek is also exceptional in
that one need not carry a lot of water for the long hike up from
the river past the junction with the Twin Spring Arm. Water runs
on the surface and then disappears, but one is never more than
forty-five minutes from water. The creek makes for very slow
walking over flood-scattered boulders, so look for stepping stones
when crossing the creek every few hundred yards. When the
water was higher than usual, I've had to wade. Take special care
of the footing as both Jorgen and I have had nasty falls here.

One thing that took me by surprise in Surprise Canyon was
the bar at its mouth. When Lake Mead was low, Jorgen and I had
trouble getting our small fishing boat over the bar into the lagoon
at the mouth. Once, when I was solo, I tied the boat outside the
bar and paddled my little inflatable about one hundred and fifty
yards to the walkable bed. Another time, floods had cut a channel through the bar, but the lake was so low that we beached our
boat just inside the bar and were able to walk on the silt bank past
the lagoon. In 1983, the lake was high enough to take a boat to the
north end of the lagoon.

Surprise Canyon has several fine overhangs that provide shelter on a wet night, especially near the top of the Tapeats and in the
Redwall near the junction with Twin Spring Canyon. There is shelter for two beds on the east side just north of the confluence with
the arm coming from Amos Spring. A shelter can be found inside
a shallow cave one hundred and fifty feet up the slope on the north
side of the confluence just beyond the Canyon on the Amos Point

7.5 minute topo. A similar cave, up from the bed of Twin Spring on the west side, north of the narrows, could sleep several.

Surprise Canyon had so many intriguing features that it became a favorite haunt of mine. For instance, there is a natural bridge on the east side about a third of a mile up the bed from the west border of Amos Point 7.5 minute topo. From a short distance, this place looks like a simple overhang with no big drainage above it. The first time Jorgen and I came here, we found it. I completely missed it on two or three later trips. About a ten minute walk upstream from the bridge, we went up on an east side terrace and found two mescal pits, as well as some cowchips near the wall. We knew that there must be an easier way to come from the plateau than the one Billingsley had found when he and his companions had to swim through a pool in the Green Spring Arm.

Jorgen and I spent several hours inspecting the arm that comes down from Amos Spring. The pockets of water that we found may not be permanent. Three barrier falls called for detours. We could only go a short way into an impressive narrows before coming to a large chockstone wedged at the brink of a small fall. Perhaps one of us could have boosted the other past this, but without a rope, the upper man couldn't have helped the lower. We decided not to attempt this move, although the bed seemed wide above. I wanted to return with a good climber and a rope. It would also be interesting to try coming down the Redwall from above. Our farthest point was less than a half-mile above where "Plateau" is printed on the map.

The next side canyon we looked at was the west side tributary whose mouth was just south of the word "Canyon" on the map. The steep jumble of big rocks in the bed was our greatest difficulty. After returning, we used the clay slope above the bed. About halfway from the main bed to our highest point, Billingsley had marked my map with the suggested Redwall route. This place on the west side didn't look too promising for my type of climbing.

Billingsley had also marked another possible Redwall route just north of the word "Surprise." It looked a lot more promising. Trying it solo, I couldn't make it, but I think that there is a better route than the one I attempted, should I try it again. The route Billingsley had marked went up to a high bench below the upper sheer cliff, then east and south around the end of the promontory before going on up the rest of the Redwall. If one can do this, the way should be clear to walk up through the Supai to the spring shown on the Devils Slide Rapids 7.5 minute topo. It would be an exciting part of a through-canyon route!

The west side tributary, whose mouth is northeast of the word "Canyon," is surely worth a visit. Both forks of this canyon have fantastic Redwall narrows with impossible barrier falls, but not before one sees solid beds of mimulae hiding the footing and banks of ferns on the walls. Seeps flow permanently in the bed. About a half-mile upstream from this tributary, there was another coming from the southeast. I was able to scramble up it for only a short way, but it was interesting and very scenic.

The much larger one on the same southeast side, about a half-mile farther, has more possibilities. I was stopped by a barrier fall less than a half-mile up from the bed of Surprise, but when I tried going up the Redwall rather close to the mouth on the west side, I succeeded quite easily. There were bighorn droppings along the way and it was surely a lot safer than the way Billingsley had suggested for getting out to the west of Surprise Canyon.

Short on time, I turned back. From my turnaround spot, I could see a way up the Supai and would assume from the map that one could walk from the bed of Surprise to Amos Spring in a day. Thus, this would be a strategic line in a through-canyon route.

From the cowchips in lower Surprise, I had hoped to find a much better route from the rim than the one used by Billingsley, which involved a bit of swimming. I tried Twin Spring Canyon. There was water in this canyon for only about the first twenty minutes and I erred by leaving my canteen behind. Soon, I reached the narrowest and deepest Redwall gorge that I had ever seen.

Standing with my feet apart, I could lean and touch the wall on one side and then, without changing my footing, lean and touch the opposite wall. At this point, the Redwall is approximately five hundred feet deep. Coming to a large chockstone wedged between the walls with about fifteen feet of clearance beneath, I was prepared for an impossible barrier around the next bend. Instead, I could walk up a gentle grade for the next forty-five minutes and find the upper part of Redwall opening out. One could climb to the top either to the east or the west here.

The bed goes through another boxing for a twenty minute walk to the top of the Redwall. In this upper narrows, Jorgen and I spent two nights in a neat cave about ten feet up from the canyon bed. Bits of charcoal on the floor suggested that others had preceded us. We had water from a rain pool, but it had almost sunk into the gravel by the next morning. We took two day-hikes from this base camp up on the Supai Plateau, both to the east and the west. We passed through the last of the Redwall and the Supai to the east by going a little north of our cave. For the other trip, we went to the upper end of the main narrows and then followed the Redwall rim south for about a mile before going up the Supai on the south side of a side canyon.

After learning that the Twin Spring narrows goes clear through, I returned in January with hopes of walking up to the rim near Twin Spring. It went smoothly for the most part, except when I walked up the wrong fork in one place. When it became steeper after a few hundred yards, I then knew that the other arm would be the correct one. In the open valley, I could identify landmarks along the rim. Impressive towers delineated the headlands, and the snow above added a touch of grandeur.

Just south of the elevation 5,725', at the northwest corner of Suicide Point, I thought I saw a possible route to the rim and another in the area between figures 5,256' and 5,871'. Upon reaching the side canyon below Lower Spring, the snow became deeper and deeper. I decided to postpone the rest of this project until the end of April when I could make a planned approach from Burnt Canyon.

Lost Creek

Lost Creek is on the other side of the lake heading downstream about a half-mile from the mouth of Surprise Canyon. There is a tamarisk jungle at the mouth making it impossible to land from a boat and walk up the bed. I had to take my time getting along the steep slope on the west side to come down into the clear bed.

As in several of the western Grand Canyon tributaries, there is a good little spring about a quarter of a mile above the lake. Beyond the bed it is dry. Short on time, I could not follow the bed to its upper end, where by all indications the walk would end in a sheer wall. I came to a broken slope on the south side that went to a notch in the Redwall. With my limited time, I went up about a third of the way to the skyline notch. Subsequent map study indicated that one might come down into a nameless canyon to reach this notch.

I checked this idea by driving on the Buck and Doe Road from Peach Springs. At that time, I lacked the detailed Horse Flat 7.5 minute topo of the area and didn't want to chance getting stuck in the mud on an obscure side road. Parking the car, I walked down a broad valley to a big clay tank, which probably accounts for "Lost Creek's" other name — "Clay Tank Canyon." A road paralleled the deepening bed of the wash. When the road climbed away from the bed, I continued down the bed. After several hours, I realized that I must be in the upper bed of Lost Creek itself, rather than the route I really wanted — up the nameless canyon farther east that goes by the notch.

I had hoped to find water pockets in this bed, but had to camp that night using melted snow and ice. It was handy that most of the ground was bare, and suitable for spreading out my bed. However, there were plenty of snow patches in the shade.

On the second day, I returned to the road and followed it east to a big metal tank. Beyond was a jeep road and the meanders of the wash fit precisely with those on the Spencer Canyon 7.5 minute topo. I needed only to climb about eighty feet from the bed to find the view down into Lost Creek from the notch. On a terrace halfway up to the notch was the largest mescal pit I have ever seen. I was able to scramble down to where I had been before and still return to the car that afternoon.

It is an interesting trip and one would have spring water down near the lake on a two-day round-trip from the car. Using the Horse Flat 7.5 minute topo, and if the dirt roads aren't too muddy, it would be possible to drive much closer than I succeeded in doing.

Reference Point Creek

This is the next big canyon on the south side of the lake. It is also called Horse Flat Canyon. I gave myself a half day for an inspection. It was still harder to get started in the clear dry wash away from the lake than at Lost Creek.

I had to work my way along the steep slope on the west side and then struggle through thickets of willows for some distance in the narrow, winding, and rather steep bed where a little stream flows. One might do better by going up the slope on the east side for quite a long way and then come down the bed. The head of the canyon was still a long way ahead and out of sight when I had to turn around. I was impressed by a huge geological fault through here. Rocks on the southwest side of the lake are much higher than the identical strata on the other side. This fault explains the notch in the Redwall of the Lost Creek route.

Salt Creek

Salt Creek is the side canyon north of the lake in line with the fault noted in the Reference Point Creek description. I gave it only a four-hour inspection and surely didn't check it out too thoroughly for a possible route to the Sanup Plateau. With its sheer walls and towers along the skyline, it impressed me as being particularly scenic. I found bighorn prints and droppings going up the wash and Billingsley had seen a prehistoric ruin in this canyon. I suspect that there is a route to the top where the wall is somewhat broken by this fault, but from a distance, I couldn't see how one could get up a wall near the base of the western arm of the canyon. I stayed over on the east side since it was possible to walk on higher ground there, but had to finally stop where the talus met the sheer wall.

Burnt Canyon

This big north side canyon furnishes an easy route to the top of the Shivwits Plateau. There is an extensive tamarisk jungle where the quiet water has deposited a silt terrace at the mouth, but it is one of the few side canyons where there is a convenient path above the delta on its east side. This starts at a mysterious tin-roofed shack hidden from the lake by a rocky outcrop at the headland. The rock layers are much lower here than at the mouth of Surprise and you are on the Tapeats as you walk the path about fifty feet up from the lake level. Again, there is a spring in the bed with good water for the first half-mile above the lake. The footing is a lot better in Burnt Canyon than in Surprise Canyon, and one can reach the confluence of the east and main arms in about two and a half hours.

In the Redwall, the east arm forks again, but these striking narrows soon terminate at impossible falls. George Beck, a caver who has spent a great deal of time in the Grand Canyon, found a cave high on the north wall of the east fork. In this cave there was a split twig figurine, a sign that people had been in the area 3,500 to 4,000 years ago. Ohlman and Kirschvink climbed up to what must have been Beck's cave, but without a light, were unable to find and indications of an artifact.

In recent years, cattle have been wandering loose in the lower canyon. Although no difficult detours are needed in going up the bed, we doubted that any rancher would bother coming down here to round up a half-dozen cattle.

The map makes the hike to Burnt Canyon Spring in the upper Supai look quite long, but one can walk from the river to the spring in six hours. During wet seasons, water flows below the springs past the fork for a quarter of a mile. The water drops over a ten-foot fall with a cowpath bypass, and there are overhangs which offer good rain protection. In 1982, I found a pool fifteen

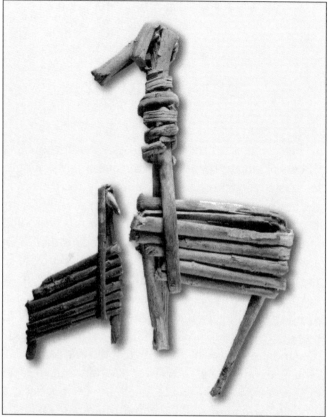

Split twig figurines. (Grand Canyon Museum Collection, 3909)

inches deep formed by a concrete dam which closed off a recess on the west side of the bed. I believed that even if the trickle of water in the bed should dry up, this pool would be reliable. However, when Jorgen and I went back in 1983, we discovered this little reservoir had filled with gravel.

When Ohlman, Kirschvink and I were here, we found that ranchers had built a trail from the Supai rim down into the bed a little north of the spring. There is a sketchier trail down from the Sanup Plateau to a spring in the west fork at this same level, about a hundred feet below the top of the Supai. For a forenoon hike, we went west and climbed all the humps on the shale ridge called Red Point. In the afternoon, we located a way to the top of the Shivwits directly east of the spring.

While alone here in 1982, I went up this break and east to the road that runs south on Twin Point. I walked north to the park boundary and then down the ravine that becomes Twin Spring Canyon. A rough road, now somewhat overgrown, goes down to where a short trail leads to the spring, a fine pool in a small cave fed by a seep in the ceiling. One looks down on a wild glen of sheer walls and crazy towers, but there is a fair cowpath down through some breaks on the north side below the spring. By 11:15am, I was down to where the deep snow had slowed my progress during the previous January. I returned to my pack at Burnt Canyon Spring after a ten and a half hour day, a gratifying effort for a man of seventy-five.

On that solo trip, I also spent a short day to see how easily I could walk around the south end of Twin Point. Red Rock Spring is located on the south edge of the Tincanebitts Point 7.5 minute topo. I made sure that I could get that far in a day by going over halfway from Burnt Canyon Spring to Red Rock Spring.

When Visbak and I headed for Red Rock Spring, we were uncertain as to the best route across the Sanup Plateau. Visbak took a higher route while I preferred the flatter lowlands. He had to wait for me at the head of the east arm Supai gorge, but hikers of equal strength probably would have come through in a tie. The Supai rim looked particularly sheer from here on south. For miles, it seemed to drop several hundred feet without even a ledge. It was very upsetting when we found Red Rock Spring. It was nothing more than a pale seep coming out of the wall, one hundred and fifty feet of vertical drop below the rim and fifty-feet up from the talus below. Even if we could have found a round-about way to get below, there was no pool. It is quite misleading and should be deleted from the map.

Luckily, the weather had been wet. Jorgen and I had seen a few small rain pools on the bedrock gulches on the way out to the spring, so we would not be in dire straits for water. Since it was only 3:30pm when we reached Red Rock Spring, we continued walking. We began to wonder whether we might have misinterpreted the map. When we were about a half-mile into the Devils Slide Rapids 7.5 minute topo, Jorgen went west to look down from the end of a promontory. There appeared to be water about 450 feet below in the bed of a draw. Jorgen found a safe route through a ravine formed by a volcanic dike.

We enjoyed two nights of camping by a little stream that may only run during wet weather. After being kept awake by showers during most of the second night we spent here, I found two good overhangs where we could have slept dry and warm. One is a shallow cave just west of where the dike ravine reaches the talus.

After our first night here, Jorgen and I took a dayhike to the springs south of Twin Point where the map shows a corral and pack trail. Walking was comparatively easy on cowpaths most of the way. When we reached the vicinity of the head of Salt Canyon, we had smooth walking on a well-established cowpath.

When we arrived at the juniper forest, we didn't see a corral, but we did find signs that someone had camped there. An old bucket had been left tied up in a tree. This time the springs were very accessible with a constructed trail going down the draw. The only catch was that the dozen or so cattle we encountered had completely fouled the water.

The map shows the trail going down to the junction of the two forks, but we saw no signs of a trail that far. We lunched at the confluence which was free and clear of any evidence of cattle. We could see that the Supai would be fairly easy going east into Surprise Canyon.

There wasn't enough time to investigate this route or to inspect the Redwall beyond. It would be entirely possible to walk north along the east side of Twin Point and come down into Twin Spring Canyon. In ten hours of walking, at a fast pace, one could come here from Burnt Canyon Spring and it wouldn't take much longer to go from this cow spring to water near the mouth of Twin Spring Canyon.

National Canyon

National Canyon is the first large tributary west of Havasu Creek. To reach its upper end, we left the Supai Road where a sign promised "National Tanks," about fourteen miles northeast of the Frazier Well Road. About a mile beyond the tanks, if the road is dry, drive into the National Canyon drainage. At the end of the road, a stock trail goes on through the Kaibab and down the Coconino. At the base of the Kaibab, the trail passes a large shelter cave where hikers and ranchers have scratched their names. A little farther north is a most peculiar ruin on a high shelf. It seems inaccessible, but names and dates written in charcoal show that modern climbers had reached it. Perhaps they threw a rope over a pole that projects from a wall and pulled themselves up.

A short distance from where the trail goes down through the Coconino, a spur trail goes up to the base of the cliff on the west. It leads to a seep spring and there are tools nearby for cleaning the pool.

There are other ways for getting into National Canyon farther north. On my second trek into this canyon, I left the car near the north boundary of Section 15 on the old National Canyon 15 minute topo (now divided into four 7.5 minute topos: National Canyon SW, Gateway Rapids, Vulcan's Throne and Vulcan's Throne SE) and got down into the bed in Section 9. Billingsley, McComb, and their companions found a more direct way into lower National from farther north. Their route goes down into the bay at the north end of the straight road along the east side of National Canyon.

The Hualapai Indians run cattle in the open valley and there are also some wild horses here. I found a metate near an overhang where the Supai begins to show, and there are indications in the Redwall gorge that the Ancestral Puebloan also lived in this valley. Just north of where red lines on the topo map cut the area into sections, the bed makes a big sweep to the east. At this first bend, a tributary comes from the northwest and a trickle of water comes over this high fall. We slowly collected water after building little mud dams. There was a much better flow right in the bed, an hour's walk north of here. The amount of flow changes with the season, but there should always be some water near the bottom of the Redwall.

On my third visit, I was with Allyn Cureton who showed me how to bypass a chockstone that had proven to be an obstacle in the past. We stayed on a bench to the west of the bed, and finally came out about two hundred feet above the river. The McCombs succeeded in getting down National to the river and when I came down the Colorado with Ken Sleight, I walked into National from below and learned how this can be done. Either with the aid of another man or by leaning a driftwood log against the wall, I could get up the lowest eight feet and then scramble up to the bench where Allyn and I had been. Thus, National is a possible route to the river, and it is most scenic — well worth the daily fee that the Hualapais charge hikers.

Mohawk Canyon

Mohawk Canyon, along its lower part, is also shown on the old National Canyon 15 minute topo. It is about as close to being a twin for National as two canyons can be. The turn off along the main Supai Road is a little less than five miles north of the Frazier Well Road. About nine miles along this side road, turn north at a sign for Mohawk Canyon. There is a cabin about a mile before the road ends. At the trailhead, there is a corral and another shack. The trail is quite distinct and passes by a shelter cave like the one in National. In the bed below this cave there is a pothole of presumably permanent water. Down in the Coconino, a spur trail goes up to the west. It continues to a seep spring at the base of the Coconino similar to the one in National.

In Section 13 of the old National Canyon 15 minute topo, the bed starts cutting into the Redwall. In Section 12 of the same map, I was able to walk on the Esplanade to the east. In Mohawk Canyon, I didn't see any evidence of use by the Ancestral Puebloan, until I found a mescal pit up there. Continuing north to a point, I had a fine view of Stairway Canyon across the river. Back in the main bed, I descended through the Redwall only to have a chock-stone stop me in the Devonian rock. To continue down the bed, one needs to do a thirty-foot rappel. Just above this there is a hole in the limestone ledge that has had more than enough water the four times I have been there. On three of those occasions, there was a running spring in the bed. Once in June it was dry, how-ever, there was a seep farther up the bed.

The first time I was here I spent the end of a hiking day going along the bench on the west. I realized that I wouldn't get to see the river that day, so I turned back to reach my campsite by day-light. If I had continued five more minutes, I would have found the route to the bottom of the canyon that Billingsley discovered

236236236236236

236

some years later. He and Jensen were looking for three missing hikers — Jim Sears, John Wehrman and Sue Varin. They were supposed to be picked up at the rim of Tuckup, any time between Monday evening through Friday. They had gone down Mohawk, crossed the river on air mattresses, and had climbed out via Stairway, on a route that was supposed to be impossible. Billingsley and Jensen went down Mohawk and found the rope they left at the rappel site. They also found two cairns at the river, the sign that the three were going to cross. On his way back up Mohawk, Billingsley checked a possible bypass for the rappel and found that the prehistoric Indians had installed a log ladder at the most difficult place. After I found out about this ancient route, I was able to walk down to the river one day and return the next.

In his book, *Havasu Ethnography*, Leslie Speer passed along a story of raids and fighting between the Paiutes of the north rim and the Hualapais on the south side of the Colorado. They went down to the river through a canyon called Moho. Norman Imus, a Hualapai, told me that Moho was the same as Mohawk Canyon.

Granite Park Area

There is a great deal of fine wilderness between Mohawk and Granite Park. Scattered roads which lead to cattle tanks are about the only signs of "civilization," and after the Indians take care of ranching chores, mending fences and rounding up cattle, they go back to live in town. Billingsley has led a fine exploratory trip north to the river near Hundred and Ninetythree Mile Canyon, but the mesa across the river from Parashant Canyon may be the least visited place in the entire canyon country.

The head of Granite Park Creek is reached by leaving the road to Supai at Frazier Well. At a fork, we took the branch which on the map showed the Ridenour Mine as the farthest destination. This winds down a ravine through a fault scarp to Prospect Valley. In the valley, we took the fork that went up a ridge to the head of Granite Park Creek. North of the valley, the road went up on a mesa and followed the rim to the west. A trail goes down from the west rim of the mesa and this is probably the best way to start into Granite Park Creek. I took the more obvious, but longer way down the valley. A road also goes down to the valley, but I was afraid it might be in poor condition, so I parked at the head of the valley and walked. There is a spring near the head of the Redwall section, and some climbing must be done to pass some minor falls.

This region is known to have a complicated system of faults. Just as I thought I had come down through most of the Redwall, I would reach a fault and find that I was still near the top part of the Redwall to the west. When I finally got below the Redwall near the river, I checked my altimeter which indicated that I had been in the Redwall for 2,600 vertical feet. I followed the bed until I came to a high fall which was passed by taking a long detour to the south. While getting back into the main bed below the fall, I passed a cave with smoke stains and a projectile point on the floor. The bed from here goes down to the northwest but the easy walking ends at another high fall where a chockstone as big as a house has come to rest. On my first attempt, Jorgen Visbak and I went west over the high spot at elevation 3,832' on the Granite Park 7.5 minute topo, and climbed down the tributary. At the bottom, I walked back up the main bed and found a good bypass around the fall with the big chockstone, so Jorgen and I came out this way. From distant observation, I have come to the conclusion that the best way to Granite Park is to come off the mesa north of the valley and stay north of the bed all the way to the river. Granite Park itself is a wide, flat bed beside the river. There are some ruins and mescal pits dating back to the time when the Ancestral Puebloans were very adventurous colonizers. It was probably in Spring Canyon, upriver a few miles on the other side, that Powell's men raided an Indian garden and made off with some squashes.

Diamond Creek

The head of Diamond Creek is at the south end of Prospect Valley. A descent from the south is possible, but there is a more direct approach. The easiest way to get into the wonderful Redwall valley of Diamond Creek used to be from the Peach Springs Wash Road. After parking where the road reaches the perennial stream of Diamond Creek, one can walk up through an eerie narrows in the Archaen, that Donald Davis called the "Black Aisle." Where once the walking was easy, with the exception of one short scramble, it now seems to be impossible. Floods come through here ten feet wide and thirty feet deep, and the bed seems to have been blocked by debris. Though I haven't thoroughly investigated it, a bypass above the Black Aisle along the south wall might be a possible alternative.

There are other ways down into the valley below the Redwall. I came down one ravine on the west side of the Robber's Roost Arm and spotted another way into this tributary from the ridge that divides Robber's Roost Canyon from the main arm of Diamond Creek. This eastern side of Robber's Roost is reached via a road that turns off the Supai Road about ten miles north of the highway. It is marked by a sign, "Wilder's Spring, Catchment #10." This road, after one fork, goes south of a lava capped butte and then turns north. It ends near a large cave. Allyn Cureton and I left this road before the end and found our way down into Robber's Roost Canyon from the dividing ridge. On another occasion, I found an old horse trail that goes down into Diamond Creek from the north side of the same ridge.

The charming quality of the Redwall valley of Robber's Roost and Diamond Creek is accentuated by many springs and groves of trees. Davis called my attention to the walnut trees with odd-looking crucifixion thorns. Hikers and climbers seeking more adventure can look for additional routes from the rim into

Harvey in Diamond Creek area. (Photo: Jorgen Visbak)

the canyon. Wild horses roam the plateau above and are also found in the canyon. They must be descending by routes we have yet to discover.

Doug Shough, a teacher in Tuba City, and I walked up through the Black Aisle and on through the main valley. We could see two or three skyline windows through the Redwall rim. When the Redwall gorge was narrowing at the upper end, we came to a vein of calcite, several inches thick in a sort of dike that went up both walls as far as we could see. With a bit of route finding, we managed to climb out the upper end into Prospect Valley. The Hualapais know that they own a good thing as hikers will gladly pay a small fee to visit Diamond Creek Canyon.

More fine hiking can be found downriver along the Tonto from Diamond Creek. One can reach the Tonto through a ravine south of the mouth of Diamond Creek, or by a trail that goes up to the west along the river below the mouth of the creek. Walking the Tonto is easy along here because of a well-established burro trail. Burros are common along both sides of the river in the western Grand Canyon, and surprisingly so are the bighorn sheep. Experts insist that burros drive the sheep out of an area, but they seem to coexist quite peacefully in the lower Grand Canyon.

Some of the boat operators end the Grand Canyon traverse at Diamond Creek and their customers get the idea that there are no rapids of consequence downriver from Diamond. This is far from the truth and it used to be still more erroneous before Lake Mead was formed. The Powell party was divided over whether or not it would be suicide to run Separation Rapids. Lava Cliff Rapids at the mouth of Spencer Canyon once had a reputation for ferocity. Glen and Bessie Hyde, the young newlywed couple who were to make a name for themselves by running the entire Colorado River, safely ran all of the famous rapids and then lost their lives, probably at Mile 232. Bessie did make history as the first woman to run all of Cataract Canyon and most of the Grand Canyon, though it was unfortunate that she didn't live to enjoy her accomplishment.

Six months after they were married in April 1928, Glen and Bessie embarked on a journey down the Colorado River, from Green River, Utah with a final destination of Needles, California. In a flat-bottom scow built by Glen, they packed in everything they would need for the lengthy journey — food, tools, a stove, even a mattress and bed springs — almost everything. They did not take life jackets, believing that their strength as swimmers would keep them from running into any trouble on the river. Even when Emery Kolb offered life jackets to them on their stop-over at Bright Angel, they refused to take them.

When days, then weeks passed, and they hadn't materialized at their final destination in Needles, an air and ground search was initiated by Glen's father with the help of the U.S. Army, and later joined by Emery and Ellsworth Kolb. Glen and Bessie's boat was found floating peacefully in an eddy at Mile 237 — with the mattress, bed springs, stove and other items laying in it untouched — but full of water.

The hike along the Tonto west of Diamond gives one a bird's eye view of several fine rapids in lower Granite Gorge. There are several places where one can get down to the river along here and also west of Bridge Canyon. There are also places where the walls are steeper, blacker, and shinier than they are in the upper Grand Canyon.

There are still many routes for future hikers to find. I walked past Mile 228 Canyon without making a decision as to whether or not there was a way to go from the Tonto out to the top of the plateau. Boaters have already found a way to come up from the river via Travertine Canyon, but it is still a challenge. As an example of the possibilities, consider the story of Jim Ervin and his partner. They were trying to get jobs at Hoover Dam which was under construction in 1931. Tired of getting thrown off freight trains, they decided to walk down Peach Springs Wash and float downriver to the construction site. They found an abandoned boat, but after an upset, they realized that their project might be suicidal. At Mile 233.5 they landed the boat and Ervin climbed to the Tonto and found a good spring in the east arm of Two Hundred and Thirtyfour Mile Canyon. He scaled the Redwall at a point which the local sheriff's deputy would later called impossible. Traveling without a canteen, he was nearly dead from thirst when he finally reached an Indian dwelling in upper Peach Springs Wash. When the rescue party went out to Bridge Canyon with horses, got down to the trail, and over to where Ervin had left his partner at the river, both boat and man were gone, never to be seen again. The river had claimed yet another life. No one seems to have repeated Ervin's Redwall climb. To my eyes, it seemed almost impossible. However, John Evans, one of the first party to reach the highest summit of Antartica, thinks it very well possible. Ervin could have walked back along the Tonto Platform, finding water at several places on the way to Diamond Creek, but Evans thought it was still too far to go without food.

Bridge Canyon to Separation

Bridge Canyon is reached from the Buck and Doe Road which connects Peach Springs with Meadview, the residential development at the upper end of Lake Mead. A spur goes to the rim of Hindu Canyon and sometimes, one can go down into the valley by car and up to the head of the trail into Bridge Canyon. For many years, Bridge Canyon was linked to a controversial dam project, and at one time, this road could be followed past the trailhead to a viewpoint above the proposed damsite. To build the dam, they would probably have constructed an aerial tram down to the Tonto. The dreamers at the Bureau of Reclamation even had a map showing a highway going down through Bridge Canyon across the top of the dam, and up through another canyon to the Shivwits Plateau.

Jim Ervin introduced me to this area. At age sixty-six, he wanted to walk down and photograph the place where he had scaled the Redwall nearly forty years earlier. He decided to join me for part of a trip on which I was going to hike down Bridge Canyon, then float down the Colorado to Separation. At Separation Canyon, I was to meet up with Jorgen Visbak and Homer Morgan who were floating downriver on surfriders from Diamond Creek. Jim planned to accompany me to the river, then would hike back out on his own. It was late afternoon by the time we started away from Jim's car on the rim of the Hindu Canyon. He wasn't equipped for backpacking, and on this particular trip he had only a quart of milk for sustenance. Soon after we started, he decided to head back to his car and asked me to photograph the location of his famous Redwall ascent.

I continued on and went up the wrong ravine in search of the head of the trail. By the last daylight, I could see that I was east of the trailhead so I walked down to the right place and camped.

The next day, Jim talked to the residents at Peach Springs on his drive back to the highway and learned that I had been looking for the trail in the wrong place. He became alarmed and notified the search and rescue men of Mohave County about my "disappearance," who in turn placed a call to my wife, Roma. When they learned from Roma that I was an experienced canyon hiker, carrying six quarts of water and was planning to spend several days down in the canyon, things quieted down.

Hindu Canyon drops into Spencer over a high fall, but hikers have found a bypass to the south which is then followed down the ridge along the east side of Milkweed Canyon. The Bridge Canyon Trail starts at the low point separating Hindu from Bridge. The trail is obvious down to a spring at the east side of the upper end of the open valley. A flood must have covered a former concrete basin to catch the water. We had to build small earthen and rock dams to collect any water.

Going down the bed to the river is quite easy. Not far from the river one can look southeast up a tributary and see the rather unimpressive natural bridge that gives the canyon its name. About halfway from the spring to the river, trails go up to the Tonto in both directions. It was one long day's walk for me to go from Bridge Canyon to Diamond Creek. It took a half day to walk from Separation to Bridge. There used to be a spur trail from the Tonto down to "Bridge Canyon City," a couple of shacks where the men lived while they were test drilling the dam site. There are other ways from the Tonto to the river, Gneiss Canyon being one. A few years earlier, Jorgen, Homer and Homer's brother, upset a powerboat in Mile 232 Rapids. Homer clung to the boat's bowline and stayed with the boat until it lodged on the bottom of the river with the bow just above water at Gneiss Canyon. Jorgen and Homer's brother spent the rest of the day and part of the next getting down to where Homer was sitting on the bank. Homer wrote a distress message and sent it downriver in an ice chest. It was picked up by two boaters who alerted the rangers. The three of them were picked up later.

I took the pictures that Jim wanted of his ascent route up the Redwall at Two Hundred and Thirtyfour Mile Canyon and then continued back to Bridge Canyon, proceeding with the plan to float down to Separation Canyon. I soon discovered that I couldn't stand the cold water for very long and couldn't land at will in rough water. When I did get to shore and had thawed out, I decided to wait there for a river party from Las Vegas, that was scheduled to come up that far the next day.

Separation to Spencer Canyon

Jorgen and Homer succeeded in floating on their surfriders in the frigid river water from Diamond Creek to Separation Canyon. In the meantime, I was picked up by the party from Las Vegas and reunited with Jorgen and Homer at Separation. After a fine dinner and breakfast furnished by the boaters, Homer, Jorgen and I walked up Separation Canyon through the Redwall. We knew we would have to follow the east arm to get out on the Shivwits Plateau.

Then the three of us floated down the quiet 6.4 miles from Separation to Spencer Canyon, taking several breaks to warm up. Spencer has permanent water from a spring south of the junction with Meriwhitica Canyon. At the mouth of Spencer, we had to struggle through thick brush. After the first hundred or so yards, it was an easy walk over gravel and boulders. We inspected the travertine terrace built by the Spencer Spring and explored a hundred foot cave in the deposit. Homer also showed us a small opening leading back to a hive of wild bees. We also saw wild burros coming down the dry bed of Spencer. Hikers have entered this valley from the south on a ridge just east of Milkweed Canyon.

The travertine deposit from the spring in Meriwhitica Canyon is amazing. This little flow, surfacing at the south end of the grove of cottonwoods, seems to be the source of more natural cement than is contained in any man-made dam in the world. The exposed east end of the deposit seems to be about three hundred and fifty feet deep and a half mile across. The travertine beneath the scanty surface soil must extend a great distance west of the exposed end. The little creek supports a narrow oasis of dense growth about fifty yards wide and several hundred yards long before it disappears into the barren travertine to the north. Many birds, some rabbits, and a family of kit foxes are at home here. There are even tiny fish in the short brook. One wonders how they got started here. Five hundred feet up the slope on the north side of Meriwhitica Valley there is a large shelter cave containing a number of prehistoric ruins. Mixed with the authentic petroglyphs are signatures of pot hunters in charcoal. As early as 1879, these Kilroys arrived. A white man tried to homestead near the grove, and the ruins of his rock house and barbwire corral are still evident. A good trail goes out to the south several miles west of the oasis. The approach from the Buck and Doe Road is marked by a sign for Meriwhitica Tank.

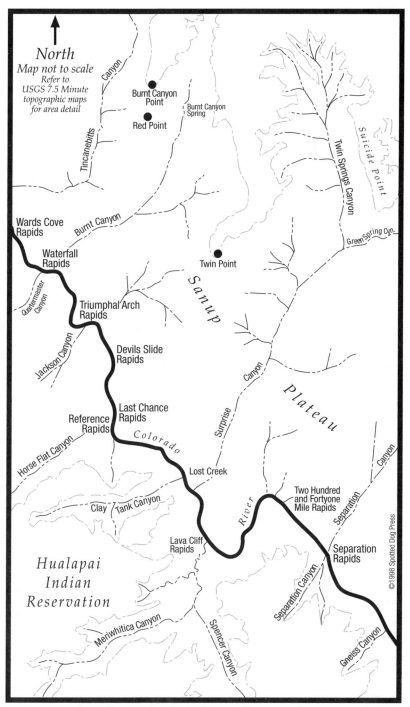

North
Map not to scale
*Refer to
USGS 7.5 Minute
topographic maps
for area detail*

Tincanebitts Canyon

Burnt Canyon Point

Red Point

Burnt Canyon Spring

Suicide Point

Twin Springs Canyon

Green Spring Cyn.

Wards Cove Rapids

Burnt Canyon

Waterfall Rapids

Twin Point

S a n u p

Quartermaster Canyon

Triumphal Arch Rapids

Jackson Canyon

Devils Slide Rapids

Surprise Canyon

P l a t e a u

Canyon

Last Chance Rapids

Reference Rapids

C o l o r a d o

Horse Flat Canyon

Lost Creek

Two Hundred and Fortyone Mile Rapids

Separation

Clay Tank Canyon

R i v e r

Lava Cliff Rapids

Separation Rapids

Hualapai Indian Reservation

Separation Canyon

Meriwhitica Canyon

Spencer Canyon

Gneiss Canyon

©1998 Spotted Dog Press

Sanup Plateau area – Gneiss Canyon to Tincanebitts Canyon

Spencer and Milkweed Canyons

Since my first trip, I have learned a lot more about this area. Unfortunately, over the years, the Hualapai Indians have become quite reluctant to allow hikers on their reservation, even at several dollars a day per person. Perhaps they will change their stand and hikers will again be able to see more of these fine areas.

A good way to reach Spencer is by boat from Pearce Ferry. There are no water sources here so plenty of water must be carried when walking the dry bed south of Spencer Spring. Taking the east fork, Spencer Canyon proper, we did find water in the steeper bed as we neared the junction with Hindu Canyon. Hindu joins Spencer with an impressive sheer fall with no bypass. The bed of Spencer rises rapidly in a very scenic narrows, and we were soon stopped here too. However, across from the mouth of Hindu, there was quite a bit of travertine and we found that we could climb up there. We discovered an interesting route clear through the Redwall and reached the end of the road at Bender Tank.

The west fork is called Milkweed Canyon and this drainage is much larger than the area drained by Spencer itself. About two miles from the junction of Milkweed and Spencer, we went east on a steep, but not difficult, walker's route to the plateau. Continuing up the bed of Milkweed, we soon came to permanent water above ground.

The open valley is now replaced by spectacular narrows and one reaches a barrier fall. Jorgen and his friend worked out a rough, challenging bypass high on the east side to get around the barrier. I found an easier, but longer, bypass on the west. There were signs of an old camp in one valley on this side. I could go down the valley into the main bed above the barrier or continue south over the hills coming to the main bed higher up.

The canyon is a broad valley for several miles and then one approaches a section where volcanic rock has formed more high falls. Here again, Visbak took to the steep and difficult slope on the east side of the fall. The ridge between Milkweed and the tributary called West Water Canyon is much easier. In fact, one can find an old Indian trail suitable for horses on this side. This probably follows the high ground clear to the end of the road from the Buck and Doe Road to Milkweed Springs. Coming in by this road to the corral, we followed the bed down to where a power line crosses the canyon before going up and finding the horse trail to lower Milkweed.

Quartermaster Canyon

There are several big canyons on the south side of the river between Meriwhitica and Quartermaster, but I don't know whether or not they are accessible from above. We had heard that Quartermaster has a trail down to it, and Donald Davis got me interested in the area. Bill Belknap and Jorgen Visbak had been down the trail, but Davis was unable to locate it. He had checked out Jeff Canyon, the big tributary from the east. He also looked into the head of the south arm. He found that he could climb down to the open lower valley through the unlikely looking west arm. There is an old Indian trail at the upper end down to a big pothole of water, but the bed below is cluttered with great fallen blocks and dominated by awesome towers. I knew that Donald had done this arm and that it would go. I was greatly relieved when I found that I could get to the lower open area using this same route.

Driving near the head of the Quartermaster Trail was very confusing. I parked on the road going north to the Bat Cave Overlook and walked to the place. I had no more luck than Donald did in finding the trail. I should have gone out on the promontory between the west and south arms of Quartermaster and looked over toward the east wall of the south arm. The trail is obscure as it goes below the east rim, but well above the lip of the high fall. Around the corner on the bench, it is well preserved except where fossil bearing limestone chips have obscured it locally. Near the junction of the south and west arms are a couple of shelter caves with prehistoric pictographs laced with more contemporary initials. There is also a mescal pit beneath the canyon wall on the west side. Dominating the fall of the bed to the river level is a blunt cone of travertine that marks a substantial spring. Although most of the soil is gone, travertine lined irrigation ditches stand out above the general surface. You can still see some barbed wire and Bill Belknap reported seeing some fig trees. The way to the river is west of the fall. River runner Harry Aleson had a wilderness home in a cave down here.

There is still plenty to see in the lower Grand Canyon. One can climb into the Bat Guano Cave at Mile 266.2 and inspect Muav Cave at Mile 273.8. The giant ground sloths lived here before man drove them out. Columbine Falls at Mile 274.3 is another real attraction and the canyon above the fall is really wild and beautiful. One can get above the fall on the west side of the cove and inspect some caves and tunnels in the next cliff. The spring is near the top of the narrow glen in this same formation. It is a rough walk of over an hour to a barrier fall in the Redwall.

A trail goes up to Rampart Cave at Mile 275. The dark half circle of the entrance can be seen from the lake five or six hundred feet up on the south side. It has been studied by scientists and a locked grating preserves it for future study.

Pearce Canyon on the north side of the lake is another fine subject for real exploration. One day is hardly enough to get to the top of the plateau and back to the lake, but if attempted soon after a rain, there is some rainwater in the bedrock depressions and camping is possible. There are shelter caves and plenty of inviting routes that seem to go clear to the top even before the end of the trail through the main bed.

Tincanebitts Canyon

Quartermaster is the canyon just west of Burnt Canyon. More recently, Jorgen and I have used the open silt flat on the east side of the mouth for camping and have found two good shelters for our beds in shallow travertine caves.

Tincanebitts is the next big canyon coming in from the right, 3.5 miles down the lake from Quartermaster. At some lake levels it is hard to get a boat to solid ground and then it is slow walking along the rough slope to the bed above the delta jungle. Jorgen and Ed Herrman were in here before Bruce Braley and I inspected it, and it was Ed's opinion that one of the arms might lead out to the top. Bruce had done some gnarly climbing in Ticanebitts Canyon on a route that is now impassable.

When we came to the confluence with the steeper west arm, it appeared that the main bed might be better. We were able to go quite a distance into the Redwall and found some plunge pools of fairly deep water.

Finally, we were stopped by impossible falls. Trying the east arm, we soon came to a steep scramble up a sloping rock. Just beyond this difficult spot, the route turned sharply to the left up a ravine that had been formed when a volcanic dike split the Redwall and the Supai. There were a couple of hand-and-toe climbs where I would want to pull a pack up with a rope, but with Bruce to go ahead, I was able to get out on the Sanup Plateau. We were on a one-day hike away from the boat, so we only had time enough to walk out on a promontory with a view down the main canyon. Once, one could come up here from the lake, but a recent rockfall makes this route an impossibility.

The road down here from St. George, west of Mt. Dellenbaugh, seems to be much better than the one going southeast of the mountain. If one came up here at the right time of the year, it would be relatively easy to go to Twin Spring Canyon, Burnt Canyon, and Tincanebitts by car.

About a mile down from the lake at the mouth of Tincanebitts, Dry Canyon comes in from the right. It is a long and scenic canyon, but I was stopped by steep drops in the Redwall. At a fork, I took a longer, more gradual east arm. Billingsley, after an aerial observation, thinks that there is a good chance for a route out on the top over to the west. As I didn't then know this, I failed to check it out.

Less than a mile down the lake from Dry Canyon, a nameless gorge comes in from the left at Mile 265. When Billingsley went out to the Bat Cave Tram, he spotted a possible route down this canyon to the river. He checked it down through the Redwall and turned back before he was stopped. At the time, he went down a dike ravine and then had to detour to the east where he found a passage along a bench south again to the main bed.

When Donald Davis came through the Grand Canyon with a river party, he stopped here long enough to climb up into the Redwall. So, it seems appropriate to call this the "Billingsley-Davis Route." Davis agreed with Billingsley that bighorn sheep use this route, but he didn't understand how they could go up a thirty-foot cliff where he had to do his best hand-and-toe climbing. I have been up into the Devonian from the river, but I didn't get to the thirty-foot cliff. It seemed to be one of the most direct and interesting routes from the plateau to the lake.

Columbine Falls and Cave Canyon

This beautiful canyon is called Cave Canyon on the map, but most river runners associate it with Columbine Falls. I mentioned it in a previous chapter, but stated that one comes to an impossible barrier in the lower Redwall. Visbak and Belknap have been by here, and when I came back with Ohlman and Kirschvink, I found that I also could get up to the west of the blunt tower near the barrier fall. To surmount this obstacle, we used meager grips in the steep limestone. Once over the steep limestone, we arrived at a bench that led back into the bed above the barrier fall. In a few hundred yards, we used a longer detour up the slope to the east.

On a one-day hike we came up from the river past these barriers and reached the main fork near the top of the Redwall. We had passed a shelter cave on the west where Visbak and Belknap had seen prehistoric artifacts. To complete this investigation, Bill Mooz and I came in by car to New Water Spring. We were able to drive along a faint track into the upper end of the east arm where Visbak and Belknap had gone down. There is no real barrier, but a lot of the walking was over rough boulders. At the fork, I went up to the west while Mooz went down to try to find the artifact cave. I went on up where the west arm forked again and then we returned to the car by the route we had used coming in.

After a second night at the New Water Spring, we walked down the middle fork. It was similar to the east arm except for one thing. We came to a high fall where the bypass was not clear. We tried following a bench around to the right and we soon came to a steep ravine where we could go to the bottom of the fall. A little farther on, we came to the confluence with the west branch and here I found my own footprints from the previous day. With a little able-bodied climbing, we passed all of the barriers in this arm. The map shows another possible route up the short westernmost arm that drains the rough country just east of Grand Wash Cliffs.

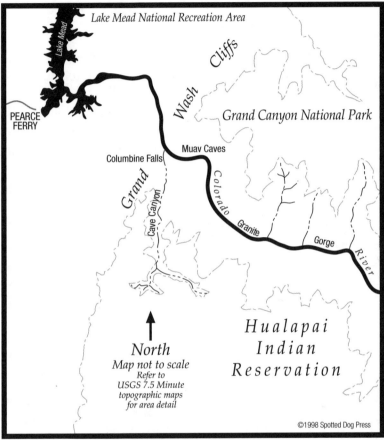

Lake Mead National Recreation Area

Cliffs

Wash

PEARCE
FERRY

Grand Canyon National Park

Muav Caves

Columbine Falls

Grand

Cave Canyon

Colorado

Granite

Gorge

River

Lake Mead

↑
North

Map not to scale
Refer to
USGS 7.5 Minute
topographic maps
for area detail

*Hualapai
Indian
Reservation*

©1998 Spotted Dog Press

Pearce Ferry area and Lake Mead

Pearce (aka Pierce) Canyon

Pearce Canyon, across the lake from the Pearce Ferry launching ramp, was mentioned briefly in a previous chapter, but it does deserve more attention. In 1876, Harrison Pearce established a ferry here to carry people from Utah into Mohave County. The original ferry landing and out buildings have since been covered with the waters of Lake Mead. It also should be noted that the name Pearce has also been spelled "Pierce" on maps. One can leave a boat at the mouth of the wash and walk up the bed, but it is a little faster to moor in the cove between the words "Lower Granite" of the Snap Canyon West 7.5 minute topo. A good burro trail follows the high ground from here northeast and can be followed down into the bed south of the end of the word "Canyon." A mescal pit can be located through the "D" of the name "Grand" on the map. A barrier fall in this ravine calls for a bypass. There is an easy ravine only a few minutes walk to the west.

With a little attention to route finding, we walked up this ravine and then out of it to the west of the headland at elevation 4,123'. There is another mescal pit here and one can follow the easy hillside walk to the saddle of elevation 4,187'. I ran out of time and turned back shortly after I found a break and had climbed through a ravine to the top of the Sanup Plateau on the northwest side of a huge depression in the Sanup Plateau. The surface of this huge bowl is Supai sandstone, but Billingsley thinks that it has slumped into a broad cavern in the underlying Redwall.

When I was sixty-five, with only my lunch and a canteen, I was able to walk from the boat in the cove and climb out to the plateau near the upper end of Pearce Canyon and still return to the boat by daylight. My route was on the south side opposite the draw that drains the middle of the block marked "29" on the Snap

Canyon East 7.5 minute topo. When I used it again, I noted that at the hardest part of the climb near the rim, ancient Indians had left a juniper log as a ladder. When I got up there and back to the boat in the same day, I only had time to walk east and noted that the bed of Pearce ended below an impossible cliff. John Green got out of the bed to the north just east of my route up the south side. He went up the talus east of a sheer drop in the bed of a short draw that is near the east border of block "29." He got onto a bare bedrock terrace below a twelve-foot fall. Trying this route a couple of months after he had told me about it, I was completely stopped at the wall. Where I turned back, he climbed up and found a good rain pocket of water and a constructed trail up at the rim of this little basin.

After I got on the south side I walked around to Fort Garrett, a ruined one-room rock house with a fireplace. I then walked north past a cattle tank containing some repulsive water and on to inspect the trail Green had found.

The trail goes down on the east side of a little bay to a campsite under an overhang. There was a little camp trash left here, including a box with a hinged lid. At nearly seventy-six years of age, I didn't feel quite up to my announced project — walking from Fort Garrett over to Joe Spring and beyond in upper Tincanebitts Canyon. Instead, I followed Green's example and climbed Snap Point. In talking with Green later, I found that I had used his route to climb to the top, from Fort Garrett through the letter "W" in the name "Grand Wash Cliffs." With shallow snow and mud everywhere on top, walking was not the easiest. I recognized the jeep road to the top and was soon enjoying a terrific view of colorful canyons and endless blue skies.

I made faster time going back to the boat at the mouth of Pearce Canyon. I stayed on top and headed northwest through the "N" of the word "Sanup" on the Snap Canyon East 7.5 minute topo. From the saddle just below this "N", I went south to the bottom of Pearce Canyon, arriving at the boat by 3:30pm. This arm is a steep, short route to the saddle where I turned south into the main arm. About ten minutes up the north arm is a permanent rain pool. The descent from the saddle shows rock fractured by a fault. The the ravine lined up with this route on the south side of the main bed is also a possible route to the top of the Sanup Plateau. When I was going up here to check this, I encountered several bighorn sheep. It is all great wilderness and I am not overly concerned with the fact that a dozen or more cows were grazing on the plateau southeast of Fort Garrett.

Some river runners take out at Diamond Creek, but when they do, their clients miss one of the most scenic parts of the entire canyon. Inability to appreciate the sublimity of the looming three thousand feet of towers and walls could only mean that one has been made numb by days spent in the upper Grand Canyon. There are one-day and overnight tours to show the public the wonders of Lake Powell, but it puzzles me that there are no comparable tours from Pearce Ferry up to Separation Canyon and back. The Norwegian fjords, the Straits of Magellan and the inlets of New Zealand have no greater attractions than one can see from a boat in the lower Grand Canyon.

In Retrospect...

People have asked me if there is any part of the Grand Canyon which I have not seen or where a person could go and feel as if they were the first to be there. I would have to quickly respond by saying that we might all be cautious in claiming a first because native people have been in the Canyon for at least 4,000 years and seem to have been everywhere. As hunters of bighorn sheep, gatherers of mescal and farmers, they really got around.

The largest areas of the old Matthes-Evans Grand Canyon map that are free of lines showing routes that I have covered, are the two sides of Powell Plateau down on the Esplanade. These have been visited by modern hikers, but perhaps by only four or five. I have only gotten a smattering of personal knowledge of the Esplanade all the way from Kanab Canyon to the Grand Wash Cliffs. However, the one area that seems like the greatest challenge of all is the rough mesa across the river from Parashant Canyon. Canyons such as Mile 193 and Mile 205 penetrate this rough area, but no one that I know has tried to explore it. Perhaps one can reach the top at 6,450 feet, but how? I will probably never get there myself, but would like to hear from anyone who does make it!

Hike When It's Cool

Best time to hike: October to April

Below its cool, forested rim, the Grand Canyon is a desert
with little water or shade, where daily summertime temperatures
can easily reach triple digits by noon. During late spring and
summer, the average daytime temperatures in the Grand Canyon
rival those of Death Valley by only a few degrees, with the latter
holding the record for the hottest temperature in the western
hemisphere. For this reason, anyone planning a backcountry trip
to the Grand Canyon should consider spring, fall, or winter to
avoid hiking during the heat of summer.

There are many benefits to hiking the Grand Canyon when
the weather is cool. The most important benefit is that the chance
of succumbing to a number of heat-related illnesses decreases.
During the summer, it is too hot during the day to do much of
anything, except perhaps read a book or take a nap beneath the
shade of a juniper tree. Dehydration and physical overexertion
can quickly escalate into more serious conditions such as heat
exhaustion or heat stroke. These two medical conditions alone,
account for most of the summertime rescues and approximately
twelve deaths per year in the Grand Canyon, all of which could
be avoided by selecting a cooler time of year to hike.

As the physical need for water increases during hot weather,
enough water must be carried for the duration of any dayhike or
overnight trip. Reliable water sources are not plentiful in the
Canyon. At least two to three gallons of water are required for an
average three-day waterless backpack. One quart of water
weighs just under two pounds and a gallon weighs nearly eight
pounds, all of which adds up to a lot of water weight. It is important to add a packet of ERG (electrolyte replacement with glucose)
to every quart of water. ERG is an efficient way to replace the

body's water, glucose, salts, electrolytes and Vitamin C lost during rigorous activity such as hiking or mountaineering. We have found Gookinaid to be the smoothest flavored, with the lowest amount of sodium and highest amount of essential nutrients, though Gatorade is also recommended and available at most supermarkets in the powdered drinks section. For people who hike in the desert, carrying all of their own water for a dayhike or backpacking trip is as an accepted routine as carrying a water filter and a quart bottle into the Sierra Nevada or Appalachian Mountains, where water is very plentiful and easy to find.

Seasonal water is found on the Bright Angel Trail from the South Rim (at Indian Gardens) and the North Kaibab Trail off the North Rim (at Bright Angel Campground and seasonally at Cottonwood Campground). In addition, one might carry a lightweight water disinfectant like iodine crystals or potable aqua if the need to drink Colorado River water arises. Water filters are the most reliable solution for water treatment, but they weigh more than their chemical counterparts.

During the winter months, from late November to February, the upper trails on the South Rim tend to be snow-covered and icy, while the North Rim is completely inaccessible by car due to winter road closures. Depending on winter conditions, some trails might require the use of an ice axe or instep crampons for balance and stability. Winter storms are unpredictable and can last for a couple of days or longer.

Average Temperatures in the Grand Canyon

	South Rim Max/Min Fahrenheit/Celsius	Inner Canyon Max/Min Fahrenheit/Celsius	North Rim Max/Min Fahrenheit/Celsius
Summer	82(28c)/51(11c)	103(39c)/75(24c)	75(24c)/44(7c)
Fall	64(18c)/37(3c)	83(28c)/58(14c)	58(14c)/31(-1c)
Winter	43(6c)/20(-7c)	58(14c)/38(3c)	39(4c)/18(-8c)
Spring	60(16c)/32(0c)	82(28c)/56(13c)	53(12c)/28(-2c)

Basics

Hazards, Risk and Responsibility

It is not possible to mention all of the potential hazards that hikers face in the backcountry, but knowing about some of the most important ones can help prevent them. Planning a backcountry trip begins with the right equipment and proper physical and mental preparation. Responsible hikers and climbers realize that their pursuit is inherently risky — they don't climb beyond their ability, and they do not let personal desires, ego or goals outweigh good judgment. Those who choose to head out into the wilderness will constantly be faced with decisions that will ultimately affect their well-being, perhaps even their lives. In doing so, they must accept complete responsibility for their decisions and their actions.

First Aid Kit

Every pack or daypack should have a basic first aid kit. Some suggested items for a compact first aid kit are: roll of one inch waterproof tape (good for preventing blisters); moleskin; 2.25" x 3" adhesive gauze pads; Band-Aids; one or two rolls of gauze; an antibacterial ointment; potable aqua tabs or iodine crystals for emergency water purification; aspirin; antacid; mosquito repellent; sunscreen; alcohol pads or biodegradable soap; whistle; mirror; emergency blanket; spare packets of ERG; ankle brace (for sprained ankles) and a pair of tweezers (for removal of cactus spines or ticks).

The Ten Essentials

The Mountaineers, a Seattle based mountaineering club, developed a list of ten essential items which should be the mainstay of every pack. In addition to this list, additional and appropriate gear must be carried depending on the route and trip duration.

The basic ten essentials are:
1. Map (USGS 7.5 minute topos recommended)
2. Compass
3. Flashlight/spare batteries
4. Food and water
5. Clothing
6. Pocket knife
7. Matches in a waterproof container
8. Sun glasses, sunscreen
9. Hat
10. First aid kit

Water, Electrolytes and a Granola Bar

Harvey Butchart and his companions spent most of their time hiking in the Canyon between October and April, and rarely hiked during the heat of summer. When they did find themselves in the Canyon during the summer, they carried a lot of water, from one to five gallons a person depending on how long the trip was and whether or not there were any known, reliable springs along the route. Never depend upon a natural water source for your water supply. What a map may show as a spring, may only be a seep in a crack on a vertical wall, 150 feet above your head. Likewise, unless you are familiar with the terrain, have been there before, or know that the spring on your route has consistent year-round flow, it is better to carry enough water for the duration of your trip or until you can reach the Colorado River, or a known, reliable water source.

This might be a good place to mention ERG or electrolyte glucose replacement. ERG is a powdered supplement that comes in a packet and is added to your water bottle. With flavors like fruit punch and cherry, they can be purchased from outdoor retailers or the supermarket and are the most efficient way to replace the body's lost salts, minerals and vitamins. ERG can also help prevent a debilitating condition known as hyponatremia, which has occurred with more frequency in the Grand Canyon in recent years. Hyponatremia is caused by drinking only water and too much of it, while not eating enough. The result is a big time electrolyte imbalance. Symptoms are similar to those of heat exhaustion — extreme fatigue, headache, nausea, vomiting, and unconsciousness. This experience can be avoided by eating and adding ERG supplements to your water which will help replenish needed electrolytes.

Granola bars, power bars or other carbohydrate rich snacks should be to a pack like a spare tire is to a car. Don't go anywhere without stashing a few in your pack. A good rule of thumb is to take at least a five-minute drink and snack break every hour of hiking. Past experience has shown that the body's metabolism functions better with regular snack and water breaks throughout the day.

Heat-Related Illness & Hypothermia

Hiking in the Grand Canyon can be compared to climbing a *desert* mountain, but in reverse. Note the emphasis on *desert*. The hazards and challenges found on a desert mountain are completely different from those found on a mountain with more annual precipitation, like the Sierra Nevada or the Alps for instance. Like a desert peak, the Grand Canyon is an essentially waterless environment where yucca, jagged limestone, and basalt replace pines, meadows, and cool flowing streams filled with trout.

Like a desert peak, there is elevation, loss, gain and round-trip mileage on each trek into the Grand Canyon. Unlike a desert peak, the elevation gain is done on the way out instead of on the way in, making it more difficult for most people to judge just how strenuous a hike will be down into the Canyon.

An hour's drive south of the Grand Canyon is Humphreys Peak in Flagstaff, which at 12,633' is the highest mountain in the state of Arizona. The round-trip elevation gain and mileage from the Humphreys Peak trailhead (located just past the ski resort parking area) to the summit is 3,100 feet of elevation gain and nine miles round-trip on trail. All water must be carried since there are no water sources along the trail. Even though it is considered a moderate seven-hour round-trip trail walk, most hikers wouldn't even think about starting up the trail to Humphreys Peak without at least two quarts of water, food, a first aid kit and other items necessary for survival. Records indicate that the majority of people who hike down the Bright Angel Trail do so with even less preparation. Many of these same people probably would never even consider hiking to the summit of Humphreys Peak if given the opportunity, even though the mileage and gain to the top of Humphreys Peak is the same as a hike from the South Rim of the Grand Canyon down the Bright Angel Trail to Indian Gardens.

Every day, many visitors to the Grand Canyon, eager to see the Colorado River or to make the claim that they have hiked the Canyon, rush right off the edge of the rim with little thought or preparation, and head down the Bright Angel Trail with the lofty goal of reaching the Colorado River and returning to the rim in the same day. The round-trip mileage just from the South Rim to Indian Gardens via the Bright Angel is 9.2 miles with 3,060' of loss. The hardest part of the hike, is the 3,060' of elevation gain, which begins on the way back to the rim. It isn't surprising that an average of 450 people a year are rescued from this part of the Canyon.

Avoiding Dehydration and Heat-Related Illness

Dehydration and heat-related illness account for most of the injuries and rescues in the Grand Canyon throughout the year, and occur with the greatest frequency during the summer. The best way to avoid heat-related illness, is to drink plenty of water mixed with an ERG supplement, take short five-minute water and snack breaks, every forty-five minutes to an hour of hiking and wear a light-colored broad-brimmed hat. During late spring, summer and early fall, when the daytime temperatures inch up above the eighties, hike when the trails and canyons are shaded, usually from dawn to late morning or from late afternoon to dusk. Avoid hiking in the sun and in particular, do not hike uphill during the hottest part of the day.

Heat-Related Muscle Cramps

Muscle cramps in the legs or abdomen can result from loss of water and electrolytes. To reduce or prevent cramping — rest, eat, drink water with an ERG supplement, stretch and massage the legs.

Heat Exhaustion

Heat exhaustion is a serious heat-related illness which occurs when the body rate of heat gain is greater than the rate of heat loss. The best way to avoid heat exhaustion is to drink adequate water with electrolyte additive. There are a number of factors that can cause heat exhaustion. Dehydration (not drinking enough water) and physical overexertion when it's hot are the two biggest causes. Symptoms include physical weakness, dizziness, nausea, vomiting, minimal or no urination and headache. As soon as symptoms are identified, the victim should be moved out of direct sunlight. He or she should sit or lie down, preferably with feet elevated, and slowly drink a fluid, such as water, containing ERG. Movement should be limited until the body's fluids are fully restored.

Heat Stroke

Heat stroke occurs when the body's internal temperature rises above 105 degrees, and can result in death if not treated immediately. Hikers or mountaineers who are not used to hot temperatures like those found in the inner Canyon, may suffer from "exertional" heat stroke if they prolong their activity. Their initial symptoms will include pale, damp, cool skin even when their internal temperature has reached dangerous levels — followed by confused, irrational, even aggressive behavior and physical collapse. Many visitors to the Grand Canyon, who are not hikers or mountaineers, might suffer symptoms of "classic" heat stroke. Their skin will be hot and dry to touch with dangerously high internal temperature. In both cases, the goal of treatment should be to quickly reduce the body temperature. Place victim in the shade, remove or loosen tight clothing and aggressively cool the victim by pouring water over them, or swabbing them with water-soaked cloths or bandannas and fanning. If the victim is conscious, have them drink water in sips. The victim must be carried out and hospitalized.

Hyponatremia

Hyponatremia or water intoxication occurs when a person drinks an excessive amount of water without replacing lost electrolytes either by not eating or not including an electrolyte replacement supplement in the water. Initial symptoms are similar to those of heat exhaustion — physical weakness, dizziness, nausea with frequent urination, which can result in seizures, collapse and unconsciousness.

Hypothermia

Hypothermia is something to look out for during winter in the Grand Canyon, or any period of cold, wet weather. Caused by exposure to cold and moisture, if ignored, hypothermia can cause death. Hypothermia occurs when the body experiences heat loss causing the body's core temperature to drop, impairing brain and muscular functions. The most common way to get hypothermia is by not dressing warmly enough to insulate the body from adverse environmental elements including, but not limited to, exposure to cold, rain, snow and wind. Initial symptoms include feeling very cold, numbness of skin, minor muscular impairment. As the body temperature drops, the muscles become increasingly uncoordinated, there is mild confusion, slowness of pace, apathy or amnesia. If not treated immediately, it can progress to unconsciousness and eventually death.

Preventing hypothermia requires warm dry clothing, food and water. Once again, drinking water and snacking on foods high in carbohydrates at frequent intervals will provide and restore energy supplies for physical activity and production of body heat. Most importantly, dress in layers. Wool and polyester are the best insulators. A layer of polypropylene long underwear, tops and bottoms, followed by wool or synthetic sweater and pants, topped off with a waterproof, breathable layer of nylon — jacket and pants which can double as rain and wind protection. The final critical item is a wool or polyester weave hat since a large percentage of heat loss occurs at the head. Include on the list, a warm pair of gloves and socks. If a person comes down with hypothermia, removing their wet clothing and warming them with another human body can be a life-saver. If a sleeping bag is handy, climbing into the sleeping bag with them can help restore their body temperature.

Backcountry Use

Grand Canyon National Park has developed a system of classification known as "backcountry management zones" to identify areas in the backcountry by accessibility and usage. Each of these backcountry management zones — *corridor, threshold, primitive* and *wild* — provide an unique wilderness experience for visitors. Because many of Harvey's routes are outside the park boundaries, they are not included in the management zone maps provided by the Prk Service; however, this system of identification has been applied to each area listed in this book to give an indication as to the difficulty level that might be expected. Some areas may also have easier or more difficult routes, yet undiscovered. With the exception of the *corridor* routes, almost all of the areas can be expected to have very rugged terrain and at a minimum, *threshold* or *primitive* ratings. USGS 7.5 minute topo maps are highly recommended for use on all routes.

Backcountry Management Zone Designations
   Corridor: The corridor areas or zones are identified by their high density usage, where there is potential for continuous contact with other people. Visitors will find, depending on location, some structural improvements including ranger residences, maintenance buildings, restrooms, piped purified water, interpretive signs, bridges, trails and emergency phones. Corridor trails are recommended for hikers who do not have previous hiking experience in the Grand Canyon or in desert mountaineering.
   Threshold: Threshold identifies areas with medium density usage, where there is potential for frequent contact with others. Visitors will find non-permanent structures, restrooms and signs. Trails are not maintained and infrequently patrolled. Water is scarce. Threshold trails are recommended for hikers with some

previous hiking experience in the Grand Canyon or some desert mountaineering background.

Primitive: Primitive describes an area with low density usage and infrequent contact with others. Water is scarce to non-existent. Routes consist of unmaintained trails or are cross-country, requiring navigation and route-finding ability. There may be a certain amount of exposure on routes that will require comfort climbing on exposed rock. A rope and other artificial climbing aid may be required. Recommended for highly experienced Grand Canyon hikers, with a background in desert cross-country travel and mountaineering.

Wild: Wild identifies areas with very low density use, where there is the potential for no contact with others. Cross-country routes are indistinct or non-existent through rugged terrain and require excellent navigation and route-finding ability. Water sources are scarce to non-existent. A rope or other artificial climbing aid may be required. Recommended for highly experienced Grand Canyon hikers with a background in desert cross-country travel and mountaineering.

Flash Floods

The canyons and washes of the southwest are prone to flash flooding all year long though certain times of the year are more prone to flooding than other times. To minimize the risk of being caught in a flash flood, prior to embarking on your trip, check conditions with the Back Country Office of the National Park Service or with local authorities. Also check local weather reports. During the summer of 1997, many lives were needlessly claimed by flash floods across the southwest. Several people from a tour group were killed after venturing into a slot canyon north of Grand Canyon National Park, even though local residents from the Navajo Reservation attempted to stop them. Never completely discount information the local residents may offer, and avoid canyon hiking when thunderstorms or clouds are within a fifty mile radius. Lives have been lost in flash floods that have been caused by storms miles away.

Maps

When Harvey Butchart first wrote this series of books, many of his canyon hiking friends asked him not to include maps. At that time, their motive was to discourage droves of people from venturing into their favorite areas. Anyone who travels into the backcountry of the Grand Canyon must use a USGS 7.5 minute topo which covers the area in which they are planning their trip. No map in a book will ever come close to interpreting the features of the landscape like a 7.5 minute topo. There are some very good maps on the market, however, we recommend the USGS topos. A compass is absolutely necessary, and being able to use it is required. If you don't know how to take a bearing, stay on the known trails until you've accrued some considerable time and experience in field navigation and route finding.

Difficulty Ratings for Routes

It would take the editor at least a lifetime or two to attempt to scout every one of Harvey Butchart's routes and apply a rating of difficulty to each one. Many of the routes may start off with easy walking, but can quickly become more difficult. If a route begins to get difficult beyond your abilities, it's better to turn around at the onset, instead of continuing on and getting in over your head.

In the 1930's, the Sierra Club, which was actively leading large numbers of people into the backcountry of the Sierra Nevada, developed what is known as the "Yosemite Decimal System." Still used today, with some modifications, it numerically rates the difficulty of hikes or climbs. For example under the system, Class 1 would define a route which requires no more than hands-in-pockets trail walking. Class 2 would include more rugged terrain, like scree (loose, sandy rock) or talus (larger rocks and boulders, rockslide areas) where the hands and feet must be used for balance. Class 3 is defined by steeper terrain where boulders and other obstacles are encountered. The arms and legs are used for climbing, not just balancing. Handholds are usually easily identified. There is exposure, meaning that there is a possibility of falling or being injured. People who have hiked only on trails will not feel comfortable with the exposure and may want or need a roped belay on third-class sections. It is fair to say, that many of the routes Harvey describes in this book fall within second and third class. Class 4 is steep and exposed, with most people wanting a roped belay. A great degree of skill and a thorough knowledge of climbing procedure, including belaying for safety is necessary. Handholds are less defined and the risk of falling is greatly increased. Class 5 is bonafide rock-climbing, which requires the use of equipment — ropes, seat harnesses, helmets, runners and assorted hardware — and experience, skill and knowledge of climbing procedure to assure a safe and enjoyable climb free from injury. Class 6 requires the use of additional aid for climbing like a ladder or an unusual arrangement of climbing hardware.

This system, in conjunction with the backcountry management zone designations, has been applied to the routes listed on the following pages to give the reader an idea of the difficulties that may be encountered on any given route. Because the actual geology of the routes is constantly changing or the routes themselves are rarely traveled, it is next to impossible to apply the exact rating to each route. Those routes containing Class 4 to 5 type climbing have been listed as technical, while those that involve Class 3 to 4 have been listed as having exposure. Those routes that have not been identified with exposure or as technical, can still be expected to involve navigational ability, with climbing difficulty ranging from Class 1 – 2, with some possible sections of Class 3 climbing. Routes will be more or less difficult depending upon the experience of each hiker. On the other hand, just because there is one technical segment on a route doesn't mean the entire route has to be abandoned. For example, the upper third of Mohawk Canyon to Moss Spring is a fine Class 2 route. However, to reach the river past Moss Spring, a rope is needed to bypass at least one dry waterfall, which under this rating system, would give the route a Class 5 rating.

Butchart route ratings:

(Please read previous pages for more information and descriptions).

Corridor: Main trails, high density usage. Restrooms and other
                 facilities. Some water may be available. (Class 1)

Threshold: Medium density. Unmaintained trails, some restrooms.
                 Scarce water. (Class 1-2)

Primitive: Low usage, unmaintained trails, requiring navigation,
                 route-finding. Scarce water. (Class 1-2, possible Class 3+)

Wild: Low usage, potential for no human contact; cross-country routes
                 are indistinct or non-existent. Rope or other climbing aid may
                 be required. Scarce water. (Section(s) of Class 4-5 possible)

Exposure: Class 3-4, some exposed sections where a roped belay
                 may be required. (Section(s) of Class 4-5 possible)

Technical: Class 4-5, exposed or technical sections where a rope or other
                 aid may be required for climbing. (Section(s) of Class 6 possible)

The Park Service recommends NOT using routes identified as primitive or wild during
the summer due to heat and lack of reliable water sources.

The Main Trails

Bright Angel Trail	Corridor
Bright Angel Campground	Corridor
Kaibab Trail	Corridor
North Kaibab Trail	Corridor
Phantom Canyon Route	Primitive, exposure, technical
Grandview Trail	Threshold

Marble Canyon Area

Lee's Ferry	Threshold
Echo Peaks	Primitive
Lee's Ferry to Soap Creek	Primitive
Soap Creek to Rider Canyon	Primitive
Rider Canyon Area	Primitive
Downriver from Rider	Primitive
Left Bank Below Mile 21.7	Primitive
Eminence Break Area	Primitive
Shinumo Wash to Tatahatso Canyon	Primitive
Saddle Canyon to Buck Farm Canyon	Primitive, exposure, technical
Along the River to Buck Farm Canyon	Primitive, exposure
Buck Farm Canyon to Nankoweap	Primitive, exposure, technical
Upriver from President Harding Rapids	Primitive
Downriver from President Harding Rapids	Primitive

Eastern Grand Canyon

Nankoweap Basin	Primitive, exposure
Kwagunt	Wild, exposure
Chuar Valley	Wild, exposure, technical
Unkar Valley	Wild, exposure, technical
Comanche Point Route	Wild, exposure, technical
Routes Away from the Tanner Trail	Primitive
Tanner Trail	Primitive
Papago Canyon Route	Primitive, exposure, some technical
New Hance Trail	Primitive
Hance Trail	Primitive
Grapevine Canyon Routes	Primitive, exposure, technical
Shoshone Point Route	Primitive, exposure, technical
Clear Creek Trail	Threshold
Redwall route in Kwagunt, Vishnu and Clear Creek Canyons	Threshold, exposure
Hermit Trail	Threshold
Upper Boucher Creek	Primitive, exposure, technical
Bass Trail	Primitive
Esplanade West of the Bass Trail	Primitive
Point Huitzel Route	Primitive, exposure, technical
Enfilade Point Route	Wild, exposure, technical
Colonnade Route	Wild, exposure
Haunted Canyon Route	Wild, exposure, technical
Trinity Creek	Wild, exposure, technical
Following Stanton in 1890	Wild, exposure, technical
Hindu Amphitheater	Wild, exposure
Rescuing the Parachutists in 1944	Wild, exposure, technical
Shinumo Amphitheater	Primitive, exposure, technical
Powell Plateau	Primitive
Tapeats and Deer Creeks	Primitive – Threshold, exposure, some technical
Deer Creek to Kanab Canyon	Primitive, exposure, technical

Western Grand Canyon

From Great Thumb to Supai	Wild, exposure, technical
Routes to Havasu Canyon	Primitive, exposure
Kanab Creek	Primitive, exposure, technical
Toroweap Area	Primitive, exposure, technical
Whitmore Wash and Parashant Canyon	Primitive
Whitmore Wash to the Shivwits Plateau	Primitive, exposure
Shivwits Plateau	Primitive
Green Spring Canyon	Wild
Surprise Canyon	Wild, exposure
Lost Creek	Wild

Reference Point Creek	Wild
Salt Creek	Wild
Burnt Spring Canyon	Primitive
National Canyon	Primitive, exposure
Mohawk Canyon	Primitive, exposure, technical
Granite Park Area	Primitive, exposure
Diamond Creek	Wild
Bridge Canyon to Separation	Primitive
Separation to Spencer Canyon	Primitive
Spencer and Milkweed Canyons	Primitive, exposure
Quartermaster Canyon	Primitive
Tincanebitts Canyon	Wild, exposure, technical
Columbine Falls & Cave Canyon	Wild, exposure
Pearce (aka Pierce) Canyon	Primitive

Leave No Trace

Minimum Impact Camping

The ultimate goal of everyone who makes a trip into the backcountry should be to come and go without leaving any trace of their presence upon the fragile terrain of the Grand Canyon's desert wilderness. Begin by keeping your hiking group small. The maximum number of people allowed on a backcountry permit is two on many of the trails below the rim.

Hiking on exposed mineral soil like the sand or gravel found in washes or on plateaus causes the least impact, as does camping in established campsites away from fertile soil and vegetation. Walk abreast on cryptobiotic crust to avoid damaging its anti-erosional and nitrogen enriching qualities which are integral to the future development of desert plant communities. In addition, the Grand Canyon Backcountry Office asks the following of all backcountry users.

1. Plan your trip well. Know where you are and where you are going.

2. Good campsites are found not made. Camp at least 200' away from water sources. Fill your water bottles during daylight and avoid using natural water sources at night since most desert animals are nocturnal and congregate at water sources after dark.

3. Stay on established trails. Don't cut switchbacks, which erode and damage trails.

4. Pack out what you pack in, which includes toilet paper and all trash.

5. Fires are not permitted below the rim.

6. Pets are not permitted in the backcountry (there are several kennels on the South Rim).

7. Bury human waste at least 200' from any water source in a hole four to six inches deep with the same diameter.

Wash dishes, yourself and anything else at least 200' away from any water source.

8. Don't burn toilet paper! Bury it or pack it out in a zip-lock plastic bag. Devastating fires have been caused by burning toilet paper.

Archaeological Site Etiquette

Visitors to the Grand Canyon need to know that all archaeological sites are very fragile and easily disturbed. They must be treated with care and respect, and left intact so that they may be enjoyed and experienced by those who follow. The following guidelines have been established for visitation to archaeological sites:

1. Viewing a site from a distance will reduce the impact a site receives. Stop, look and think before entering a cultural site. Locate the midden area (the trash pile) to avoid walking on it. Middens are very fragile and contain important archaeological artifacts and information about the ancient residents.

2. If a trail has been built across a site, stay on it to reduce the effects of destructive erosion. Don't camp near ruins.

3. Leave artifacts in place. Make a note of their location and report them to rangers or visitor center personnel.

4. Enjoy rock art by sketching or photographing it, but don't touch, chalk in the outline, take rubbings or latex molds, or otherwise touch rock art. The slightest touch will leave damaging acids and oils from the skin on the rock.

5. Walk carefully when visiting ancient or historic structures to avoid damaging archaeological and structural features of a site. Climbing on roofs or walls could, in a moment, destroy what has lasted hundreds of years.

6. Leave all objects, including seemingly insignificant broken bits in place. The relationship of artifacts to each other and to their natural surroundings is important to any archaeological investigation.

7. Writing, spray-painting, drawing on, or scratching into the surfaces of prehistoric rock art found on walls, caves or in other environments is punishable by federal law.

8. Collecting artifacts on the surface or by digging is against the law.

9. Notify rangers or other authorities if you witness any illegal activity. The Archaeological Resource Act of 1979 provides stiff penalties and a reward for information that leads to a conviction.

10. Archaeological sites are places of ancestral importance to Native Americans and must be treated with respect.

Backcountry Permits

Permits and use fees are required for all overnight trips in the backcountry of Grand Canyon National Park. As of this writing, permits are not required for dayhikes. Permission to drive across tribal lands should obtained from the appropriate Tribal Offices. For more information on obtaining permits, contact the Grand Canyon Backcountry Office:

Backcountry Office
Grand Canyon National Park
P.O. Box 129
Grand Canyon, Arizona
(520)638-7875

Hike with a Group

For those wanting to learn more about desert backcountry hiking or climbing, or who want to enjoy the companionship of others in the great outdoors, we suggest going with a group that offers trips and/or training specific to the desert.

Many organizations offer a variety of day and weekend trips to the desert — from car camps, desert backpacks, dayhikes and peak climbs to rafting trips. A few of these, are listed below, and depending on the organization, trips are either free or range in cost from a nominal fee to several hundred dollars.

Grand Canyon Field Institute
The field seminar program for the Grand Canyon Association. Classes explore the natural and cultural history of the Grand Canyon through dayhikes, van camping, and river trips.

For information contact:
Grand Canyon Field Institute
P.O. Box 399
Grand Canyon, Arizona 86023
(520)638-2485

Arizona Mountaineering Club
Established in 1962 by a group of Arizona climbers to teach people how to climb. Offer rock climbing classes and outings which include rock climbing, hiking, canyoneering, alpine climbing, backpacking and mountain biking.

For information contact:
Arizona Mountaineering Club
P.O. Box 1695
Phoenix, Arizona 85001-169
www.dtek.chalmers.se/Climbing/Guidebooks/NorthAmerica/Arizona/amc.html

Desert Peaks Section, Sierra Club
Mountaineering-based group that climbs and explores the desert
mountain ranges of the southwest and Baja California while aid-
ing in the preservation of desert wilderness areas. Trips are led
by volunteers and rate in difficulty from Class 1 to Class 6. A list
of peaks is available for a nominal fee. For information contact:
    Desert Peaks Section
    Angeles Chapter, Sierra Club
    (Ask for a contact number for Desert Peaks Section outings)
    3345 Wilshire Blvd., #508
    Los Angeles, California 90010
    (213)387-4287
    www.edgeinternet.com/dps/

Desert Survivors
Committed to experiencing and preserving the desert's unique
beauty and value. Explore the desert canyons and mountains of
the southwest, primarily California and Nevada.
    For information contact:
    P.O. Box 20991
    Oakland, California 94620-1706
    (510)769-1706
    www.desert-survivors.org/oasis/index.html

References

Black, W.J., *Grand Canyon of Arizona*, Passenger Department of the Santa Fe, Poole Brothers, Chicago 1906

Euler, Robert C. and Tikalsky, Frank, *The Grand Canyon – Intimate Views*, The University of Arizona Press, Tucson, Arizona 1992

Grand Canyon Natural History Association, *Inner Canyon Hiking*, Grand Canyon, 1970

Hughes, Donald, *The Story of Man at the Grand Canyon*, Grand Canyon Natural History Association, Grand Canyon 1967

James, George Wharton, *The Grand Canyon of Arizona*, Little, Brown and Company, Boston, 1910

Kolb, Ellsworth, *Through the Grand Canyon from Wyoming to Mexico*, The Macmillan Company, 1952

Lavender, David, *River Runners of the Grand Canyon*, The University of Arizona Press, Tucson, Arizona 1986

Leydet, François, *Grand Canyon: Time and the River Flowing* Sierra Club, San Francisco 1964

Lister, Robert H. and Florence C., *Those Who Came Before*, The University of Arizona Press, Tucson, Arizona 1983

Peattie, Roderick, *The Inverted Mountains: Canyons of the West*, Vanguard Press, New York 1948

Powell, John Wesley, *Exploration of the Colorado River and Its Canyons*, Dover Publications, New York 1961

Quinn, Michael, *Oral History Interview with Dr. Harvey Butchart, Grand Canyon National Park 75th Anniversary Celebration*, Albright Training Center, Grand Canyon National Park, Arizona, 1994

Thomas, David Hurst, *Exploring Native America – An Archaeological Guide*, Macmillan, New York 1994

Wilkerson, Dr. James A., *Medicine for Mountaineering*, The Mountaineers, Seattle 1985

Place Names Index

I N D E X

© 1995 Spotted Dog Press

OTHER BOOKS BY SPOTTED DOG PRESS

CLIMBING MT. WHITNEY
BY WALT WHEELOCK AND WYNNE BENTI

*The original classic with up-to-date permit
and route information, local history, photographs, and maps.*

CLOSE UPS OF THE HIGH SIERRA
BY NORMAN CLYDE

*"Close Ups of the High Sierra" is a journey to the exquisite
and remote backcountry of the Sierra Nevada as told by
Norman Clyde, the greatest California mountaineer of all time,
who was credited with making more first ascents
than John Muir, Clarence King, and
William Brewer combined.*

AVAILABLE FROM YOU LOCAL BOOKSTORE.
IF THEY DON'T HAVE IT, HAVE THEM ORDER IT FOR YOU!